The Original Position

At the center of John Rawls's political philosophy is one of the most influential thought experiments of the twentieth century: which principles of justice would a group of individuals choose to regulate their society if they were deprived of any information about themselves that might bias their choice? In this collection of new essays, leading political philosophers examine the ramifications and continued relevance of Rawls's idea. Their chapters explore topics including the place of the original position in rational choice theory, the similarities between Rawls's original position and Kant's categorical imperative, the differences between Rawls's model and Scanlon's contractualism, and the role of the original position in the argument between Rawls and other views in political philosophy, including utilitarianism, feminism, and radicalism. This accessible volume will be a valuable resource for undergraduates as well as advanced students and scholars of philosophy, game theory, economics, and the social and political sciences.

Timothy Hinton is Professor of Philosophy at North Carolina State University, Raleigh, North Carolina. He has published numerous papers on political philosophy, ethics, and the philosophy of religion in journals including *Philosophy and Public Affairs*, *Analysis*, and *Journal of Social Philosophy*.

Classic Philosophical Arguments

Over the centuries, a number of individual arguments have formed a crucial part of philosophical enquiry. The volumes in this series examine these arguments, looking at the ramifications and applications which they have come to have, the challenges which they have encountered, and the ways in which they have stood the test of time.

Titles in the series

The Prisoner's Dilemma
Edited by Martin Peterson
The Original Position
Edited by Timothy Hinton

The Original Position

Edited by

Timothy Hinton

CAMBRIDGE UNIVERSITY PRESS

CAMBRIDGE
UNIVERSITY PRESS

University Printing House, Cambridge CB2 8BS, United Kingdom

Cambridge University Press is part of the University of Cambridge.

It furthers the University's mission by disseminating knowledge in the pursuit of
education, learning and research at the highest international levels of excellence.

www.cambridge.org
Information on this title: www.cambridge.org/9781107627512

© Cambridge University Press 2015

First published 2015

Printed in United Kingdom by TJ International Ltd. Padstow Cornwall

A catalogue record for this publication is available from the British Library

Library of Congress Cataloguing in Publication data
The original position / edited by Timothy Hinton.
    pages   cm. – (Classic philosophical arguments)
Includes bibliographical references and index.
ISBN 978-1-107-04448-7 (Hardback : alk. paper) –
ISBN 978-1-107-62751-2 (Paperback : alk. paper)
1. Political science–Philosophy.   2. Liberalism–Philosophy.   I. Hinton, Timothy, 1964- editor.
JA71.O675 2015
320.01–dc23   2015020040

ISBN 978-1-107-04448-7 Hardback
ISBN 978-1-107-62751-2 Paperback

Contents

Contributors

Amy R. Baehr is Associate Professor of Philosophy at Hofstra University. Her work has appeared in journals including *Ethics, Law and Philosophy, Hypatia: A Journal of Feminist Philosophy*, and *The Journal of Political Philosophy*. Her papers have also appeared in anthologies including *The Philosophy of Rawls: A Collection of Essays* (edited by Henry S. Richardson) and *Feminist Interpretations of John Rawls* (edited by Ruth Abbey). She is editor of *Varieties of Feminist Liberalism* (2004) and author of "Liberal Feminism" (*Stanford Encyclopedia of Philosophy*).

David O. Brink is Distinguished Professor of Philosophy at the University of California, San Diego, Director of the Institute for Law and Philosophy at the University of San Diego School of Law, and editor of the journal *Legal Theory*. He is author of *Moral Realism and the Foundations of Ethics* (Cambridge, 1989), *Perfectionism and the Common Good* (2003), and *Mill's Progressive Principles* (2013).

Gillian Brock is a Professor of Philosophy at the University of Auckland in New Zealand. She is the author of *Global Justice: A Cosmopolitan Account* (2009) and editor or co-editor of *Current Debates in Global Justice* (with Darrel Moellendorf, 2005), *The Political Philosophy of Cosmopolitanism* (with Harry Brighouse, 2005), *Necessary Goods: Our Responsibilities to Meet Others' Needs* (1998), and *Global Heath and Global Health Ethics* (with Solomon Benatar, 2011). She has published in journals including *Ethics, The Monist, American Philosophical Quarterly, Philosophy, Canadian Journal of Philosophy, Journal of Social Philosophy, Analysis, The Journal of Ethics*, and *Utilitas*.

John Christman is Professor of Philosophy, Political Science, and Women's Studies at Penn State University. He is the author of *The Myth of Property: Toward a Theory of Egalitarian Ownership* (1994) and *The Politics of Persons: Individual Autonomy for Socio-historical Selves* (Cambridge, 2009). He is also the editor of *The Inner Citadel: Essays on Individual Autonomy* (1989) and *Autonomy and the Challenges to Liberalism: New Essays* (with Joel Anderson, Cambridge, 2004).

Matthew Clayton is Associate Professor of Political Theory at the University of Warwick. He is the author of *Justice and Legitimacy in Upbringing* (2006) and has co-edited *The Ideal of Equality* (with Andrew Williams, 2000) and *Social Justice* (with Andrew Williams, 2004).

Joshua Cohen is 'on the faculty at Apple University and a Senior Distinguished Fellow at the School of Law, the Department of Philosophy, and the Department of Political Science at the University of California, Berkeley.' His recent publications include *Philosophy, Politics, Democracy* (2009), *Rousseau: A Free Community of Equals* (2010), and *The Arc of the Moral Universe and Other Essays* (2011).

David Estlund is Lombardo Family Professor of Humanities, in the departments of Philosophy and Political Science at Brown University. He edited the collection *Democracy* (2001) and is the author of *Democratic Authority: A Philosophical Framework* (2008). He is also the editor of *The Oxford Handbook of Political Philosophy* (2012).

Gerald Gaus is the James E. Rogers Professor of Philosophy at the University of Arizona. He is the author of a number of books, including *On Philosophy, Politics, and Economics* (2008), *Contemporary Theories of Liberalism* (2003), *Justificatory Liberalism* (1996), and *Value and Justification* (1990). He was a founding editor of *Politics, Philosophy and Economics*. His most recent publications include *The Order of Public Reason* (Cambridge, 2011) and with Fred D'Agostino he edited *The Routledge Companion to Social and Political Philosophy* (2013).

Timothy Hinton is Professor of Philosophy at North Carolina State University in Raleigh. He has published articles in journals including *Philosophy and Public Affairs, Analysis, Social Theory and Practice*, and *The Philosophical Forum*.

Andrews Reath is Professor of Philosophy at the University of California, Riverside. He is the author of *Agency and Autonomy in Kant's Moral Theory* (2006) and editor of *Reclaiming the History of Ethics: Essays for John Rawls* (with Barbara Herman and Christine Korsgaard, Cambridge, 1997) and *Kant's 'Critique of Practical Reason': A Critical Guide* (with Jens Timmermann, Cambridge, 2010).

John Thrasher is a lecturer in philosophy at Monash University in Melbourne, Australia. His published work has appeared in *Philosophical Studies, The Journal of Moral Philosophy, The European Journal of Philosophy, Ethical Theory and Moral Practice*, and *The Adam Smith Review*.

Jeremy Waldron is University Professor in the School of Law at New York University. 'From 2010 to 2014, he was' also the Chichele Professor of Social and Political Theory at the University of Oxford. His books include *Liberal Rights*

(Cambridge, 1993), *The Dignity of Legislation* (Cambridge, 1999), *Law and Disagreement* (1999), *Torture, Terror, and Trade-offs* (2010), *The Harm of Hate Speech* (2012), and *Dignity, Rank and Rights* (2012).

Paul Weithman is Glynn Family Honors Collegiate Professor of Philosophy at the University of Notre Dame. His most recent book is *Why Political Liberalism? On John Rawls's Political Turn* (2011), which won the David and Elaine Spitz Prize for the best book on liberal democratic theory published in 2010.

Acknowledgments

The editor gratefully acknowledges the assistance of Allison Freeman, Kenneth Peters, and Ann Rives in preparing the manuscript for publication. Thanks are also due to North Carolina State's College of Humanities and Social Sciences for a Scholarship and Research Award that helped to fund research for the book. Finally, the editor wishes to record his deep gratitude to Allison Freeman, Hilary Gaskin, and Michael Pendlebury for their indispensable advice and encouragement.

Abbreviations

The following abbreviations are used for John Rawls's works:

TJ	*A Theory of Justice* (Harvard University Press, 1971)
TJR	*A Theory of Justice*, revised edition (Harvard University Press, 1999)
PL	*Political Liberalism* (Columbia University Press, 1993)
LP	*Law of Peoples* (Harvard University Press, 1999)
CP	*Collected Papers*, S. Freeman (ed.) (Harvard University Press, 1999)
LHMP	*Lectures on the History of Moral Philosophy* (Harvard University Press, 2000)
JFR	*Justice as Fairness: A Restatement* (Harvard University Press, 2001)
LHPP	*Lectures on the History of Political Philosophy* (Harvard University Press, 2007)

The following abbreviation is used for Robert Nozick's work:

ASU	*Anarchy, State, and Utopia* (Basic Books, 1974)

Introduction: the original position and *The Original Position* – an overview

Timothy Hinton

John Rawls's idea of the original position – arguably the centerpiece of his theory of justice – has proved to have enduring philosophical significance for at least three reasons.[1]

First, it offered a fresh way of thinking about problems of justification and objectivity in political philosophy. At the heart of these difficulties is the need to find an objective point of view from which to deliberate about matters of basic justice. Here "objective" implies "not mired in partiality" and "not biased by one's particular position in the social world." The original position is a hypothetical contractual situation in which parties who are ignorant about crucial features of themselves (such as how wealthy or talented they are, and what their vision of the best way to live is) are to select the principles of justice to regulate the basic institutions of their society. In selecting those principles, the parties are thought of as entering into an agreement that binds them to honor whichever principles they choose. By specifying that the parties are ignorant of matters that would allow them to favor themselves, Rawls vividly and unforgettably captures a widely shared sense that principles of justice cannot be justified by appealing to morally irrelevant considerations.

The original position is important in the second place because of the many interesting philosophical questions it raises. As soon as Rawls's argument had been fully digested, many philosophers felt that something was amiss with it. Questions abound. How could the fact that I would have agreed to certain principles in a special situation of choice give those principles binding authority over me?[2] Is it true that Rawls's two principles in particular are

---

[1] Rawls's first published paper "Outline" (1951) focused on the question of justification in moral philosophy. He went on to present an early version of his two principles of justice in two papers entitled "Justice as Fairness" (1957, 1958). The idea of the original position as a way of justifying those principles only emerged in his 1967 paper "Distributive Justice."

[2] Rawls himself considers and responds to this objection in *TJ*, at pp. 21 and 587. It was taken up by Ronald Dworkin in his review of *TJ*, "The Original Position," and more recently Habermas raises it.

the most rational choice that could be made in the original position?[3] Are the assumptions needed to get the device off the ground really as weak and untroubling as Rawls seems to have thought?

Finally, the original position is significant because of its evident traction: it has inspired other philosophers to take up alternative positions, to rethink it, and to conceptualize afresh the philosophical problems to which the idea was initially addressed.[4] The vast literature on Rawls's idea – and the use he himself made of it in his subsequent work – are testament to its capacity to inspire further philosophical reflection.

In this introduction, after briefly describing its role in *TJ*, I shall lay out the main features of Rawls's argument from the original position as presented in that text.[5] I will then indicate some of the ways in which Rawls's use of the original position changed in his subsequent work. I shall end with a description of the chapters that make up the volume.

0.1 The place of the original position in *TJ*

In the preface to *TJ*, Rawls tells us that he considers his theory of justice to be a systematic alternative to utilitarianism. The theory Rawls presents – which he names *justice as fairness* – is a form of contractualism he describes as "highly Kantian in nature" (*TJ*, p. viii). What recommends justice as fairness over utilitarianism, according to Rawls, is both that it more faithfully reflects our considered beliefs about justice and that it "constitutes the most appropriate moral basis for a democratic society" (*TJ*, p. viii).

Let's take each of these claims in turn. What exactly are the considered beliefs that Rawls has in mind? They are the claims that first, justice is the most important virtue of social institutions; and second, that justice confers on each person an inviolable status. Together these constitute what he calls "our intuitive conviction" that justice has primacy (*TJ*, p. 4). Rawls wants to know: are we justified in thinking this? And what are the strongest reasons we can give for thinking it? Rawls's theory of justice is meant to answer these questions: it is intended to explain why we are justified in thinking that justice is so basic by uncovering the foundations of that belief.

But we should not lose sight of Rawls's second reason for taking justice as fairness to be superior to utilitarianism. This has to do with the highly

---

[3] For an examination of some of these issues, see Harsanyi, "Can the Maximin?"
[4] T. M. Scanlon provided a famous alternative form of contractualism in "Contractualism."
[5] For an excellent discussion of the original position, see Freeman, *Rawls*, Chapter 4.

practical nature of Rawls's overall project: he wants to find a moral justification for the institutions that comprise a constitutional democracy, and he
wants us – you and me – to find in his theory of justice grounds that could
justify our own (presumed) commitment to a democratic society.

If we put these thoughts together, we can formulate a basic question. What
conditions must a democratic society satisfy in order to count as perfectly
just? The basic hypothesis driving both the argument of *TJ* and much of
Rawls's subsequent work is that the traditional idea of a social contract, with
appropriate modifications, has a fundamental role to play in answering this
question. Rawls wants us to think of the basic principles of democratic justice
as ones that would be agreed to by "free and rational persons" who sought to
"further their own interests" while they were tasked with selecting those
principles in a completely fair choice situation (*TJ*, p. 11).

It is important to bear in mind that the original position is embedded in the
broader coherence-driven conception of justification that Rawls named
"reflective equilibrium." Rawls is assuming that all our beliefs, including of
course our beliefs about justice, form a systematic whole, which, in the ideal
case, would be fully governed by rational standards. Justification is a matter of
finding the right kind of coherence among the elements that make up this
system, including those elements that tell us what it is for our beliefs to be well
justified. In the course of seeking an appropriate ordering for our system of
beliefs about justice in particular, Rawls says, we need to set out from certain
basic convictions that we treat as "provisional fixed points" in our reasoning.
As examples of the kind of beliefs he has in mind, Rawls mentions our
confidence that "religious intolerance and racial discrimination are unjust"
(*TJ*, p. 19). To decide *which* of our considered judgments to take as provisionally fixed, we can set aside those about which we feel hesitant, as well as
those made when we are fearful or upset. With these provisional lower-level
judgments in place, the aim then is to find more general or abstract principles
which, in conjunction with our knowledge of the relevant facts, would
support these very same judgments. We could put this by saying that the
principles we are after ought to be able to function as the normative major
premises in an argument whose conclusions were the basic judgments from
which we began.

In the method of reflective equilibrium, the original position functions
as an intermediate step. It stands between our initial basic convictions and
the more abstract principles to which inference will be made. This is why
Rawls insists that it be as fair as possible: in effect, it works to filter out
unreliable or biased reasons that might be proposed in support of candidate

principles of justice. It explains why the parties in the original position should be ignorant about such things as their socioeconomic status, their ethical or religious commitments, and their native endowments, including their strength and intelligence.

Because they are ignorant about these matters, Rawls describes the parties in the original position as being behind a "veil of ignorance" (*TJ*, p. 136). In addition, they are understood as enjoying perfect equality: none has any more information or bargaining power than any other. Furthermore, the parties are neither altruists nor egoists, nor are they spiteful or malicious. As Rawls puts it, they have no "interest in one another's interests" (*TJ*, p. 148). Crucially, they are rational: they want to do as well for themselves as they can, given their situation. As a result, they want to choose whichever set of principles will best advance their interests. This presupposes that they know they have certain interests of their own: they want to ensure that, once the veil of ignorance is lifted, they will be in a position to live out their lives as best they can. They are trying to find principles that will enable them to meet these goals. But since they do not know what their own values and life plans are, they are forced to make a choice under uncertainty.

Of course, Rawls wants us (you and me, here and now) to be persuaded that the set-up of the original position makes sense. This is why he suggests that we will agree with him on the most reasonable way to go about creating the original position. In other words, Rawls hopes that we will agree that the constraints to which the parties in the original position are subject are ones that we ourselves find reasonable. Rawls hopes that even if we do not initially accept these conditions,

> perhaps we can be persuaded to do so by philosophical reflection. Each aspect of the contractual situation can be given supporting grounds. Thus what we shall do is to collect together into one conception a number of conditions on principles that we are ready upon due consideration to recognize as reasonable. (*TJ*, p. 21)

But it is important to bear in mind that Rawls insists that the stipulations that set up the original position are all open to reflective re-examination, and, where necessary, to rational revision:

> We begin by describing it so that it represents generally shared and preferably weak conditions. We then see if these conditions are strong enough to yield a significant set of principles. If not, we look for further premises equally reasonable. But if so, and these principles match our

considered convictions of justice, then so far well and good. But presumably there will be discrepancies. In this case we have a choice. We can either modify the account of the initial situation or we can revise our existing judgments, for even the judgments we take provisionally as fixed points are liable to revision. By going back and forth, sometimes altering the conditions of the contractual circumstances, at others withdrawing our judgments and conforming them to principle, I assume that eventually we shall find a description of the initial situation that both expresses reasonable conditions and yields principles which match our considered judgments duly pruned and adjusted. (*TJ*, p. 20)

The parties in the original position are trying to choose the most basic principles that will regulate their society, that is, the basic principles of justice. Rawls argues that in this choice situation, the parties would choose the following pair of principles:

The Equal Basic Liberty Principle: Each person is to have an equal right to the most extensive system of equal basic liberties compatible with a similar system of liberty for others. (*TJ*, p. 250)

The Second Principle (which comes in two distinct parts, and in which the first part has lexical priority over the second): (a) The Fair Equality of Opportunity principle: Social and economic inequalities are to be arranged so that they are attached to offices and positions open to all citizens under conditions of fair equality of opportunity; (b) The Difference Principle: Social and economic inequalities are to be arranged so that they work to the greatest expected benefit of the least advantaged group in society. (*TJ*, p. 83)

0.2 The core of the original position argument

In my discussion of the argument by which Rawls derives these principles from the original position, I shall, for the sake of simplicity, consider the case in which the parties are making a single pairwise comparison.[6] Here, they are choosing between Rawls's two principles and

---

[6] In both *TJ* and *JFR*, Rawls presents the argument in two distinct stages. In the latter text, he describes these as "the first fundamental comparison," in which his two principles are paired with the principle of average utility, and "the second fundamental comparison," in which his two principles face off against "an alternative exactly the same as those principles except in one respect. The principle of average utility, combined with a suitable social minimum is substituted for the difference principle" (*JFR*, p. 120).

The principle of average utility: All social goods – such as rights, opportunities, income and wealth – are to be distributed in such a way as to maximize the average utility of the members of society.

In his first main line of argument, Rawls suggests that it is useful to think of his two principles as "the maximin solution to the problem of social justice" (*TJ*, p. 152). This involves an appeal to

The maximin rule: Choose that alternative whose worst outcome is better for you than the worst outcome of any other alternative (in a slogan: Maximize the minimum).

Rawls's intention is to characterize the original position in such a way that it is rational for the parties to employ this rule in making their choice. Once this has been done, he says, somewhat optimistically, "a *conclusive* argument can ... be constructed for these principles" (*TJ*, p. 153, my emphasis).

Rawls believes that it is rational to use the maximin rule in making a decision under uncertainty if the following conditions are met:

1 there is strong reason for discounting the probabilities attached to the various possible outcomes;
2 one has a conception of the good involving a threshold *t* which is such that it is much better to be at *t* than to be anywhere below *t*; however, once *t* is achieved, further gains above *t* either have very little or no significance at all;
3 the situation involves "grave risks": the outcomes one rejects by using the rule are very bad indeed.

In making a case that condition (1) holds in the original position, Rawls reasons as follows. Since the parties do not know any specific facts about their society, they have no way to determine how likely it is that they will end up in any given position. (For example, they have no idea what the possible social positions are, nor do they know how many people occupy any particular position.) Rawls also emphasizes here that the parties (as individuals with continuing lines of descendants) have to be able to justify their choice to others.

In arguing that condition (2) is satisfied in the original position, Rawls appeals to the fact that his two principles seem to guarantee a "satisfactory minimum," while the principle of average utility does not. The first principle guarantees basic liberties for all, while the second principle gives the least advantaged as much as it is possible for them to have. Of course, some people (say, those at the top end of the income scale) might do better in a utilitarian society than in a Rawlsian one. But, being ignorant about where one will end up makes it rational, Rawls insists, to secure a decent minimum in liberties, opportunities, and income and wealth, rather than taking a gamble in which one might end up much worse off.

Finally, when it comes to condition (3), Rawls argues that none of the social positions that would be permitted by his two principles would turn out to be intolerable, while the possibilities that they rule out would clearly be so. After all, among the possibilities allowed by the principle of average utility could be slavery and serfdom.

In his second main original position argument in *TJ*, Rawls considers what he calls "the strains of commitment." Recall that the parties know that they have a sense of justice. Knowing that they will see themselves as bound by whichever principles they end up choosing, they know that they "cannot enter into agreements that may have consequences they cannot accept" (*TJ*, p. 176). So each of the parties must consider the impact which any chosen principles will have on the lives of people in the society to which they apply. Each must be able to say sincerely: I could commit myself to acting on these principles irrespective of where I ended up as a result of their workings.

With this in mind, Rawls suggests that it would be easier to commit to his principles than to the principle of average utility because, in doing so, the parties would thereby rule out the possibility of having to live with "the worst eventualities" (*TJ*, p. 176). Indeed, he wonders whether anyone could rationally commit themselves to abide by principles whose outcome might involve a loss of important freedoms simply in order to secure greater utility for other people.

Another significant feature of this part of Rawls's argument is its invocation of the importance of publicity in choosing a conception of justice. In the context of the original position, Rawls connects this with the suggestion that what he calls a "stable" conception of justice is a more desirable choice. He explains that such a conception is stable when public awareness of its having been fully realized in a society will lead its members to develop a desire to act in accordance with its principles. Rawls suggests that the parties will be moved by facts about ordinary human motivation to see that utilitarianism "seems to require a greater identification with the interests of others than the two principles" (*TJ*, p. 177). This level of identification, he thinks, would place undue strain on one's ability to remain faithful to the principle of average utility.

There are two further features of the publicity condition. The first appeals to self-respect. Rawls believes that having a lively sense of your own worth is a condition of achieving your ends in life. Unless you are confident that other people respect your standing in society, you are unlikely to feel that your projects are fully worthwhile. A democratic polity shows proper respect for its members, Rawls says, when it ensures that they have sufficient access to what he calls the social bases of self-respect.

When a society follows the two principles of justice, each person's advantage is taken into account and each takes part in a cooperative scheme of mutual benefit. Since each knows that his or her good is being protected, each can have confidence that he or she is being treated as an equal. This connects with the idea of an underlying moral equality between people that is part of the deep structure of Rawls's view.

Rawls's appeal to publicity in his original position argument also invokes the Kantian principle that people are ends in themselves and ought never to be treated as mere means. Rawls gives this a contractualist gloss. On his view, we treat someone as a mere means just in case we treat her in ways that she would not have consented to being treated had she been asked for her consent in a perfectly fair choice situation. Although it is not entirely clear what this comes to, perhaps we can take Rawls's line of thought to be something like the following. To treat others as ends in themselves is to be willing to forgo a larger share of goods like rights, opportunities, and income and wealth, if having that larger share oneself would mean that someone else would end up with fewer of those goods than anyone needs to have.

Recall that, for Rawls, what matters most when it comes to justifying principles of justice is our status as free and equal persons, each with a conception of the good and a capacity to act on the principles of justice. When I view the social world from the perspective of the original position, Rawls holds, I see only free and equal persons engaged in social cooperation. I would want that social world to be one in which no one could be better off than anyone else simply as a result of factors which are arbitrary from the point of view of justice. The factors which are arbitrary in this way include people's social class, their natural talents, and the values and plans that animate their lives. This conception of the original position – which Rawls calls its "intuitive" understanding (*TJ*, p. 22) – is tied to the very moving lines with which Rawls ends *TJ*:

> to see our place in society from the perspective of this position is to see it *sub specie aeternitatis*: it is to regard the human situation not only from all social but also from all temporal points of view. The perspective of eternity is not a perspective from a certain place beyond the world, nor from the point of view of a transcendent being; rather it is a certain form

of thought and feeling that rational persons can adopt within the world. And having done so, they can, whatever their generation, bring together into one scheme all individual perspectives and arrive together at regulative principles that can be affirmed by everyone as he lives by them, each from his own standpoint. Purity of heart, if one could attain it, would be to see clearly and to act from grace and self-command from this point of view. (*TJ*, p. 578)

0.3 The original position after *TJ*

To understand the main shifts in Rawls's thinking about the original position in his writings after *TJ*, it is helpful to bear in mind an important feature of the broader reflective framework in which the device is embedded. Recall that in *TJ* Rawls wanted his conception of justice to clarify and, if necessary, to correct our basic convictions about justice. By doing so, he hoped to justify those convictions, and to help make sense of our commitment to a democratic society.

In that work, however, Rawls thought of the process of achieving these goals as broadly speaking Socratic. For there, the original position was deployed in a fundamentally first-personal search for principles that one ought to accept. This goal is Socratic mainly because Rawls took the search for principles of justice to involve critical self-reflection on one's own beliefs – the kind of reflection in which neither one's initial judgments nor the subsequent principles to which inference is made are to be treated as sacrosanct. One should stand ready to revise either or both under the pressure of sound reasons. So, framed by the Socratic question, the point of the original position is to enable us to figure out what each of us taken individually should believe about justice.[7]

Beginning with the Dewey and Tanner Lectures, delivered in the early 1980s, Rawls set out in a new direction, in which the aim of justice as fairness was somewhat refigured, and, as a result, a second, non-Socratic method come to the fore.[8] What begins to dominate Rawls's thinking is a focus on certain deep and important political difficulties confronting contemporary democracies, difficulties which he hopes his theory can address, and quite

---

[7] Compare Scanlon's remarks on "Rawls" in Freeman, *Cambridge Companion*, p. 142.

[8] The Dewey Lectures, delivered in April 1980 and published in the *Journal of Philosophy* 77 (1980), 515–72 as "Kantian Constructivism," were re-written for *PL*, appearing there as Lectures I–III. Rawls presented the Tanner Lectures in April 1981; they appear in *PL* as Lecture VIII.

possibly, resolve. This political focus took two main forms during the later part of Rawls's career.

In its first iteration, the practical worry that exercised Rawls concerned the competing claims of freedom and equality in a democratic society. As a result, he adapted justice as fairness to work out a view of justice

> which is congenial to the most deep-seated convictions and traditions of a modern democratic state. The point of doing this is to see whether we can resolve the impasse in our recent political history; namely, that there is no agreement on the way basic social institutions should be arranged if they are to conform to the freedom and equality of citizens as persons. (*PL*, p. 300)

As this passage suggests, Rawls began to employ the original position as part of what might be called an interpretivist method, where the device is put to work in a program of identifying principles of justice that count as the best overall interpretation of the beliefs, practices, and traditions of modern liberal democracies.

In its second iteration, the basic practical worry that shaped Rawls's revised application of the original position was what he called the fact of reasonable pluralism.[9] This is the idea that a plurality of different conceptions of the good is an enduring feature of any democratic society. This is related to an explanatory claim that Rawls advances, namely that such a plurality exists because of the nature of human reason: when human beings think about the ultimate questions of life (like whether or not there is a god or what the meaning of human life is) they are bound to reach different answers. The questions are hard to answer and human reason is such an imperfect thing that we cannot but arrive at different positions. Provided that there is no state-sanctioned religion which all citizens are forced to profess, this kind of plurality is inevitable. A free society always produces it. But, Rawls wants to stress, many of the doctrines that people formulate are "perfectly reasonable": not only can reason not settle which is of them is correct, but in fact many of these views involve no errors from the standpoint of reason (they involve no errors that a reasonable person would never make).

Along with the shift to interpretivism, Rawls began to describe the original position as a *device of representation*, by which we can take him to mean two things. First, the parties to the agreement are now to be thought of as

---

[9] For some of Rawls's key thoughts about the fact of reasonable pluralism, see *PL* introduction and Lecture I.

representing the interests of others, rather than their own interests. In particular, they represent the interests of citizens who will end up living in a society whose basic institutions are shaped by the principles that the representatives choose. One important effect of this change is that it places much greater stress on the parties being able to justify their choices to the citizens they represent. As we might put it, the parties need to ensure that those they represent would have no reasonable grounds of complaint against them once the principles were chosen.

Second, the original position is a device of representation because it is a theoretical model – it represents our deliberations about justice in a certain way. Here it must be emphasized that Rawls insists that he is not presenting a model of human nature – or moral persons – as such, but rather he is modeling the core features that characterize the citizens of a liberal democracy: their capacity for a conception of the good and their ability to act on the principles of justice. In *JFR*, Rawls tells us that the original position models both our conception of what a fair agreement should look like, and our conception of the kinds of reasons that are "acceptable" as grounds for deciding between competing principles of justice (*JFR*, p. 80).

Rawls's later conception of the original position had many important consequences. But two seem especially worth mentioning. The first is that it enabled Rawls helpfully to clarify a distinction he worked with in *TJ* between the reasonable and the rational. As Rawls later put it, in the original position argument, the reasonable "frames" the rational.[10] I take this to mean that the set-up of the original position is meant to capture our beliefs about what it is reasonable to think about the principles of basic justice and their proper justification, while the deliberations within it are meant to embody a relatively uncontroversial conception of what it is rational for people to decide.

The second consequence – obviously tied to the later Rawls's embrace of interpretivism – is the scaling-down of his ambitions for the original position. We saw that in *TJ* Rawls pictures the original position as an Archimedean point from which the social world can be envisaged from afar, a way of viewing our place in society from the perspective of eternity. With his move to political liberalism, and its consequent insistence on the need to bracket out our particular ethical views of the world, this inspiring vision is apparently, if not left behind, given a secondary status.

---

[10] See *PL*, pp. 48–66.

In the last years of his career, Rawls used a version of the original position to address questions of international justice, where it played a key role in the construction of what Rawls called the law of peoples.[11] Here, a number of innovations are on offer, including picturing the parties as representatives of whole peoples rather than as representatives of individuals.

0.4 The contents of this volume

In the first chapter, David Brink reconstructs and assesses Rawls's contractual argument for his two principles of justice, and in particular, for what Rawls calls the special conception of justice. Brink focuses on the case Rawls makes for his principles over against utilitarianism and so-called mixed conceptions that accept the same prior principles as Rawls (equal basic liberties, fair value of basic liberties, and fair equality of opportunity) but distribute the remaining primary goods according to principles other than the difference principle. Brink distinguishes between Rawls's more modest aim of defending the special conception against traditional forms of utilitarianism and his more ambitious aim of defending it against all plausible rivals, including mixed conceptions. Brink argues for three principal conclusions. First, he holds that Rawls's arguments provide a better fit with his general conception of justice, rather than his special conception, even for the circumstances of moderate scarcity for which Rawls designed the special conception. Second, Brink thinks it is not obviously reasonable for contracting parties to use the maximin rule, and this makes difficulties for Rawls's more modest aim of defending his special conception in preference to unrestricted average utilitarianism. Finally, Brink believes, even if Rawls could defend his more modest claim, he could not defend the more ambitious claim that the special conception should be preferred to all plausible rivals, including various mixed conceptions. In mixed conceptions, prior principles set a decent social minimum below which no one can fall and limit social and economic inequalities above this minimum. This means that even if unrestricted average utilitarianism countenances possible outcomes that are unacceptable to the worst off, mixed utilitarianism does not. Similarly, most forms of sufficientarianism prioritize establishing a decent minimum for all, which means that Rawls's best argument against unrestricted average utilitarianism is not a good argument against sufficientarianism.

[11] See *LP*, pp. 30ff.

In their chapter, Gerald Gaus and John Thrasher argue that what defines the original position arguments of both John Harsanyi and John Rawls is the belief that the justification of principles of justice must be rational from the point of view of some specified set of choosers. They call this the *Fundamental Derivation Thesis*, emphasizing that for Rawls and Harsanyi the original position is a model of rational choice, not a form of counterfactual justification or hypothetical consent. They also emphasize that the original position is not intended to be an epistemological device for identifying true or justified principles. Instead, it is a model that links the rationality of individual choosers with a set of principles evaluated from the moral point of view.

In Chapter 3, Jeremy Waldron takes up Rawls's strains of commitment argument, which, as we have seen, is one of the main planks of the original position derivation of the two principles. Waldron thinks that Rawls is actually on safer ground appealing to the strains of commitment than he is when he relies on the maximin in rule. This is because the parties need to be confident that they will be in a position to honor their losses, as it were, if their gamble turns out badly for them when the veil of ignorance is lifted. This is, as Waldron puts it, a question of gaming *morality* rather than gaming *rationality*. Waldron responds to two important objections to the strains of commitment argument. One he calls the malcontents objection. This says that even under the governance of Rawls's two principles, there will be some people who would have been better off had the principle of average utility been chosen. Perhaps they too will chafe under the strains of commitment. The other worry Waldron calls the model-theoretic objection. In essence, this is the complaint that the strains of commitment argument mistakenly imports features of an abstract choice situation – the original position – into our reasoning about justice in the real world.

Robert Nozick mounted one of the earliest and most subtle critiques of the original position argument and the principles that Rawls claims arose from it, in particular the difference principle. In the fourth chapter, John Christman points out that Nozick wove together several lines of argument both against what he took to be the redistributive policies endorsed by the difference principle and the use of the veil of ignorance – specifically the bracketing of knowledge of persons' "natural endowments" – to justify those policies. In particular, Nozick claimed that Rawls's procedure illegitimately ruled out any "historical" principles of entitlements, such as his own libertarian schema for distributive justice.

Unlike most commentators, Christman focuses directly on Nozick's critique of the original position itself. He suggests that the various strains in

Nozick's critique derive their power from his claim that Rawls illegitimately regarded natural talents as arbitrary from the point of view of a theory of justice. Christman argues that Nozick's claims about arbitrariness are not justifiable and, in fact, depend on a misunderstanding of Rawls's original view. In addition, he suggests that one way to understand the motivation behind Rawls's claims about the arbitrariness of people's personal and social endowments is one that Nozick should embrace, in some form, when his own full theory of distributive justice, including his principles of rectifying unjust transfers, is taken into account.

Given that Rawls's device of the original position uses hypothetical reasoning to identify the demands of justice, in Chapter 5 Matthew Clayton asks why, and in which circumstances, hypothetical choices actually help us to identify justice. Clayton explores Ronald Dworkin's engagement with Rawls on these questions. In his early review of *TJ*, Dworkin argued that Rawls's original position argument for the two principles might be sound, but if it is sound that is because the original position enables us to draw out the implications of every citizen's fundamental right to equal concern and respect. However, in developing his own conception of distributive justice, equality of resources, Dworkin deploys hypothetical reasoning in a different way from Rawls. In his hypothetical insurance scheme, Dworkin allows his hypothetical choosers knowledge of their own view of how to live well as well as knowledge of the society-wide distribution of good and bad luck. This contrasts with Rawls's original position in which representatives are ignorant of their clients' conceptions of the good and of any information about the probability of their clients being burdened by misfortune. Clayton explores the similarities and differences between Rawls's and Dworkin's conceptions of the role of hypothetical reasoning within an account of justice. He seeks to explain the differences between their views of the appropriate hypothetical-choice context for the purposes of identifying justice by reference to the fundamental ideas that animate their respective views of political morality. Dworkin's conception is presented as raising a forceful challenge to Rawls's view, a challenge that defenders of Rawls should confront.

Amy Baehr, in the sixth chapter, suggests that the original position's principles are in reflective equilibrium with some important feminist considered convictions about justice, but not with others. In addition, she thinks, a well-ordered society may well be characterized by significant gender injustices – even those recognized within the original position – because the coercive measures needed to prevent such injustices may be disallowed by other parts of Rawls's theory. Baehr holds that certain feminist uses of the original position (such as that of Susan Okin) better accommodate the feminist considered convictions; but they fail to accommodate feminist concerns about dependency. She asks whether a feminist re-design of the original position could accommodate feminist considered convictions while remaining part of an overall liberal view. Baehr thinks it would be premature to conclude that justice as fairness is a defense of injustice since, insofar as we are contractualists, we may no more assume that the feminist considered convictions are true than assume that Rawls's original position is the correct interpretation of the initial situation. Rather, in the chapter, she takes up Rawls's invitation to engage in the process of reflective equilibrium.

In his chapter, David Estlund explains and critically examines G. A. Cohen's elaborate and illuminating critique of John Rawls's method and conclusions in his theory of justice. Estlund considers three lines of criticism. The first is a formal criticism that Rawls must erroneously deny that there are fact-free foundational principles on which the principles of justice must be grounded. Second comes a substantive criticism of the method of the original position on the ground that it would allow the content of justice to be determined by matters that bear on appropriate social regulation, but not on social justice proper. Finally, Estlund examines a third somewhat underdeveloped suggestion in Cohen that the method of the original position must adapt the principles of justice to fit the case of morally bad facts such as poor motives or behavior.

In Chapter 8, I take up a radical critique of the original position. I show how Rawls's political philosophy is animated by certain key assumptions about history and social theory that radicals can and should contest. Because these deeper assumptions shape our understanding of questions of principle, I treat them in tandem with a substantive dispute between liberals and radicals over the content of constitutional liberties. My aim in the chapter is to use the lens of the original position as a way to scrutinize these important assumptions, in order to bring out their relevance to the principles of justice.

I begin by examining Rawls's original position argument for a set of distinctively liberal freedoms. After this, I interrogate some of the key background stipulations that work to support Rawls's case for those freedoms. I then indicate how radicals can reasonably contest those stipulations, proceeding to show how that contestation would play out in an original position framework more congenial to radicals.

In "Contractualism and utilitarianism," T. M. Scanlon distinguished his moral contractualism from Rawls's social contract theory of justice. In Chapter 9, Joshua Cohen argues for a view like Scanlon's. He argues that it was a mistake for Rawls to model the informal contract idea of a *reasonable agreement* among individuals as a view – which Cohen calls the Rational Advantage Model – about what individuals, under a veil of ignorance, would *rationally choose* to advance their good. In defense of the original position, with its Rational Advantage Model, Rawls says that it is a "device of representation," a representational device that models fair conditions of agreement and acceptable restrictions on reasons for defending principles of justice. Cohen explains why the Rational Advantage Model cannot plausibly be defended simply as a device of representation. Focusing on self-respect and its social bases, he shows how the form of representation – which models arguments about the requirements of justice as arguments about what is good for us – forces on us substantive claims that arguably weaken the arguments it aims to model. In the course of his discussion, Cohen distinguishes two kinds of individualism that we find in contractualist views: *judgmental* and *substantive* individualism. Rawls's Rational Advantage Model embraces a particular form of substantive individualism, as well as judgmental individualism. But in scattered passages in *TJ*, Rawls also suggests a form of contractualism – continuous with Rawls's later notion of public reason – that is judgmentally individualistic, without being substantively individualistic. In the final part of the chapter, Cohen discusses Scanlon's moral contractualism in light of the judgmental/substantive distinction. Scanlon rejects the Rational Advantage Model, but his notion of reasonable rejection does endorse an alternative form of substantive individualism. The chapter ends with some reflections about why this endorsement may not be an advantage of Scanlon's contractualism. Judgmental individualism may be the only individualism we want to preserve at the foundations of our ideas of justice.

In Chapter 10, Andrews Reath explores the Kantian roots of the original position and of justice as fairness more generally. In §40 of *TJ*, Rawls tells us that the original position may be viewed "as a procedural interpretation of Kant's conception of autonomy and the categorical imperative within the framework of an empirical theory." By "Kant's conception of autonomy" Rawls means Kant's thesis that moral principles originate in the rational volition of the agents who are subject to them. In "Kantian Constructivism in Moral Theory," Rawls develops the Kantian basis of justice as fairness in much greater detail, explaining it as a form of Kantian constructivism in which a conception of persons as free and equal moral agents forms the basis of a "procedure of construction" – the choice in the original position – that is used to justify and produce consensus on principles of justice for the basic structure of society. Reath examines both the Kantian basis of the original position and the structural parallels between justice as fairness and Kant's moral conception, with a focus on the ways in which each conception is driven by a certain conception of the person. He provides an overview of Kant's thesis of autonomy (one that to be sure draws on Rawls's own interpretive work on Kant), as well as an overview of the original position that brings out the structural parallels with Kant's categorical imperative, and a brief discussion of ends with *TJ* §40.

In the penultimate chapter, Paul Weithman focuses on the idea that Rawls intended his conception of justice to be *self*-stabilizing. He argues that it is illuminating to think of stability as effected, not by Rawls's *principles* them-selves, but by *the agreement upon them*. More precisely, Weithman suggests, it is illuminating to read Rawls as arguing that justice as fairness would stabilize itself because the agreement reached in the original position is a special kind of "self-enforcing agreement."

One advantage of this reading, according to Weithman, is that it offers a clear and economical way of understanding what it is for a conception to be self-stabilizing. Another advantage is that it allows a precise understanding of Rawls's transition to political liberalism. Rawls said he made the turn to political liberalism because he came to think that the stability arguments of *TJ* failed. Weithman's reading explains that failure as the failure of the agreement reached in the original position to satisfy two of the conditions of self-enforcement. This reading also helps us understand the account of stability that Rawls offered in *PL* by displaying new conditions of self-enforcement and by showing how the later Rawls could maintain that the agreement reached in the original position satisfied them. Finally, Weithman suggests that his interpretation helps to answer the much-controverted question of whether the original position is essential to Rawls's theory. In short, Weith-man holds that it does so by identifying a crucial premise in both of Rawls's accounts of stability that depends upon his reasons for devising the original position construction.

In the final chapter of the volume, Gillian Brock examines Rawls's reliance on original position reasoning to answer important questions about inter-national justice. These include: what kinds of principles should guide liberal peoples in their international affairs, especially when dealing with peoples who are not apparently committed to liberal values? And what responsibilities do affluent developed societies have to those that are poor and developing? Brock shows how Rawls's original position-derived views concerning both duties to address global poverty and how to interact with non-liberal societies contain many deep insights that have not been adequately acknowledged.

1   Justice as fairness, utilitarianism, and mixed conceptions

It would be hard to overstate the philosophical significance of John Rawls's *TJ*.[1] It articulates and defends an egalitarian conception of liberalism and distributive justice that consists of two principles of justice: a principle of equal basic liberties and a principle that distributes social and economic goods and opportunities so as to be to the greatest benefit of the least advantaged. Rawls defends this liberal egalitarian conception of justice primarily as an alternative to utilitarianism.[2] He situates his defense of this liberal egalitarian conception of justice within the social contract tradition by arguing that his principles of distributive justice would be preferred to utilitarianism and other

Thanks to David Estlund, Tim Hinton, Theron Pummer, and Paul Weithman for comments on an earlier draft. I learned much of what I know about the appeal and resources of justice as fairness while I was at MIT in the late 1980s and early 1990s, especially from interactions with John Rawls, Tim Scanlon, Derek Parfit, and my (then) colleague Joshua Cohen. This essay develops ideas in lectures that I gave on justice as fairness during that period, which Tim Hinton attended and discussed with me.

[1] Unless otherwise noted, all references to Rawls will be to *TJ*. The second edition (*TJR*) was published in 1999. Because the section numbering is the same in the two editions, I will refer to *TJ* using section numbers as much as possible. Rawls offers a restatement and reinterpretation of justice as fairness in *JFR*. Though *JFR* corrects *TJ* in places, its main point is to reinterpret justice as fairness as part of a specifically *political* conception of liberalism that aims to justify liberal essentials by identifying an overlapping consensus among different comprehensive religious, moral, and political commitments. This political reinterpretation of justice as fairness seems largely orthogonal to my main concern with the contractual argument for justice as fairness in *TJ*. I will take notice of *JFR* only insofar as it seems to bear directly on the reasoning within the contractual argument.

[2] Rawls also defends justice as fairness against libertarian conceptions of justice. The libertarian conception gives moral significance, as justice as fairness does not, to the morally arbitrary effects of the natural and social lotteries – the distribution of natural talents and of social class and advantage (§§12–13). The argument against libertarian conceptions is an important part of the case for justice as fairness. Nonetheless, Rawls regards utilitarianism as the main rival to justice as fairness, both inside and outside the contractual argument, and the argument against libertarianism is largely a contract-independent argument. So in reconstructing and assessing Rawls's contractual argument for justice as fairness, I will focus on the contrast with utilitarianism, largely ignoring his interesting and important discussion of libertarianism.

rivals by parties to a social contract in which they were represented fairly, that is, as free and equal moral persons. This explains why Rawls calls his conception *justice as fairness* and the importance of the hypothetical *original position* as a way of modeling a fair initial position from which principles of justice might be selected. Rawls thinks not only that justice as fairness would be preferred to utilitarianism in a fair social contract but also that it provides a better reconstruction than utilitarianism of our considered views about individual rights and justice. Though Rawls's primary focus is on the justice of the basic structure of society, his critique of utilitarianism, his contractualist methodology, and his defense of equal basic rights have had much wider philosophical influence, extending to a variety of issues in ethical theory and normative ethics. In this way, the publication of *TJ* transformed and reinvigorated ethics as well as political philosophy.

Any assessment of justice as fairness must address the adequacy of Rawls's contractual argument for his two principles of justice and against utilitarian rivals. In this context it is worth noting that Rawls has two kinds of ambition. On the one hand, he has the substantial but comparatively modest ambition to defend a more egalitarian alternative to utilitarianism. He would succeed in this ambition insofar as parties in the original position would indeed prefer his two principles of justice to traditional utilitarian rivals. On the other hand, Rawls also has the more ambitious aim of showing his two principles of justice to be uniquely plausible, that is, to be superior to all reasonable alternatives. He would succeed in this ambition insofar as parties in the original position would prefer his two principles of justice to any plausible rival. Basically, the more ambitious claim consists in claiming that Rawls's two principles are superior to a greater number of rivals. Of special interest here is the possibility of rivals to Rawls's two principles that differ from traditional forms of utilitarianism (whether classical or average) but nonetheless combine elements of utilitarianism with elements of liberal egalitarianism. Rawls calls these hybrids *mixed* conceptions (*TJ*, §21).

So one question is whether Rawls's contractual argument succeeds against mixed conceptions, as well as against traditional utilitarian conceptions. Of course, the more modest claim that justice as fairness is superior to traditional forms of utilitarianism is a very important claim, whether or not Rawls can support his stronger claim that justice as fairness is uniquely plausible among reasonable alternatives. Moreover, the more modest claim would be positively relevant to establishing the stronger claim. But it is worth noticing that Rawls might succeed in the more modest aim without succeeding in the more ambitious claim if there are other rivals that justice as fairness does not defeat. Rawls himself distinguishes between these two ambitions in the second edition of *TJ*, where he reasserts both ambitions but expresses greater confidence in the more modest comparative claim than in the more ambitious one (*TJR*, p. xiv).[3] It is worth distinguishing these modest and ambitious claims not just to display logical possibilities. In fact, Rawls's ambitious claim turns out to be much harder to justify than the more modest one, and his main contractual arguments for justice as fairness fail to demonstrate that it is uniquely reasonable, whether or not they succeed against more traditional utilitarian rivals.

In section 1.1 I will provide a brief reconstruction of the main elements of justice as fairness. In section 1.2 I will contrast Rawls's general and special conceptions and ask whether something like the general conception isn't a more plausible conception than the special conception, even when we restrict our attention to the circumstances that Rawls thinks justify adoption of the special conception. Then in section 1.3 I will reconstruct and assess Rawls's specifically contractual arguments for his special conception of justice, focusing on the contrast between Rawls's conception and traditional utilitarian principles. In section 1.4 I will focus on the adequacy of Rawls's argument against a larger range of alternatives, including mixed and other conceptions. I will argue that even if Rawls can defend his more modest claim that justice as fairness is superior to traditional utilitarianism, his more ambitious claim that it is superior to mixed conceptions is problematic.

1.1 Justice as fairness: the two principles

One of the most distinctive features of justice as fairness is that Rawls develops an egalitarian conception of social justice that he defends by appeal to a hypothetical social contract, which he claims fits within the social contract tradition of Locke, Rousseau, and Kant. The contractual argument represents the basic structure of society and its provision of liberties, opportunities, and rights as just insofar as it satisfies principles that would be chosen in fair initial conditions in which contracting parties were represented as free and equal moral persons. It is essential to this sort of social contract that the contract be both *hypothetical* and *moralized*. The contractual argument

---

[3] Similarly, in Part III of *JFR* Rawls distinguishes two "fundamental comparisons," which correspond to the moderate and ambitious claims respectively. Though he still thinks that justice as fairness is superior to both unrestricted average utilitarianism and restricted average utilitarianism, he is more confident about the first comparison than the second.

requires Rawls to specify (a) fair initial contractual circumstances and (b) the principles that would be chosen in these circumstances.

We might begin with a preliminary specification of the principles that Rawls thinks would be chosen in this hypothetical contract. We will discuss issues introduced by Rawls's distinction between general and special conceptions of justice later (section 1.2 below). But his primary focus is on the circumstances of justice faced by societies in conditions of moderate scarcity in which there is sufficient economic development and security to make possible a decent minimum standard of living for all (§26). For these conditions, Rawls defends what he calls the special conception of justice, which consists of two main principles (§§11, 46):

1 Each person is to have an equal right to the most extensive total system of equal basic liberties compatible with a similar system of liberty for all [equal basic liberties].
2 Social and economic inequalities are to be arranged so that they are both (a) to the greatest benefit of the least advantaged, consistent with the just savings principle, [the difference principle] and (b) attached to offices and positions open to all under conditions of fair equality of opportunity [fair equality of opportunity].

The currency of distributive justice for utilitarians is utility or well-being. For others, it is resources, or capabilities, or income. For Rawls the currency of distributive justice is *primary goods* – maximally flexible assets that it is supposed to be rational to want whatever else one wants (§15). Rawls adopts primary goods as the currency of distributive justice so as to avoid traditional worries about the basis for interpersonal comparisons of utility and to make the public deployment of his conception of justice easier, involving less complex calculations. Rawls understands primary goods to include rights and liberties, opportunities and powers, income and wealth, and the social bases of self-respect (cf. *JFR*, §17).

Notice that the three component principles here regulate the distribution of different goods: the equal basic liberties principle regulates basic liberties; the fair equality of opportunity principle regulates opportunities; and the difference principle regulates other kinds of social goods, including income.

The equal liberties principle concerns specific basic liberties, such as freedom of expression, conscience, religion, and association, rather than liberty *per se*. Insofar as liberties are prior to other primary goods, the most extensive system of equal liberty would lead to a form of libertarianism that would not permit restrictions on liberty to prevent harm or nuisance. Because this is not Rawls's claim, he must be concerned with specific liberties that seem fundamental.[4] The first principle concerns those liberties relevant to the two primary capacities of citizens in a well-ordered society: (a) their sense of justice and (b) their interest in pursuing a conception of the good. Presumably, this includes liberties of thought, expression, and association, and political liberties, such as the right to vote, to campaign, and to run for office (cf. *JFR*, §13).

Rawls's considered statement of the second principle emerges from a comparison of different interpretations of the more general idea that there be equality of opportunity and that any inequalities be to the advantage of all (§§12–13). Here Rawls describes a natural progression through several conceptions motivated by the idea that the terms of social cooperation should not make some worse off than they would otherwise be as the result of factors over which they have no control. This principle gives rise to worries about the system of natural liberty that combines laissez-faire with the idea that careers should be open to talents. The moral arbitrariness of the social lottery should force us to recognize the ways in which the idea of equal opportunity should constrain the unfettered accumulation of wealth across generations. But the same principle should make us skeptical of the system of liberal equality that allows unearned natural talents to determine a person's social and economic prospects. The correct interpretation of opportunity and equality, Rawls thinks, should lead us to treat the distribution of natural talents as a common asset and insist on a conception of equality of opportunity that aims for reasonable accommodation of differences in native endowment.

The difference principle does treat the distribution of natural talents as a common asset (cf. *JFR*, §21). Robert Nozick believes that this implies that the community has property rights in the talents and powers of individuals, so that the community could compel talented individuals to work on the community's terms.[5] But Nozick's criticism seems to conflate the following distinct ideas:

1 I am entitled to possess my natural endowments, though they are unearned.
2 I am entitled to exercise my natural endowments (in acceptable ways).
3 I am entitled to benefit from the exercise of my natural endowments (assuming they are productively employed).
4 I am entitled to the benefits that accrue from my exercise of my natural endowments in an unregulated market.

---

[4] See Hart, "Rawls."   [5] Nozick, *ASU*, pp. 225, 229.

Rawls does not deny (1)–(3), only (4). Another way to see this involves distinguishing between rights of self-ownership and rights of worldly owner-ship, which we get from the Lockean tradition that Nozick embraces. Rawls does not think that the moral arbitrariness of the natural lottery raises questions about the rights of self-ownership of the talented, as Nozick seems to assume. Rather, Rawls thinks that the arbitrariness of the natural lottery affects the rules by which the talented can generate property rights in the world from the productive employment of the talents in which they have rights of self-ownership.

Rawls identifies two kinds of priority in his special conception of justice. The first principle is lexically prior to the second, so that liberty can only be restricted for the sake of liberty and the other goods cannot be distributed in ways that upset the demand for equal basic liberties. Moreover, the second part of the second principle is lexically prior to the first part, so that other social goods, including income, cannot be distributed in ways that upset fair equality of opportunity. Elsewhere, Rawls mentions another principle, which he calls the fair value of political liberties (§36). His idea here is to distinguish between the existence of a political right or liberty and its worth or value, where its worth or value can be affected by one's absolute or comparative level of resources. We might have equal rights to make private expenditures on political campaigns, but this right will be of very unequal value to the rich and the poor. Rawls thinks we have compelling reason to care about the value of these political liberties. He does not insist on maintaining the equal value of basic political liberties, only on prohibiting unfair inequalities in their value. Rawls seems to think that ensuring the fair value of basic political liberties should be part of the priority of the first principle. Notice that Rawls refers to this principle as the fair value of *political* liberties. Since it is not clear why the concern with the worth of liberty should be restricted to political liberties, I will assume that it should be extended to all of the basic liberties.

If we were to display the components of Rawls's special conception in a way that distinguishes different claims and reflects their priority relations, we might do it this way:

1 equal basic liberties;
2 fair value of basic liberties;
3 fair equality of opportunity;
4 the difference principle.

Rawls offers two very different kinds of defense of this conception of justice. He takes utilitarianism to be the chief rival to his more egalitarian conception of justice. Some of Rawls's arguments are arguments of overall comparative plausibility, independent of the contract argument. Some of these contract-independent arguments are quite powerful and have proved influential. But Rawls's most distinctive arguments are contractual arguments that his principles of justice would be preferred to utilitarian rivals in the right sort of hypothetical moralized contract. Before focusing on these contractual arguments, it might be worth identifying some of the contract-independent arguments.

Utilitarianism, Rawls thinks, extends the decision procedure appropriate for intrapersonal contexts to interpersonal contexts. In doing so, it treats different lives as if they were parts of a single life, in which it makes sense to make individual sacrifices for the good of the whole. But whereas intra-personal aggregation and sacrifice are acceptable, interpersonal aggregation and sacrifice fail to take seriously the separateness of persons. This is why utilitarianism has trouble recognizing individual rights, which trump utilitarian reasoning. In contrast with utilitarianism, justice as fairness places a limit on the sacrifices that some might have to make in order to improve the position of others and so recognizes rights as inviolable (§§5–6).

This is a complex and striking argument for Rawls's liberal egalitarianism that deserves and has received extensive discussion elsewhere.[6] In describing this as a contract-independent argument, I don't mean to imply that it couldn't play some role within his contractual argument. For instance, the critique of utilitarianism could enter into the contractual argument for Rawls's two principles insofar as it might bear on the comparative strains of commitment and stability of rival schemes that contractors must assess (§§29, 76). My point is only that this critique of utilitarianism does not depend for its force on the contractual argument; it affects the overall comparative plausibility of Rawls's conception and utilitarian conceptions.

This brings us to Rawls's contractual argument for his liberal egalitarian conception of justice. The general form of the contractual argument is well known. Because the contract proceeds from a fair initial situation in which contractors are represented as free and equal moral persons, the bargaining situation is hypothetical and shaped by considerations of fairness. In particu-lar, Rawls appeals to an *original position* that excludes factors that seem arbitrary from the moral point of view or that might be used to select principles favoring one group at the expense of another (§20). Parties in the

---

[6] See e.g. Brink, "The Separateness."

original position are placed behind a *veil of ignorance*, which deprives them of information about their identities and attributes, including their identity, gender, race and ethnicity, social class, level of social capital, generation, natural talents, attitude toward risk, and conception of the good (§24).

The deficits that the contracting parties operate under may make one wonder if they have the basis for preferring any principles and outcomes to others. However, the parties do have positive characteristics. They are mutually disinterested, but concerned to advance their own prospects; they use primary goods, which are maximally flexible social assets, to measure their prospects; they evaluate representative social positions, rather than individual lives; they display instrumental, means–ends, rationality; and they have general social knowledge about the forms of social, political, and economic organization (§§11, 24, 25).

The negative and positive attributes of the contracting parties combine to yield the following sort of choice situation:

> Knowing all of the possible representative social positions that she might occupy in all possible societies at all possible points in time, a contractor should choose principles of justice that set terms of social cooperation that will best promote her stock of primary goods.

It is important to recognize that the original position is not supposed to be a description of how people actually are. It is an analytical device in which the characteristics of parties, considered together, represent a fair contractual situation such that any principles chosen in those circumstances to regulate the basic structure of society would be just. The parties in the original position do not represent Rawls's picture of human nature; their characteristics are not intended to be descriptive individually or collectively. Together, the attributes of the contracting parties are supposed to model impartial and fair choice.

The opacity of the veil of ignorance appears to imply that it makes no difference to the contractual choice who the parties are. All parties, qua parties to the contract, would appear to be in the same position. This is why Rawls claims that the choice in the original position can be represented as a problem in individual decision theory under special circumstances, rather than as a contract or bargain among several parties with potentially conflicting interests (§§4, 20, 24).

Though the parties are not making a moral choice, they realize the point of their exercise and assess the consequences of alternative principles by considering their application in a well-ordered society (§§1, 69). In a *well-ordered society*, citizens have a sense of justice and a higher-order interest in pursuing their conception of the good, whatever it turns out to be, once the veil of ignorance is lifted. Moreover, principles must satisfy a *publicity* condition, according to which the principles are recognized publicly as establishing standards of just institutional design and citizens actually assess their institutions in private and public fora by measuring their conformity to these principles (§§1, 23). Publicity, Rawls believes, imposes constraints of *stability* and *practicality* (§24).

Rawls is committed to the claim that the contracting parties will prefer his special conception of justice to utilitarian rivals. This is because utilitarianism, Rawls thinks, does not provide enough assurance against bad luck and exploitation by others. By contrast, Rawls's two principles insure against both bad luck and exploitation. Later, we will examine and assess the details of this contractual argument. But perhaps this gives us a clear enough general picture to raise some questions about the principles that Rawls thinks would be chosen in the original position.

1.2 Special and general conceptions

So far, we have accepted Rawls's focus on the *special conception*, which applies in societies above a certain developmental threshold, at which point Rawls thinks individuals care more for marginal increases in basic liberties than for marginal increases in social and economic goods. Below this developmental threshold, Rawls endorses the *general conception*, which basically distributes all goods according to the difference principle (§§11, 26, 46):

> All social primary goods – liberty and opportunity, income and wealth, and the bases of self-respect – are to be distributed equally unless an unequal distribution of any or all of these goods is to the advantage of the least favored. (*TJ*, p. 303)[7]

Notice that the special conception differs from the general conception in two ways. First, it treats the distribution of some goods as lexically prior to others. Second, the special conception applies different distributional principles to these different goods: it insists on an equal distribution for liberties, fair value for the worth of basic (political) liberties, and fair equality for opportunities, while requiring that other goods be distributed according to the difference

---

[7] Notice that this statement of the general conception does not explicitly require maximizing the position of the worst off, as the difference principle does.

principle. These two points of disagreement are independent of each other and should be assessed separately.

Rawls's rationale for the special conception is based on the priority that he imagines contractors would assign to basic liberties once a certain threshold of material well-being was assured. But this claim about the priority of liberty supports at most the first difference between special and general conceptions. It does not support different distributional principles for the different goods. In particular, Rawls thinks that it is irrational for contracting parties to prefer equality to the difference principle when considering other primary goods (*TJ*, p. 151). But, if so, why not extend this reasoning to all the primary goods, while respecting the priorities that Rawls sees among them? No matter which primary goods we are talking about, it is not clear why contracting parties should prefer an equal distribution of those goods if there is an unequal distribution that makes everyone better off.

Recall that we said that when we factor in Rawls's priority rules, we can see that the two principles that constitute the special conception are equivalent to the following ordered quartet:

1 equal basic liberties;
2 fair value of basic liberties;
3 fair equality of opportunity;
4 the difference principle.

Perhaps we should give liberties lexical priority over opportunities and other goods but distribute each by the difference principle. This would yield something like the following conception, which we might call the *extraspecial conception*:

1 difference principle for basic liberties;
2 difference principle for the value of basic liberties;
3 difference principle for opportunities;
4 difference principle for all other primary goods.

If Rawls has good reason to prefer the special conception to the general conception for circumstances of moderate scarcity, then perhaps he has good reason to prefer the extraspecial conception to the special conception.

Like the special conception, the extraspecial conception claims that in circumstances of moderate scarcity there should be strict priorities among different kinds of primary goods. But should we accept that claim? If there is a preference, above a certain threshold, for liberties over opportunities or other primary goods, surely it is not a lexical preference. Even if I wouldn't trade increases in basic liberties one-for-one with increases in other primary goods, surely I might prefer large increases in other primary goods to small increases in basic liberties? I might prefer to live much more comfortably, even if this would be purchased at a very small cost in my personal or political liberty. But if we reject both Rawls's egalitarianism about liberties and opportunities (thus accepting the extraspecial conception in preference to the special conception) and his lexical priority rules, the result is something closer to the general conception, even for societies above the material threshold.

This is significant in itself inasmuch as we want to be clear about which principles Rawls should take his arguments to support. It is also potentially significant in assessing his more ambitious claim to defend his principles in preference to mixed conceptions, because the general conception is relevantly like a form of consequentialism in which priority is given to the worse off.

1.3 The contractual argument for the special conception

Why does Rawls think that the contracting parties would choose his special conception of justice in relation to utilitarianism and other alternatives? He presents the details of the contractual argument against traditional utilitarianism and in favor of the special conception in Chapter 3 (esp. §§26–9; cf. *JFR*, §§27–40). But he is committed to thinking that the parties have reason to prefer the special conception not just to utilitarianism but to mixed conceptions as well (§49).

One obstacle to comparing justice as fairness with utilitarianism and other rivals in the original position is that some of these rivals employ different metrics for assessing distributions from Rawls's preferred metric of primary goods. Utilitarians assess distributions of utility or welfare, which would themselves be measured differently according to different conceptions of well-being. Other theories assess distributions of resources, opportunities, and functioning. We might focus on the difference between primary goods and utility. The principle of diminishing marginal utility claims that as a person increases her consumption of a given resource the marginal utility of additional units of that resource decreases. That principle ensures that distributions of primary goods and other resources do not in general reflect distributions of utility. This makes certain kinds of comparison between utilitarianism and Rawls's principle difficult. But we can try to finesse this problem by focusing on distributions of primary goods in which we stipulate that these figures also represent equivalent differences in utility.

Table 1.1

	A	B	C	D
D1	5	5	5	
D2	4	4	4	4

Within the contractual argument, Rawls takes utilitarianism to be the main rival to justice as fairness. We must distinguish between *classical utilitarianism*, which tells agents to maximize total happiness, and *average utilitarianism*, which tells agents to maximize average or per capita happiness.

Assume that D1 and D2 are two different possible distributions (see Table 1.1) and that A–D represent representative social positions, each of which has the same number of members (and D has no members in D1). Whereas classical utilitarianism endorses D2, because it has the highest total utility, average utilitarianism endorses D1, because it has the highest average utility. The contracting parties would prefer average to classical utilitarianism, because it maximizes their expected prospects (*TJ*, pp. 163–4).

Intuitively, Rawls's argument against average utilitarianism and in favor of justice as fairness is that choosing the latter represents a more reasonable attitude to adopt toward risk in one's life prospects. But this simplifies a more complex argument.

Rawls claims that for conditions of moderate scarcity the parties would prefer his two principles (the special conception) over both average utilitarianism and mixed conceptions. In arguing against mixed conceptions, he assumes that we have already satisfied the prior principles (equal basic liberties, fair value of political liberties, and fair equality of opportunity) and argues that the parties would then choose the difference principle over a mixed conception employing average utilitarianism in the role that justice as fairness assigns to the difference principle. If justice as fairness is superior to such a mixed utilitarian conception, then a fortiori it will be superior to unrestricted average utilitarianism.

Rawls makes this case by contrasting two decision rules: the *maximin* rule that instructs one to make the worst outcome as good as possible and the rule of *maximizing expected utility*. These two decision rules will evaluate possible distributions differently.

Assume again that the matrix in Table 1.2 represents possible distributions of both primary goods and utility (circumstances in which the two coincide) among three representative groups. The question is whether parties should

Table 1.2

	A	B	C
D1	10	15	20
D2	12	13	15
D3	5	15	26

maximize expected utility, gambling that they will be one of the better off in D1 or D3, or whether they should minimize risk and ensure the best worst-case scenario by choosing D2. Maximin supports adoption of the difference principle, and the principle of maximizing expected utility supports adoption of average utilitarianism.

Rawls says there are three conditions that favor the use of maximin, though it is not entirely clear whether they are supposed to be individually or jointly sufficient for this purpose (§26; cf. *JFR*, §28):

1 ignorance of the probabilities of the various outcomes;
2 a conception of the good such that one cares little, if anything, for what one might gain above a certain minimum;
3 alternative decision rules have possible outcomes that would be unacceptable.

It seems crucial to Rawls's argument that these three conditions are satisfied or approximated in the original position. So, in assessing this argument, we should distinguish two kinds of issue: whether these conditions, individually or collectively, favor maximin, and whether these conditions are satisfied or approximated in the original position in an appropriate way.

Consider (1). Standard decision theory distinguishes decisions under three different epistemic conditions:

A *Certainty* in which the probability of the outcome is 1 on a scale of 0–1.
B *Risk* in which the probability of the outcome is fixed but less than 1 or in which there is a probability space (e.g. 0.5–0.6).
C *Uncertainty* or *ignorance* in which there is no determinate information about the probability of the outcome.

Standard decision theory identifies rational decision-making with maximizing expected utility. This is straightforward in contexts of certainty – prefer more utility to less. It is also the conventional view of rational decision-making in contexts of risk. For instance, one should prefer 1/3 chance of 100 utiles to a 1/2 chance of 50 utiles to a 1/1 chance of 20 utiles. However, it is usually thought that rational decision-making is impossible or undefined for uncertainty or ignorance. Under such circumstances, the principle of maximizing expected utility has no application.

Rawls recognizes that maximin is not normally a rational decision rule (*TJ*, p. 153). If we adopted it generally, we would never take risks, no matter how low their probability or how great the possible payoff. He does not advocate using maximin in conditions of certainty or risk. But he does seem to think that maximin might sometimes be rational under uncertainty.

This is part of what makes it important that the choice in original position is supposed to be under uncertainty. John Harsanyi thought that contracting parties should assume that the various possible outcomes were equiprobable. If we make this assumption about the original position, then the choice in original position becomes a decision under risk.[8] So understood, Harsanyi argued, parties should employ the principle of maximizing expected utility and should therefore adopt average utilitarianism. However, Rawls understands the choice in the original position as one involving uncertainty, rather than risk. The contractors are not supposed to have knowledge or even beliefs about the comparative likelihood that they will occupy various representative social positions or historical circumstances. Rawls is right insofar as he claims that the argument for average utilitarianism is undermined if the choice in the original position is one under uncertainty, rather than risk.

But that leaves two potential gaps in Rawls's argument. First, even if it is not rational to employ the principle of maximizing expected utility under conditions of uncertainty, it does not follow that maximin is uniquely rational. Perhaps rationality is just undefined in these circumstances. Certainly, further argument is required to show that maximin is uniquely rational under uncertainty. Second, there is the question of whether the original position should be modeled in terms of uncertainty or risk, such as equiprobability. We might claim that insofar as our task is to model what principles free and equal persons would choose to govern the basic structure of their society we should represent the various possible outcomes and our roles in them as equally probable. Similarly, if we thought that the point of the original position was to represent members of society impartially, we might argue that this would be best achieved by asking them to treat outcomes as equally likely, whoever they turned out to be when the veil of ignorance was lifted. To block these utilitarian arguments, Rawls needs to provide a more

[8] Harsanyi, "Morality."

satisfactory rationale for claiming that fairness requires uncertainty, rather than equiprobability. Perhaps he could make use of his idea that fairness requires excluding from the original position information that could be used to form coalitions that might disadvantage some at the expense of others. But the flip side of excluding information that can be used to advantage some at the expense of others is excluding information that might prevent some from holding others hostage to their own benefit. Again, I think, the demands of fairness here are unclear.

Now consider condition (2), which stipulates that one cares little, if anything, for what one might gain above a certain minimum. As it stands, (2) does not help the case for maximin. The conception of the good must exhibit a marginal utility threshold above which one cares very little or nothing for further increments in primary goods, and – importantly – this utility threshold must be at or below the minimum that maximin would secure. If the utility threshold is above the minimum that maximin would secure, then the utility threshold won't favor maximin over maximizing expected utility. Moreover, it is not enough that above this threshold one cares less for further increments in primary goods; above this threshold, one must care absolutely nothing for further increments of primary goods. So the assumption that Rawls really needs is something like this:

2′ A conception of the good such that one cares nothing at all for increments above the highest minimum that one might receive.

In questioning Rawls's priority rules in the special conception, we have already suggested that this claim is extreme.

This poses two problems for Rawls. First, it is no surprise that this conception of the good would support maximin. If the original position were to build this assumption in, the contractual argument would be circular – we would be deriving maximin from a version of the original position that presupposes maximin. Second, Rawls stipulates that contracting parties do not know their conception of the good (*TJ*, pp. 18 and 137). A fortiori they do not know that they have this peculiar conception of the good.

The first two rationales for maximin are not very compelling. So let's consider (3)'s claim that alternative decision rules have possible outcomes that are unacceptable. This is perhaps Rawls's strongest rationale for use of maximin in the original position (*JFR*, §29). His idea seems to be that the stakes here are extremely high, because they concern one's life prospects. We accept certain risks and take gambles where the stakes are smaller and where we can absorb losses fairly easily. But as the stakes become greater,

Rawls reasons, it is harder to accept unnecessary risk. If one takes an unnecessary risk when the stakes concern one's life prospects then losses become unacceptable. Rawls seems to think that it will seem even more unacceptable to lose a gamble when there was a less risky alternative available. For example, if one gambles that one will be a master in the course of embracing the permissibility of slavery, when the option of prohibiting slavery was available, then the prospect of becoming a slave will be unacceptable or unbearable. So the idea is that in the selection of life prospects the cost of losing a gamble that one ends up as one of the Haves and turns out instead to be a Have Not is not just bad but unacceptable, especially when one could have employed maximin and ensured that the worst-case scenario was least bad. Since the contractual choice in the original position is precisely a selection of principles governing life prospects, this favors maximin, rather than maximizing expected average utility.

Though Rawls is right to call attention to the high stakes involved in the choice in the original position, this rationale for maximin is problematic. For one thing, the high stakes cut two ways. Not only is there more to lose in a gamble, but there is also more to gain. Moreover, maximin appears not to be a reasonable attitude toward risk, even when some losses are catastrophic. Suppose that I suffer from a condition that involves significant, persistent pain but that my life is otherwise worth living and valuable. Suppose, moreover, that I can have surgery performed to relieve my pain that has an extremely high success rate. Nonetheless, surgery always carries a small risk of catastrophic outcomes of various kinds. It doesn't seem reasonable to forgo the kind of surgical treatment that offers a very good chance of significant relief on the ground that some possible outcomes of the procedure are catastrophic. The risk of catastrophic outcomes that are possible but unlikely is not always or even usually unacceptable, certainly not *ex ante*.

Finally, notice that Rawls writes as if there are only two options – maximizing expected average utility in a way that tolerates considerable risk if the gains are great enough and maximin. But, of course, maximin forbids nearly all risk-taking. So it rules out not only risking catastrophic outcomes but also outcomes that are risky but where the risk is limited in various ways. It is hard to see how that degree of aversion to risk could be the product of choice in the original position unless the parties are stipulated to be highly averse to risk. But that would beg the question against less extremely risk-averse principles and would, in any case, be inconsistent with Rawls's insistence that contracting parties should be ignorant of their individual attitudes to risk (*TJ*, p. 137).

1.4 The comparison with mixed and other conceptions

This last point is relevant to assessing Rawls's more ambitious claim to provide a contractual justification of his two principles (the special conception) not just in relation to unrestricted average utilitarianism but also in relation to other possible conceptions of justice, including mixed conceptions. Recall that in the special conception of justice as fairness the difference principle is posterior to three prior principles:

1 equal basic liberties;
2 fair value of basic liberties;
3 fair equality of opportunity;
4 the difference principle.

According to the special conception, the difference principle distributes other primary goods only after and in ways constrained by the equal basic liberties, the fair value of basic liberties, and the fair equality of opportunity.

Mixed conceptions are conceptions of justice that differ from Rawls's special conception only with respect to (4). In other words, mixed conceptions must also respect these prior principles, (1)–(3). But that means we need to distinguish two different sorts of utilitarian rivals to Rawls's own special conception: (a) unrestricted average utilitarianism, which does not recognize any prior principles that constrain the maximization of expected average utility, and (b) a mixed conception, which we might call *mixed utilitarianism*, which enjoins us to maximize expected average utility in ways constrained by the three prior principles. For comparison, mixed utilitarianism would embrace this ordered quartet:

1 equal basic liberties;
2 fair value of basic liberties;
3 fair equality of opportunity;
4 average utilitarianism.

Of course, mixed utilitarianism is only one kind of mixed conception.

These distinctions are important, because Rawls's clearest contractual argument against utilitarianism works at most against unrestricted average utilitarianism. This is his argument that in the original position contractors should be loath to take the risks involved in maximizing expected average utility, because possible outcomes can be completely unacceptable. The example he gives is that it is conceivable that a slave society might maximize average utility and that we might end up as slaves in such a society once the veil of ignorance was lifted (*TJ*, pp. 156 and 167–8). Though the principle of diminishing marginal utility makes it very unlikely that a system of slavery would maximize average utility, perhaps the conceptual possibility that it might is reason enough to condemn average utilitarianism. But, of course, slavery would violate the equal basic liberties principle. Because slavery would violate a prior principle, mixed utilitarianism would necessarily prohibit these social arrangements. More generally, the prior principles constrain permissible social and economic inequalities in significant ways. Inequalities in primary goods that would affect the equal provision of basic liberties, their fair value, or fair equality of opportunity are ruled out by mixed utilitarianism. Exactly how big a substantive constraint the prior principles impose is an interesting and complex issue about which there can be reasonable disagreement. But if we think about the way in which significant differences in wealth can compromise fair equality of opportunity at a time or across generations, it seems likely that these prior principles will significantly constrain permissible social and economic inequality. Prior principles will likely both set a threshold below which people cannot fall and significantly constrain possible inequalities among people above that threshold. But then prior principles limit the amount and extent of gambling that mixed utilitarianism might countenance. If so, it is much harder to make out that contracting parties should prefer Rawls's special conception to mixed utilitarianism, because it is hard to see mixed utilitarianism tolerating outcomes that are genuinely unacceptable.

Rawls came to recognize that the argument against unrestricted average utilitarianism does not work against mixed utilitarianism, which ensures against possible outcomes that are unacceptable (*JFR*, §§27–34). He would later argue against mixed utilitarianism and in favor of his special conception by appeal to the social bases of self-respect, reciprocity, publicity, and stability (*JFR*, §§34–8). [9] But these arguments are largely independent of the contractual argument, and even Rawls recognized that they are not decisive (*JFR*, §40). It is not clear why the social bases of self-respect and reciprocity are not addressed by the prior principles that demand equal basic liberties, the fair value of basic liberties, and fair equality of opportunity. Indeed, one might wonder whether guaranteed distributional minima beyond those contained in the prior principles are fully compatible with a culture of mutual respect and reciprocity. It is hard to see how mixed utilitarianism undermines publicity

---

[9] Also see Cohen, "Democratic Equality."

any more than the special conception. While it is true that mixed utilitarianism may allow greater dispersion of income than the special conception, it severely limits permissible dispersion. So it is not obvious that mixed utilitarianism generates troublesome strains of commitment. Moreover, we must remember that precisely because it further constrains income dispersion, beyond that required by the prior principles, the special conception may give rise to its own strains of commitment among those whose life prospects would have been better had the basic structure not been required (by the difference principle) to provide guaranteed minima above those required by the prior principles. More generally, Rawls faces a challenge here explaining why these values (self-respect, reciprocity, publicity, and stability) require more constraints on economic dispersion than the substantial constraints guaranteed by mixed conceptions but fewer constraints than those imposed by an equal distribution. It's hard to see how so much could hang on threading that needle.

We might compare mixed utilitarianism with other conceptions that are structurally similar. One such mixed conception is *sufficientarianism*. Sufficientarianism focuses not on securing equality, as such, or giving priority to the worst off, as such, but rather on ensuring that people fare *well enough*.[10] There are different ways of articulating sufficientarianism, but the central idea is to recognize a *moral asymmetry, relative to some threshold level of welfare* such that all else being equal the urgency of benefits below the threshold is greater than the urgency of benefits above the threshold. Different sufficientarian conceptions will specify the threshold differently and will have to weight and combine independent variables, such as a beneficiary's distance from the threshold, the size of the benefit to be conferred, and the number of similarly situated people that can be benefitted. However these details are spelled out, sufficientarian views will disagree with Rawls's special conception and, in particular, the difference principle. All else being equal, they will prioritize benefits to the worst off but only up until the point of sufficiency. On some sufficientarian views, there might be no special concern for the worst off above the sufficiency threshold. Perhaps above that threshold, we should maximize expected average utility. Provided that the threshold established by this form of sufficientarianism is sufficiently close to the baseline established by the prior principles, this form of sufficientarianism might be quite similar to mixed utilitarianism.[11]

---

[10] See, for example, Frankfurt, "Equality"; Crisp, "Equality, Priority"; and Shields, "The Prospects." For some skepticism, see Arneson, "Distributive Justice" and Casal, "Why Sufficiency."

[11] Cf. Waldron, "John Rawls."

This and other forms of sufficientarianism provide a response to Rawls's appeal to the unacceptability of possible outcomes in his argument against average utilitarianism and in favor of the special conception. Even if that was a good argument against unrestricted average utilitarianism, it would not support the special conception, because there are other ways of ensuring against worst-case outcomes that don't require committing to the difference principle. Moreover, because the prior principles insure against many intolerable outcomes, there are also mixed conceptions, such as mixed utilitarianism, that provide viable contractualist alternatives to the special conception.

1.5 Concluding remarks

We should distinguish between Rawls's justificatory appeal to a hypothetical moralized contract to derive principles of justice and his claim that such a contract uniquely favors his form of liberal egalitarianism, enshrined in the special conception of justice as fairness. There is reason to be skeptical of Rawls's own principles. First, Rawlsian arguments might provide a better fit with his general conception of justice, rather than his special conception, even for the circumstances of moderate scarcity for which he designed the special conception. Second, it is not clear that it is reasonable for contracting parties to employ maximin, which raises questions about Rawls's more modest aim of defending his special conception in preference to traditional utilitarianism, in particular, unrestricted average utilitarianism. Third, even if Rawls could defend this more modest claim, he could not defend the more ambitious claim that the special conception should be preferred to all plausible rivals, including various mixed conceptions. In mixed conceptions, prior principles set a decent social minimum below which no one can fall and limit social and economic inequalities above this minimum. This means that even if unrestricted average utilitarianism countenances possible outcomes that are unacceptable to the worst off, mixed utilitarianism does not. Similarly, most forms of sufficientarianism prioritize establishing a decent minimum for all, which means that Rawls's best argument against unrestricted average utilitarianism is not a good argument against sufficientarianism.

This skepticism about Rawls's contractual defense of justice as fairness against utilitarianism and mixed conceptions should not obscure the philosophical significance of justice as fairness. In particular, even if this skepticism is correct, Rawls's defense of liberal egalitarianism could proceed in one of two ways. One could eschew the contractual argument and rely on contract-independent arguments to criticize utilitarianism and defend his special conception. Alternatively, one could maintain the contractual argument and its appeal to the original position and explore more fully just which principles of justice that supports, paying greater attention to the merits of sufficientarianism and mixed conceptions.

2 Rational choice and the original position: the (many) models of Rawls and Harsanyi

Gerald Gaus and John Thrasher

2.1 The original position and rational justification

2.1.1 The Fundamental Derivation Thesis

At the outset of *TJ* Rawls closely links the theory of justice to the theory of rational choice:

> one conception of justice is more reasonable than another, or justifiable with respect to it, if rational persons in the initial situation would choose its principles over those of the other for the role of justice. Conceptions of justice are to be ranked by the acceptability to persons so circumstanced. Understood in this way the question of justification is settled by working out a problem of deliberation: we have to ascertain which principles it would be rational to adopt given the contractual situation. This connects the theory of justice with the theory of rational choice. (*TJR*, p. 16)

Indeed, Rawls proclaims that "*the theory of justice is part, perhaps the most significant part, of the theory of rational choice*" (*TJR*, p. 15, emphasis added; see section 2.2.3 below). Many have refused to take this claim literally (or even seriously), by, for example, interpreting the original position analysis as a heuristic for identifying independently true moral principles (see Dworkin, "Original Position," p. 19 and Barry, *Theories*, pp. 271–82). In this chapter we take this fundamental claim of Rawls at face value. We thus shall defend:

> *The Fundamental Derivation Thesis*: the justification of a principle of justice *J* derives from the conclusion that, under conditions *C*, *J* is the rational choice of chooser(s) *P*.

On the Fundamental Derivation Thesis that *J* is the rational choice of *P* under *C* is neither *evidence* that *J* is the correct principle nor a way of us *appreciating* or *seeing* that *J* is just. Rather *J*'s justification is derivative of *J*'s status as *P*'s rational choice; moral justification derives from justification qua rational choice. Notice that we do not say that *J*'s justification is *entirely* derivative of rational choice justification, for the set of the conditions C under which the choice is made (including those that identify the feasible choice set) also has justificatory relevance.

The Fundamental Derivation Thesis also sets aside the interpretation of the original position as fundamentally justifying through appeal to hypothetical consent. Consent is not, strictly speaking, ever a concern for Rawls or for any original position theorist. When Rawls tell us that his "aim [is] to present a conception of justice which generalizes and carries to a higher level of abstraction the familiar theory of the social contract" (*TJR*, p. 10), we should not read him as saying that because J *would* be the object of consent by P under C, J *is* justified. At most, insofar as we might be tempted to read *any* claims about hypothetical consent into an original position argument (and we certainly need not), the relevant claim would be that the demonstration that J *would* be the object of consent by P under C shows that J *is* the rational choice of P, and it is this latter claim that is truly justificatory. Rawls never says that the theory of justice is part of the theory of rational consent. Henceforth we shall entirely set aside questions of consent.

2.1.2 The attraction of the Fundamental Derivation Thesis

Our aim in this chapter is not to defend the Fundamental Derivation Thesis as a philosophic commitment in theorizing about justice, but rather to show how the two most famous original position arguments – those of John Rawls and John Harsanyi – seek to follow through on it in their justifications. Nevertheless, unless the reader has at least some appreciation of the thesis's appeal, the exercise might seem pointless.

It is essential to appreciate that the Fundamental Derivation Thesis is part of a view of moral enquiry according to which models such as the original position are not epistemological, helping us to find "moral truth interpreted as fixed by a prior and independent order of objects and relations"; the original position is part of "the search for reasonable grounds for reaching agreement rooted in our conception of ourselves and our relation to society. The task is to articulate a public conception of justice that all can live with" (*CP*, p. 306). Given this, the crux of moral enquiry is to find common reasonable grounds for accepting a conception of justice. From his earliest work, however, Rawls insisted that we have conflicting ideas and intuitions about justice; arguments based on such intuitions are typically "unconvincing. They are not likely to lead to an understanding of the basis of justice" (*CP*, p. 52). Thus in the search for reasonable agreement we are led to build on a more widely shared understanding of justification – rational choice. In employing an original position argument, we suppose only that people are capable of rational choice: they know and can act on their own interests and are capable of figuring out the likely consequences of their various choices and so on. If the justification of the principles of justice derives from this prosaic, common, notion of rational choice, then we can say that the principles pass *the identification test*: actual persons, with their own interests can verify and identify with the rationality of the principles (Gauthier, *Morals*, pp. 325ff.) That is, each can see that she too would choose them under conditions of impartiality, and so can rationally identify with them. Consulting only her deliberative rationality, each sees the principles as rational. We might say that in a diverse society, the justificatory force of rational choice is our only common touchstone.

But, of course, not all rational choices constitute choice of a conception of justice. In addition to the identification test, the principles chosen in the original position must be recognizably principles *of justice*. To be principles of justice they must pass what we might call a *recognitional test* of choice in that each can confirm that the principles are chosen from an impartial moral point of view, and so qualify as bona fide principles of justice (Gauthier, *Morals*, Chapter 8).

Thus as a model of justification, the original position has two links, one to the moral point of view and the other to the point of view of actual rational individuals. Justification in the original position succeeds if the principles are chosen from a genuinely moral point of view and a rational individual can endorse them. Without the identification test, the critics of the original position would be right to see it as a complicated mechanism for generating impartial principles that do not really derive their force from rational choice (they are not what any rational agent would choose in those circumstances). Similarly, without the recognitional test, we could not be sure that the principles chosen by rational individuals in the original position were principles of justice rather than merely principles of, say, prudence or a "modus vivendi." We need to confirm that from the moral point of view, these are the rational principles of justice – that they would be chosen by an impartial legislator. Both links are essential and it is the combination of these two types of rational choice that gives original position arguments their distinctiveness and their power.

2.1.3 A social contract or an Archimedean perspective?

A long-standing question concerning Rawls's original position argument is whether the idea of a "contract" is otiose, with the real justificatory work being done by the account of a rational choice of a single chooser. Soon after the publication of *TJ*, Sidney Alexander claimed:

> The *contractarian* aspect of Rawls's device is not essential, it is even misleading. What is essential, I think, is the *choice* aspect. Whatever worthwhile principles Rawls can validly deduce from his social contract mechanism can also be deduced as the principles that a single rational man would choose, from behind the veil of ignorance, for a social system in which he was to be assigned a role after that choice. Rawls does not need the contractual aspect, as is clear from his observation that the principles would be chosen unanimously. ("Social Evaluation," p. 604)

Rawls responds to Alexander with a number of reasons why he thinks the concept of a contract is essential: (1) it "reminds" us that separateness of persons is fundamental to justice as fairness; (2) a contract "introduces publicity conditions"; and (3) "reaching a unanimous agreement without a binding vote is not the same thing as everyone's arriving at the same choice or forming the same intention" (*CP*, p. 249). None of these considerations strikes us as especially compelling; Alexander is surely correct that the critical justification is that under conditions *C* the principle *J* would be rationally chosen, and this choice can be modeled as that of a single individual, *P*. Crucially, as Rawls acknowledges, there are "no differences to negotiate" (*CP*, pp. 249 and 120), and so the choice in the original position is rational in the sense of the norms of rational individual parametric choice, not, say, non-cooperative game theory with its strategic reasoning, cooperative bargaining theory, or principles of aggregation. This is the truly fundamental point: once difference has been eliminated, the justification in the original position is via an individual principle of rational parametric choice.

We thus shall take original position arguments as necessarily seeking to reduce the choice of principles of justice to the rational parametric choice of one individual. We thus set aside an account such as Ken Binmore's *Natural Justice*, according to which there is bargaining in the original position.[1] As we shall understand it, an original position argument seeks to provide what Rawls (*CP*, p. 511) and David Gauthier have described as an "Archimedean point" for judging society:

---

[1] Although he does not describe himself as an original position theorist, Gauthier's *Morals* contractarian account qualifies. If space allowed, examining his view would be especially enlightening, since so few readers appreciate its strong commitment to an Archimedean moral choice.

Archimedes supposed that given a sufficiently long lever and a place to stand, he could move the earth. We may then think of an Archimedean point as one from which a single individual may exert the force required to move or affect some object. In moral theory, the Archimedean point is that position one must occupy, if one's own decisions are to possess the moral force to govern the moral realm. From the Archimedean point one has the moral capacity to shape society. (*Morals*, p. 233)

The original position comprises such an Archimedean point, where the rational parametric choice of one individual determines the principles of justice.

2.2 The evolution of Rawls's original position

2.2.1 The early model

As does Robert Paul Wolff in his excellent analysis *Understanding Rawls*, we identify several different versions of Rawls's original position model. Rawls first advances an initial position choice model in his 1958 "Justice as Fairness" for evaluating the justice of established social practices (*CP*, p. 52). In this model of the original position, Rawls's agents are not, strictly speaking, deliberating about first principles of justice from, as it were, an atemporal "view from nowhere." As Rawls writes, "there is no question of our supposing them to come together to deliberate as to how they will set these practices up for the first time" (*CP*, p. 53). The practices are taken to already exist. Instead, the agents are deliberating about whether any of them has a "legitimate complaint" against the practices (*CP*, p. 53). In so doing, they must also develop standards for legitimate versus illegitimate complaints, and these standards shape what will ultimately be the principles of justice.

Rawls attributes a fairly narrow utility function to the choosers: individuals are mutually disinterested, evaluating the practice in question simply on the basis of whether they believe it will be to their advantage (*CP*, p. 52). This is not a claim about the nature of humans, but a model of what a certain sort of rational actor would choose. Rawls's 1958 choosers

are rational: they know their own interests more or less accurately; they are capable of tracing out the likely consequences of adopting one practice rather than another; they are capable of adhering to a course of action once they have decided upon it; they can resist present temptation and the enticements of immediate gain; and the bare knowledge or perception of the difference between their condition and that of others is not, within certain limits and in itself, a source of great dissatisfaction. (*CP*, p. 52)

Rawls also assumes that they are situated in such a way that they have roughly similar abilities and needs and can benefit from cooperation (*CP*, p. 53). They normally are unable to dominate one another, thus ensuring that they have an interest in finding common principles (Wolff, *Understanding*, pp. 28–9).

That said, the precise specification of the preferences of the choosers in "Justice as Fairness" is unclear. Rawls claims that individuals will choose principles of justice for a practice where each has a conception of "legitimate claims" that it is reasonable for others to acknowledge (*CP*, p. 59). He also writes that in a just practice persons "can face one another openly and support their respective positions, should they appear questionable, by reference to principles which it is reasonable to expect each to accept" (*CP*, p. 59). All of this is somewhat vague; it leads to substantive constraints on what sorts of principles will be acceptable without fully specifying the basis of the choice in the original position. That is, the preferences of the choosers are set out as self-interested without specifying how that self-interest constrains their utility functions. As Rawls notes, this means that the subject of their agreement will be "very general indeed" (*CP*, p. 57).

The principles that they would endorse, according to Rawls, are: (1) each has an equal right to the most extensive liberty compatible with a like liberty for all and (2) inequalities are arbitrary unless it is reasonable to expect that they will work to everyone's advantage and that positions and offices are open to all (*CP*, p. 48). We can see the first principle as setting out a baseline of equality in rights or liberties and the second principle as justifying certain deviations from equality. The second principle endorses what we might call a strong Pareto condition that a move from a more equal to a less equal social state is justified if everyone is better off in the less equal state. At this point, Rawls's description of the choosers and their information sets provides no grounds for a single rational ranking of the set of mutually beneficial social states. Just states of affairs must be on the Pareto frontier, but this, in itself, does not specify a point on the Pareto frontier that is uniquely just.

This version of the choice situation does not employ any "veil of ignorance" to eliminate knowledge of an individual's capacities and interests. A veil of ignorance excludes from choosers' information sets knowledge of their identity, introducing uncertainty as to what choice is in their best interests. In the early model Rawls introduces uncertainty in another way:

They each understand further that the principles proposed and acknowledged on this occasion are binding on all future occasions. Thus each will be wary of proposing a principle which would give him peculiar advantage, in the present circumstances, supposing it is accepted. Each person knows that he will be bound by it in future circumstances the peculiarities of which cannot be known, and which might well be such that the principles are to his disadvantage. (*CP*, p. 53)

Here the argument is that, because he is bound by the choice of the principles over an extended period of time regulating circumstances that he cannot predict, a rational person will not seek to tailor the principles so that he gains undue advantages given his present circumstances, since these may unpredictably change, and he may end up on the losing end of rigged or inegalitarian principles. Note that this argument seeks to secure some of the results that the veil of ignorance achieves in the later formulations: it requires that a person seeks principles that are what Kohlberg was later to call "reversible": one can endorse them regardless of the position one occupies under them (*Moral Development*, pp. 190–201).

Rawls is proposing here a version of maximin reasoning. He immediately explains the upshot of his principle for choice under ignorance: "The restrictions which would so arise might be thought of as those a person would keep in mind if he were designing a practice in which his enemy would assign him his place" (*CP*, p. 54). This claim is striking; it is repeated in various formulations of the original position, including "Distributive Justice" (published in 1967) (*CP*, p. 133n) and as late as *TJR* (pp. 132–3). What is so striking is that these are the only sentences in which Rawls seems tempted to introduce multi-person strategic reasoning into the original position, even though he immediately adds "the persons in the original position do not, of course, assume that their position in society is decided by a malevolent opponent" (*TJR*, p. 133).

What is going on with this unusual appeal to strategic reasoning? Recall that the definitive argument for maximin reasoning was presented by John von Neumann, who showed maximin to be the general solution to zero-sum games (*Theory of Games*, pp. 153ff.)[2] In a zero-sum, two-person game, any gain for one player implies an equal loss for the other; if we tally up all the

---

[2] Rawls cites this work in note 9 of "Justice as Fairness" (*CP*, p. 56) but does not direct us to specific pages. He does, though, indicate that readers should consult the Luce and Raiffa *Games* chapters on two-person cooperative games and group decision-making. Rawls always recognized that his choice situation was not, in the end, properly modeled in zero-sum terms.

gains and all the losses, the sum will always be zero. The quintessential example is a game between enemies, where one player's gain is the reverse side of the other's loss. So *if* we did think of the original position as a zero-sum game, then maximin *would be* the uncontroversial solution. It almost seems as if Rawls thinks this argument is too good not to mention, even though in *TJ* he immediately rejects it as inappropriate.

2.2.2 The middle models

Rawls's original position undergoes a series of substantial changes in what we shall call the "middle models" – from "Distributive Justice" (1967) through "Distributive Justice: Some Addenda" (1968) to *TJ* (1971). There are substantial shifts in: (1) the construction of the information sets; (2) the description of the choosers; (3) the more explicit role of maximin as a principle of rational choice; and (4) a switch in the role of maximin, from primarily an argument for the egalitarian principle, to what seems to be the main argument in favor of "the difference principle," which is itself introduced in the middle models. We briefly consider each in turn.

(1) The veil of ignorance is introduced in an effort to specify the original position as a "suitably defined initial situation" wherein "no one knows his position in society, nor even his place in the distribution of natural talents and abilities" (*CP*, p. 132). Indeed, one knows nothing of one's own personal utility function (one's ends, goals, or values). Rawls describes this restriction on the information of the choosers as justified to create a fair bargaining problem. The veil prevents "anyone from being advantaged or disadvantaged by the contingencies of social class and fortune" (*CP*, p. 132). According to Rawls, this is essential to making his contract theory, and "ethics itself," a part of "the general theory of rational choice" (*CP*, p. 132). Of course, in the general theory of rational choice, there is no restriction on the knowledge that choosers have about themselves or their fellows. Indeed, in most specifications of rational choice, agents are assumed to have full information of their circumstances. But, as we saw in the early model, Rawls is explicitly seeking to develop a theory of rational choice under radical uncertainty, where the uncertainty is intended to induce impartiality among rational choosers. The veil of ignorance is critical in allowing us to see the choice from the original position as an Archimedean point (§1.3), in which rational choice must be made from an impartial point of view.

(2) Having eliminated personal knowledge about oneself, including knowledge of one's own aims, how is anyone to make a rational choice? As Rawls

notes, rationality alone is not an adequate basis for rational choice of the principles of right, since rationality only tells us to choose more of what is preferred, not what we should prefer. It specifies means, not ends. Real persons have interests, values, and goals – what Rawls calls a "conception of the good" – that orders their rational life plans and their ends. Choosers behind the veil lack knowledge of their conception of the good; they do not know who they are, what their capacities and abilities are, and what they value and care about. As Rawls argues, while his choosers "know that they have some rational plan of life, they do not know the details of this plan, the particular ends and interests which it is calculated to promote" (*TJR*, p. 123). Without a specification of ends, however, rational choice seems either impossible or chaotic: impossible if there is simply no basis for choice, and chaotic if everyone in the original position makes spurious or random assumptions about what they would want without the veil. In the second case, once the veil is lifted, individuals from the point of view of what Rawls calls "you and me" (*PL*, p. 28) would not have reason for seeing the principles justified in the original position as having any normative force.

To solve this problem, Rawls introduces the notion of "primary goods." Primary goods are goods of which it is reasonable to assume individuals want more rather than less, regardless of whatever else they want. Thus even behind the veil, individuals know they will want to maximize their primary goods. This solves the deep concern that without some conception of the good, rational choice behind the veil would be impossible. The introduction of primary goods also considerably simplifies choice in the original position. Since everyone wants more rather than fewer primary goods, and since all have the same knowledge of their situation behind the veil, rational choice is characterized so that "unanimity is possible; the deliberations of any one person are typical of all" (*TJR*, p. 232). These elements of the original position (the veil restricting information and the thin theory of the good) make the rational choice of the "parties" truly analogous to the rational choice of one suitably constructed person, and so the choice is indeed a parametric choice of one person against a background of fixed (non-strategic) options (§1.3).

(3) The middle models witness the rise of maximin – the rule that one should choose the option whose worst outcome is better than the worst outcome of all other options – as an explicit principle of rational choice under uncertainty and, indeed, its prominent role in the overall argument. Although, as we have said, Rawls continued to employ the zero-sum strategic game imagery even into *TJ*, certainly by his 1967 essay on "Distributive Justice" he was emphasizing maximin as a general principle for choice under

uncertainty, at least under conditions of long-term commitment. Rawls believed that the uncertainty engendered by the veil of ignorance makes reliance on the maximin rule compelling.

This is not simply an idiosyncratic idea of Rawls's. In 1951 Leonard Savage noted that the minimax principle was central to the theory of choice when the actor cannot assign probabilities.[3] In "Distributive Justice," Rawls directs us to Luce and Raiffa's discussion of maximin as a principle for choice under uncertainty. However, the appeal of maximin waned in decision theory as a preferred principle for choice under uncertainty after the 1950s (e.g. McClennen, *Rationality*, pp. 25–8). Just what is the best principle for rational choice under great uncertainty is a vexed issue, but certainly as a general rule maximin seems unduly pessimistic. As Binmore quips, "only a paranoiac would find maximin attractive in general" (*Game Theory*, p. 31).

Rawls denies that his use of maximin is based on any assumptions about risk aversion (*CP*, p. 245), even though Rawls himself describes it as "conservative" (*CP*, p. 133n). In *TJ* Rawls contends that three features of the choice in the original position make plausible reliance on this "unusual" rule. (i) A distinctive feature of maximin is that it entirely discounts probabilities. In the original position, choosing social structures and your position in them, and in which you must justify this choice to others (say, your descendants), it is reasonable to be highly skeptical of any probabilistic claims. (ii) Second, "the person choosing has a conception of the good such that he cares very little, if anything, for what he might gain above the maximin stipend that he can, in fact, be sure of by following the maximin rule" (*TJR*, p. 134). And relatedly, (iii) "the rejected alternatives have outcomes that one can hardly accept. The situation involves grave risks" (*TJR*, p. 134). The point here is that the *very* special features of the choice in the original position, plus further (rather strong) assumptions about the utility functions of the parties,

---

[3] In von Neumann's analysis, a solution to a zero-sum game implied that maximin leads to the same choice as minimax. Suppose Row and Column are playing a zero sum game, and payoffs are stated in terms of Row's payoffs (in a zero-sum game only one player's payoffs need to be stated, since the other player's payoffs are exactly the opposite). If Row goes first, he must choose the row with the highest minimum (maximin), since he knows that Column will, from the selected Row, choose the cell which gives Column the highest payoff, which is equivalent to that which gives Row the lowest. So, like the parties in the original position, Row is concerned with nothing but the lowest payoffs in each row. If Column goes first, she will choose the column whose maximum payoff for Row is the smallest, since Column knows that once she had chosen the column, Row will choose the cell that gives him the most. Thus the equilibrium solution is one in which maximin = minimax.

renders maximin a purely rational rule under the circumstances – one that makes the most sense given the personal aims of the parties.

(4) One of the distinctive features of the middle models is that the "maximin" criterion has two distinct meanings: as a principle of rational choice and as a principle of equity ("Distributive Justice"). Although Rawls would later come to hold that the "maximining" features of the rule of rational choice and of equity (i.e. the difference principle) constitute simply a "formal resemblance" that is "misleading" (*JFR*, p. 95), they certainly seemed systematically linked in the middle models. In the early model the second principle of justice was simply a strong Pareto condition that required that justified inequalities must fall on the Pareto frontier of mutual benefit. The principle, however, does not say anything about *where* on the Pareto frontier society must settle. By the time Rawls writes "Distributive Justice," he sees this indeterminacy as a serious problem:

> There are many such [Pareto-optimal] distributions, since there are many ways of allocating commodities so that no further mutually beneficial exchange is possible. Hence the Pareto criterion, as important as it is, admittedly does not identify the best distribution, but rather a class of optimal, or efficient distributions... The criterion is at best an incomplete principle for ordering distributions. (*CP*, p. 135)

Rawls is thus committed to specifying the second principle in a way that makes a complete ordering of social alternatives possible from the point of view of justice. Here the middle models introduce another innovation: the choosers are now making their choices from the point of view of a representative member of a specific social class.

Since the veil excludes the knowledge of individual circumstances and interests that choosers could use to maximize their expected outcome in the society, Rawls argues that some particular social position needs to be selected so that the choosers can maximize the expected outcome of that representative social class. He argues that the "obvious candidate is the representative man of those who are least favored by the system of institutional inequalities" (*CP*, pp. 137–8). Applying this analysis, the agents in the original position will choose a basic structure of society as just when "the prospects of the least fortunate are as great as they can be" (*CP*, p. 138). In this formulation of the second principle we have what he now calls the "difference principle." To arrive at the difference principle, though, several more refinements or assumptions are needed in the original position. These assumptions are "chain-connection" and "close-knittedness" (*CP*, p. 139). Rawls argues that we should assume that inequalities are "chain connected," i.e. "if an inequality raises the expectation of the lowest position, it raises the expectation of all positions in between" (CP, p. 139). Greater expectations for low-skilled workers improve the prospects of higher-skilled workers. Relatedly, the "close-knit" assumption claims that "it is impossible to raise (or lower) the expectations of any representative man without raising (or lowering) the expectation of every other representative man" (CP, p. 139). These assumptions, though empirically dubious, are essential to making this version of the difference principle consistent with the earlier, Pareto version. If it is impossible to maximize the position of the least well off without at the same time harming the better off, it is not clear that even those who did not know their position in society would choose the least well off class as the representative chooser. Why not, after all, use the median class or the average representative person as the position from which to maximize, rather than the least well off? A critical reason must involve the maximin choice rule, for the parties are primarily focused on the worst outcomes. It is no wonder that (Rawls's protestations notwithstanding) for most readers of TJ the task of the maximin rule of choice is to justify the maximin rule of equity.

2.2.3 The final model: adieu to justice as rational choice?

In his original Dewey Lectures, in PL, and in JFR, Rawls describes the original position as a "device of representation" (CP, p. 308; PL, p. 48; JFR, p. 17). The specifications and, more importantly, the rationale, of the model change again. The final model is meant to provide the answer to the question "how is it possible for there to exist over time a just and stable society of free and equal citizens who still remain divided by reasonable religious, philosophical and moral doctrines?" (PL, p. 47). To answer this, Rawls models the justification of principles of justice as what rational *and* reasonable agents would choose if put into an original position where the diversity of their beliefs and aims was abstracted away and, again, their only goal was to maximize prospective social primary goods. In the final version a central aim is to model the normative political implications of two relevant aspects of our moral personality – our sense of justice (the reasonable) and our capacity for a conception of the good (the rational) (PL, p. 52).

   This approach to the justification of principles of justice seems a significant departure from the middle models. In particular, the introduction of the reasonable as a feature of the representatives in the original position appears to signal that Rawls gave up on his bold claim that "the theory of justice is a

part, perhaps the most significant part, of the theory of rational choice"
(*TJR*, p. 15). Rawls now insists that the project of deriving the reasonable
from the rational is misguided, but his renunciation is nuanced:

> From what we have just said, this [the claim that justice is a part of the
> theory of rational choice] is simply incorrect. What should have been said
> is that the account of the parties, and of their reasoning, uses the theory
> of rational decision, though only in an intuitive way. This theory is itself
> part of a political conception of justice, one that tries to give an account
> of reasonable principles of justice. There is no thought of deriving those
> principles from the concept of rationality as the sole normative
> concept. I believe that the text of *Theory* as a whole supports this interpret-
> ation. (*PL*, p. 53n)

Is Rawls truly renouncing the fundamental derivation claim (§1.1)? It
certainly is a mistake to think that his project in *TJ* was an attempt to derive
principles of justice from one normative concept, rationality; we concur that
TJ as a whole makes this point clear. We have tried to show, however, that the
Fundamental Derivation Thesis, which is central to the rational choice
approach to ethics, does not claim that morality can be reduced to rational
choice and nothing else: as we have stressed, the circumstances *C* are also
fundamental. In the middle models, "reasonableness" is entirely modeled by
the circumstances of the choice situation: they ensured that the rational
choice could be *recognized* as a moral choice (*TJR*, p. 514). In the final model,
although the reasonable continues to be primarily modeled by the circumstances of choice, Rawls more explicitly integrates some elements of the
reasonable into the description of the choosers themselves. This in itself
would be consistent with the Fundamental Derivation Thesis. However, the
claim that the rational choice only enters into the final model in an "intuitive
way" does suggest that, at least in Rawls's eyes, the Fundamental Derivation
Thesis has been abandoned, with rational choice demoted to something more
like a heuristic role.

Certainly in the evolution from the early to the final models, we can see a
clear movement. In the early model *identification* – the ability of actual
rational choosers to identify with the principles as clearly rational choices –
looks very strong. The principles are general and abstract, and do indeed seem
rational choices for cooperative schemes facing unknown futures. But Rawls
clearly worried that the early model was lacking on the recognitional dimension: it was less clear that the contract was "moral". In addition, it did not
provide a complete ordering of social states, something that Rawls thought

important to a theory of justice. We can thus understand Rawls's later models as seeking to enhance the recognitional features of the original position – to show that it was a genuinely Archimedean point. Whether this enhancing of recognition was ultimately at the cost of identification is, of course, a fundamental worry. Gauthier thought it was: as the models develop, the chooser from the original position is so far removed from any preferences, capacities, and talents that actual individuals have little idea of what it would mean to identify with the choices of such a empty agent (*Morality*, p. 254).

2.3 Harsanyi's models

2.3.1 The original position model

There are three main differences between Rawls's middle model (which we take as the quintessential Rawlsian original position) and Harsanyi's in the way they construct the original position: (1) Harsanyi uses an expected utility decision rule rather than maximin for choice in the original position; (2) utilities are directly compared across *persons* (not classes) in Harsanyi's original position; and (3) choice in the original position selects a version of average utilitarianism rather than the two principles as the rational principle of justice. We will examine Harsanyi's original position in some detail, and then consider whether his model meets the conditions of an original position as we have laid them out in the first section.

For Harsanyi, moral choice in the original position is a species of rational choice, but rational choice over a very specific domain. Using utility theory, he argues that individuals choose rationally under uncertainty when they choose the prospects that will lead to the highest expected utility. In individual choice, these prospects and outcomes tend to be self-regarding or at least partial to a person's concerns, friends, and family ("Morality," pp. 43–4). Moral choice is distinctive because they are choosing not from their partial point of view (on the basis of their utility function) but impartially over social systems as a whole. In his most straightforward presentation Harsanyi describes a social system, say a capitalist system, of having $n = \{1,2,3\ldots\}$ possible social positions with specific utilities related to each ("Morality," pp. 45–7). These are ranked so that social position U_1 is better, from the point of view of any given member of that society, than social position U_2 and so on. Choice from the moral point of view then can be modeled so that a given individual i who does not know who she will be in that society would seek to maximize the expected value of being in that society, assuming that there is an equal probability of being any person in the society. That is, the chooser would maximize

$$\frac{1}{n}\sum_{j=1}^{n} U_j$$

or the "arithmetic mean of all individual utility levels in society" ("Morality," p. 46). Not knowing who one would be, the impartial choice would be to choose the highest expected average level of utility in the society.[4] In addition, various different kinds of societies can be compared using this method. We can, for instance, compare the expected average level of a capitalist versus a socialist society given various assumptions.

2.3.2 The axiomatic model

Harsanyi repeatedly claims ("Cardinal Utility," "Cardinal Welfare,") that his choice of the average utility principle is a result of applying standard Bayesian decision theory to choice in the original position, at one point stating that Bayesian rationality conditions, combined with a "hardly controversial" Pareto optimality condition, "entail *utilitarian ethics* as a matter of mathematical necessity" ("Morality," p. 233). But there are several essential features of Harsanyi's model of choice in the original position that reflect his aim of modeling specifically *moral* choice in the original position that deviate from standard Bayesian decision theory. To see this, it is worth looking at Harsanyi's axiomatic formulation of his model. There are four axioms that, taken together, show that genuinely moral choice is made in the original position (*Rational Behavior*, pp. 64–9):

1 rationality of moral preferences;
2 rationality of personal preferences;
3 positive relationship between the moral preferences of a person *i* and the personal preferences of all of the members of society;
4 symmetry.

The first axiom specifies that any individual choosing over social states of affairs would satisfy the standard requirements of Bayesian rationality, that is,

---

[4] Harsanyi recognizes that real individuals would know their actual positions in society. The critical point, he argues, is that a person's "value judgment will still qualify as a true moral judgment as long as he judges these social situations essentially in the same way as he would do *if he did not have this information*" (*Rational Behavior*, p. 50).

that person would have a complete ordering suitable for Von Neumann–Morgenstern transformation to a linear invariant cardinal utility scale. The second holds that one's individual preference ordering would meet the basic conditions of Bayesian utility theory. The third condition is a Pareto requirement for rational social choice. If all individuals in a society weakly prefer option A to option B in their individual orderings, the moral or social ordering should not rank option B over option A. Harsanyi argues that the first two conditions are merely rationality requirements while the third is a moral requirement, but one he thinks is "surely a rather non-controversial moral principle" ("Bayesian Decision," p. 226).

The fourth condition, symmetry or what Harsanyi sometimes calls "equal treatment," is more complicated. As Michael Moehler shows, the first three conditions, taken together, entail weighted utilitarianism but do not generate average utilitarianism and do not require interpersonal comparisons of utility ("Contractarian Ethics"). In this way, without the "equal treatment" condition, Harsanyi's description of the original position would generate a principle that reflected impartiality in the original position, but it would not reflect what he takes as fundamental to morality: universality and, more importantly, impersonality ("Morality," pp. 39–41). The weight that individuals put on their rankings of particular social states of affairs would be reflected in the overall social utility function. With the introduction of the "equal treatment" condition, all separate utility functions are given equal weight. Individuals assign the same weights to alternative rankings of social states of affairs when those rankings are made in the same utility units. This is not only a simplifying assumption: it has the substantive upshot that the only distinguishing factor between different orderings of social states is the particular individual names that would be associated with them. Individuals choose rationally in the original position when they assume they might actually have any name associated with a particular social position. Another way to put this is that an impartial rational chooser in the original position weights all individual utility functions equally. As we will see this is a key assumption for generating the equiprobability assumption that generates the average rule utilitarian conclusion.

2.3.3 Equiprobability and extended preferences

Harsanyi's proof of the rationality of average utilitarianism relies on two controversial assumptions: (1) the equiprobability assumption; and (2) interpersonal comparisons of utility or what he calls "extended preferences."

The first assumes that individuals will assign equal probabilities, when they are choosing in the original position, that they will occupy any social position in the social world they are selecting. If one is evaluating a capitalist society, for instance, one should place equal probability on person i, who is extremely poor, and person j, who is extremely rich. If there are n individuals in a society, a person in the original position will assign a probability of $1/n$ that she will be any particular person in that society (*Rational Behavior*, pp. 49–50). One chooses as if one doesn't know whether one will be Alf the teacher, Betty the factory owner, Charlie the laborer, or poor indigent Doris; one assigns equal probability to each option.

Harsanyi assumes that since the choice is made under uncertainty, that is, with no objective probability of being one person rather than another, the correct principle of choice is to assign equal probabilities to all possibilities. This is an application of Laplace's principle of indifference or insufficient reason, that if one doesn't have any reason for assuming a particular probability of one outcome over another occurring, one should assign equal probability to each outcome. As Binmore and others have pointed out, however, this doctrine of indifference is more controversial and ambiguous than it may initially seem (*Rational Decisions*, p. 128). If there are three horses running a race and one has no basis for judging their ability to win, Binmore asks, should one give the chance of a particular horse winning the probability of ⅓ by indifference (since it is one of three horses), or should one assign it a ½ probability of winning (since the horse will either win or lose and one has no more reason to think it will win or lose) (*Rational Decisions*, p. 129)? How we apply the principle of indifference in this case determines how we should bet, but the options are very different. The principle does not tell us how to apply itself.

Indeed, Rawls argues "the parties have no basis for determining the probable nature of their society, or their place in it" (*TJR*, p. 134). We have seen that Rawls argues that the parties would not use probability calculations at all, even a principle of indifference, relying instead on maximin. Rawls insists that choice in the original position should be modeled as a choice under "complete ignorance," not uncertainty, and the parties should, therefore, seek to protect themselves and their families from the worst possibilities that might befall them if they ended up in the lowest social role. Harsanyi ridicules Rawls's argument against using probabilities in the original position, arguing that it entails either (1) that we are forced to use a decision rule like maximin which is unsuited for rational choice under uncertainty and has absurd conclusions or (2) that we are being inconsistent on the basis of standard

Bayesian theories of rationality ("Can the Maximin?"). Harsanyi is quite right to point out that in standard Bayesian decision theory, subjective priors can be assigned to any gamble. The problem, as we have seen, is that the principle of indifference does not unambiguously lead to the equiprobability assumption. This does not show that Rawls is correct to object to Harsanyi's formulation of choice in the original position, only that the equiprobability assumption is not a mere extension of Bayesian decision theory. In a later essay, Harsanyi admits as much:

> In its traditional form, the principle of indifference, also called the principle of insufficient reason, asserts that when the conditions permit two or more different outcomes, yet we have no evidence favoring any particular outcome over any other, we ought to assign the same probability to each outcome. In this form, the principle is much too vague to be of any real use. It is also open to the important logical objection that it attempts to draw a positive conclusion (that of equal probabilities) from mere ignorance (from absence of information favoring any specific outcome) – an attempt that cannot possibly succeed. ("Objective Probabilities," p. 352)

Equiprobability is not an uncontroversial extension of Bayesian decision theory: it is a substantive moral assumption that makes choice in the original position impersonal as well as impartial ("Contractarian Ethics"). Harsanyi takes both of these conditions to be essential components of the moral point of view ("Bayesian Decision," p. 227).

In addition to equiprobability, Harsanyi's original position model also assumes interpersonal comparisons of utility. As with the equiprobability assumption, this is part of the "equal treatment" or symmetry assumption in the axiomatic model (section 2.3.2). Harsanyi justifies reliance on interpersonal utility comparisons as an application of what he calls "imaginative empathy" ("Morality," p. 50). We empathize with others by imagining ourselves in their position and thinking how we would evaluate a state of affairs if we were them:

> We imagine ourselves to be in the shoes of another person, and ask ourselves the question, "if I were now really in *his* position, and had *his* tastes, *his* education, *his* social background, *his* cultural values, and *his* psychological make-up, then what would now be *my* preferences between various alternatives, and how much satisfaction or dissatisfaction would I derive from any given alternative? ("Morality," p. 50)

Harsanyi argues that this imaginative empathy is not philosophically problematic for two reasons. First, human beings are so alike in psychology and so similarly situated that it is reasonable to think that we can actually empathize with others in this way. Second, he contends that in any case we must make interpersonal comparisons when we are making moral evaluations. Notice that Harsanyi is certainly making substantive modeling choices when he introduces equiprobability and interpersonal comparisons into his original position.

2.3.4 Identification and recognition

Does Harsanyi's original position meet the recognitional and identification conditions? Rawls denies that it meets the recognitional test, maintaining that the problem with utilitarianism and any view that makes the principles of justice the result of the rational choice of one impartial and impersonal observer is that they mistake impartiality for impersonality (*TJR*, p. 166). Impartial choice does not favor any particular point of view, but impersonal choice does not respect the separateness of persons and merges the distinct individuals of a society into one aggregative utility function. Much depends here on just what one thinks is characteristic of the moral point of view.

A more serious problem arises with the identification test. Regardless of whether impersonality is a reasonable assumption of choice from the moral point of view, it is hard to see how actual individuals could identify with the choice of an agent choosing to maximize average utility, rather than maximizing the expected utility of any particular person. As Gauthier points out, in Harsanyi's original position "the ideal actor, in maximizing expected average utility, is not maximizing expected utility – her own or that of anyone else" (*Morals*, p. 243). In moving from the rational choice of an agent maximizing her expected utility to the choice of maximizing expected average utility Harsanyi has "broken the link ensuring that each person would identify" with the chooser in the original position (*Morals*, p. 244). Put another way, actual individuals would not see the reasons of the chooser in Harsanyi's original position as reflecting their reasons. In this way, the justificatory link between the model of rational choice in the original position and the reasons of actual individuals in society would be severed. Individuals will not see Harsanyi's justification of average utility as a justification for *them*. If this is correct, Harsanyi's original position will not pass the *identification test* even if it does pass the *recognition test*. This is an independent reason for thinking that impersonality, as Harsanyi models it, is not a suitable standard for modeling moral choice in the original position.

2.4 Conclusion: rational choice and the Archimedean chooser

Why did Rawls and Harsanyi spend so much effort developing principles of rational choice for an Archimedean chooser – a chooser whose position is so constrained that his purely rational choice defines the moral realm for us all? Fundamental to any answer is a loss of faith that in a deeply pluralistic society the traditional sources of moral convictions – religion, tradition, or the moral insight of the elite – could provide the basis of a conception of morality or justice "that all can live with" (*CP*, p. 306). For this to be the case, each must be able to project himself into the Archimedean position. In doing so, he must confirm that he recognizes this as a genuine basis for moral choice and that he would choose in the way the theory indicates. As we have shown, these are difficult criteria to meet simultaneously. Both Rawls and Harsanyi sought to satisfy the recognitional criterion, providing an Archimedean position that could definitely impartially order feasible social states. In order to accomplish this, however, they developed choosers who possessed no determinate utility functions, who were stripped of capacities, interests, and aims. And, in addition, both resorted to highly contentious principles of rational choice – maximin and equiprobability. Real individuals, considering their own concerns and aims are apt to find these versions of the "moral point of view" alien: who knows what one would choose, with all knowledge of all aspects of one's individuality shorn away? We believe that Rawls's early model, in spite of its vagueness and indeterminacy, provides a more promising basis for connecting a rational Archimedean choice to real individual choices. That is a claim we shall have to vindicate elsewhere.

3 The strains of commitment

Jeremy Waldron

The parties in the original position "cannot enter into agreements that may have consequences they cannot accept. They will avoid those they can adhere to only with great difficulty ... [W]hen we enter into an agreement we must be able to honor it even should the worst possibilities prove to be the case" (*TJR*, p. 153).

On some readings, these propositions are key to John Rawls's argument against utilitarianism in *TJ*.[1] The principle of average utilitarianism has the potential to require that great deprivations – deprivations of liberty and material deprivations – be borne by some individuals for the sake of a greater sum of benefits to others. Anyone contemplating the choice of the utilitarian principle in Rawls's original position must take this into account and take into particular account that she may turn out to be one of those who will suffer deprivation of this kind. Utilitarianism, we know, is not constrained by any fundamental requirement that these burdens be tolerable at the individual level. But if there is a prospect of some people facing a requirement that they bear intolerable burdens, then the principle that generates such a requirement does not satisfy what Rawls calls "the strains of commitment" (*TJR*, p. 126), and the people in the original position must reject it. "Otherwise," as Rawls puts it, they "have not acted in good faith" (*TJR*, p. 153).

The strains of commitment argument operates independently of whatever rational choice argument can be made in favor of a maximin approach to decisions made in the original position. According to the rational choice argument for maximin, it is not rational to choose any principle that will lead to outcomes that are worse for certain individuals than those resulting from the application of Rawls's two principles. Rationality requires risk

---

[1] See, for example, Freeman, *Rawls*, pp. 180–3. Rawls makes it clear in *TJ* that he relies on the strains of commitment as one of the "main grounds" for the principles he favors (*TJR*, pp. 153–9). Elsewhere, however, he has said that the argument, though important, is not "clearly decisive by itself": see Rawls, "Some Reasons" (*CP*, p. 230).

aversion in the original position even if, statistically, a principle like average utilitarianism defines a better bet than Rawls's principles.[2] But this rational choice argument for maximin is precarious and it is deprecated by most commentators.[3] At worst it involves a question-begging stipulation of a risk-averse mentality for the parties in the original position. At best it relies on arguments about our inability to define rational choice for a single (one-off) bet that is supposed to shape one's life chances once and for all, as opposed to the open-ended series of bets that gaming rationality seems to presuppose. Rawls certainly pursues the latter version of the rational choice argument for maximin. He says that in order to justify the gambling approach, one would have to assume

> either that men move from one social position to another in random fashion and live long enough for gains and losses to average out, or else that there is some mechanism which insures that legislation guided by the principle of utility distributes its favors evenly over time. (*TJR*, p. 148)

But, he goes on,

> clearly society is not a stochastic process of this type . . . The pervasive and continuing influence of our initial place in society and of our native endowments, and of the fact that the social order is one system, is what characterizes the problem of justice . . . We must not be enticed by mathematically attractive assumptions into pretending that the contingencies of men's social positions and the asymmetries of their situations somehow even out in the end. Rather we must choose our conception of justice fully recognizing that this is not and cannot be the case. (*TJR*, p. 148)

That is an interesting and, in my view, important response to the argument for average utilitarianism based on gaming rationality.

However, the alternative argument used by Rawls against utilitarianism – the strains-of-commitment argument – is much more powerful. It is neither question-begging nor reliant on any gap in our theory of rational choice. It supposes that the parties in the original position approach the choice that

---

[2] Rawls acknowledges that it is a good bet for an economically rational person to gamble on coming out on the right side of inequalities justified on average utilitarian grounds. She does not need to know the probabilities: all she needs to know is that no more equal distribution would yield the same or a greater balance of average utility, i.e. total utility divided by the number of persons among whom it is to be shared (*TJR*, p. 143). So this is what has to be displaced by whatever argument Rawls can make in favor of risk aversion.

[3] See e.g. Harsanyi, "Can the Maximin?" pp. 594–606.

faces them responsibly as well as rationally. Rawls believes that the gamble that the adoption of average utilitarianism represents will be rejected in the original position, not because the parties are unsure about whether it represents a good bet, but because they cannot be confident that they will be in a position to pay up and honor their losses, as it were, if the gamble turns out badly for them when the veil of ignorance is lifted. The argument is that the parties *should* not take the risks involved in accepting a utilitarian principle, not that they could not or would not do so. I may not place a wager that I know I cannot pay up on if I lose; and people in the original position may not gamble on coming out ahead in the utilitarian stakes if they know that they will be unable to discharge their commitment to utilitarian principles should they turn out to be the individuals of whom great deprivations are going to be required for the greater good of others. Provided there is some non-zero probability of losing, I must not bet if I cannot afford to pay up if I lose, no matter how attractive (and how likely) is the prospect of winning. The point is one of gaming morality, not gaming rationality.[4]

So far, so good. But the strains-of-commitment argument faces challenges of its own. In this chapter I shall consider two such difficulties, and attempt to answer them.

The first is that the strains-of-commitment argument may prove too much. In deploying the argument against average utilitarianism, it is natural to focus on those who will turn out to be worst off under average utilitarianism and to compare the situation that they would be in under Rawls's two principles. Given the content of the difference principle, they know that they would have been at least as well off under Rawls's principles, most likely better. So they will be malcontents in a utilitarian social structure, chafing under the strains of commitment. But now consider people who turn out to be only moderately well off under the difference principle, and suppose those people are aware that, if the principle of average utility had been adopted, they could have been

---

[4] Notice, by the way, that this argument would survive the abandonment of the Rawlsian "veil of ignorance" device. The veil of ignorance means that *nobody* in the original position would sign up for the average utility principle, since all would be disturbed by consideration of the strains of commitment. Lose the veil, however, and average utility would still not be adopted. No doubt *some* people would sign up for the principle, being sufficiently convinced that there was no probability of their being losers in a society governed by such a principle. But still, not everyone would sign up; those who knew now that they were likely to be the worst off would not sign up, on account of the strains of commitment. And that is enough to scuttle average utility as a choice because of course unanimity is required for a contractarian argument; one cannot be voted into a contract.

much better off (because their society would have been in a position to sacrifice the well-being of more poor people for the sake of people like them). Then *they* will be malcontents in a social structure governed by Rawls's principles, and maybe they too will chafe under the strains of commitment. Indeed anyone who is worse off under Rawls's two principles than they would have been under some alternative arrangement – including our insidiously unequal status quo – will find it irksome to put up with the burdens that Rawlsian principles impose. Rawls himself was well aware of this difficulty, but I think we can improve on his answer to it. I will call this first difficulty *the malcontents objection*.

The second difficulty starts off as abstract and methodological, but answering it takes us to the heart of the liberal conception that characterizes Rawls's political philosophy. The difficulty is that the strains-of-commitment argument seems to involve the importation of features of the original position model into the real-life situation to which that model is being artificially applied. And maybe that is a confusion. After all, contractarian choice in the original position and the undertakings it involves are thought of as purely hypothetical: the original position is a thought experiment designed to illuminate features of a conception of justice. Even as we play with this model, we all know that "[n]o society can ... be a scheme of cooperation which men enter voluntarily in a literal sense" (*TJR*, p. 12). So why is the choice of principles constrained by a consideration that pertains to voluntary commitment in a literal sense? I shall call this second difficulty *the model-theoretic objection*.

To answer it, we have to make the case that Rawls's contractarianism is not just a way of thinking hypothetically about the choice of social principles, but also a way of thinking about what the application of social principles amounts to in well-ordered society. It is a way of thinking about what it would be for a society, in Rawls's words, to "come ... as close as a society can to being a voluntary scheme" (*TJR*, p. 12). As it stands, this is just an elusive formulation. Unless we can make sense of it in what follows, the strains-of-commitment argument will have to be abandoned as involving a confusion of levels in the theory – a sort of category mistake.

3.1 The malcontents objection

The first challenge faced by the strains of commitment argument is to find a way of dealing with the point that *anyone* who is worse off under Rawls's two principles than they would have been under some alternative arrangement will find it irksome to put up with the burdens that Rawls's principles impose. If people in the original position contemplate this possibility, they might have reason to reject the Rawlsian principles on account of the strains of commitment stemming from their dissatisfaction with the outcomes that Rawlsian principles generate for their case once the veil of ignorance is lifted.

There are two versions of the malcontents objection. On the one hand, the strains of commitment may arise under Rawlsian principles when some people reflect on how much better off they might have been under alternative principles. On the other hand, the strains of commitment may arise under Rawlsian principles when some people reflect on how much better off they would be had they not been required to live under principles of justice at all.

In *PL*, Rawls attempted to answer the second branch of the malcontents objection by something approaching stipulation. He said:

> The so-called strains of commitment are strains that arise in [a well-ordered] society between its requirements of justice and citizens' legitimate interests its just institutions allow ... These strains do not arise from a desire to preserve the benefits of previous injustice. (*PL*, p. 17)[5]

And indeed, he had said something similar quite early on. In an article published in 1974, Rawls said that "we do not consider the strains of commitment that might result from some people having to move from a favored position in an unjust society to a less favored position (either absolutely or relatively, or both) in this just society" (*CP*, p. 251). If the desire to preserve the benefits of previous injustice causes difficulties, then no doubt those difficulties can be dealt with in the transitional part of non-ideal theory (*PL*, pp. 17–18). It is primarily a problem about those who are well resourced as things stand being tempted to act unjustly, i.e. being "tempted to violate any principle of justice" (*JFR*, p. 127). Such temptations need not be taken into account in determining what justice is.

There is even a passage in the original 1971 edition of *TJ* that purports to deal with this case:

> To be sure, any principle chosen in the original position may require a large sacrifice for some. The beneficiaries of clearly unjust institutions (those founded on principles which have no claim to acceptance) may find it hard

---

[5] Rawls's use of the phrase "*so-called* strains of commitment" suggests that this is someone else's idea foisted on him by his critics or interpreters. But of course Rawls was the one who introduced the idea of strains of commitment and made it central to his conception.

to reconcile themselves to the changes that will have to be made. But in this case they will know that they could not have maintained their position anyway (*TJ*, p. 176)

– not once justice is on the agenda (which is, presumably, the presupposition of the whole enterprise).[6]

The other version of the malcontents objection raises the possibility of strains of commitment arising under Rawlsian principles when some people reflect on how much better off they might have been under alternative principles, i.e. under some alternative bona fide conception of justice. For example, some people may believe – quite reasonably – that they would be much better off under Robert Nozick's principles than they are under Rawls's.[7] Even in the original position, they will know that if they turn out to be acquisitively talented when the veil of ignorance is lifted, then Rawls's principles will likely generate a much worse outcome for them than Nozick's principles. This possibility they must surely take into account when they are contemplating the choice of Rawls's principles: in the original position, they have to reflect on how they will feel when the veil of ignorance is lifted and they turn out to be acquisitively talented. Such reflection may lead them to refrain from committing to Rawls's principles because they know they will be malcontents in this eventuality. And this they may put down to the strains of commitment.

The answer to this difficulty, as I see it, is that we must not confuse the strains of commitment with mere dissatisfaction that one did not secure what would have turned out to be a more advantageous choice. The strains of commitment are supposed to reflect the genuine difficulty that people may have in bringing themselves to comply with a given set of principles of justice, the genuine difficulty that they will have in playing the part assigned to them in the institutions that such principles define. The difficulties in question are not just preferential; they are supposed to represent a healthy acknowledgment of physical and psychological realities. A starving person may not be able to bring herself to pass by an open store of food without taking some for herself or her family; a person maltreated as a slave may not be able to prevent herself from striking back or running away. People in the original position

---

[6] In "Reply to Alexander and Musgrave," Rawls announced that this passage in the original edition of *TJ* was incorrect: "The bottom lines of *A Theory of Justice*, p. 176, are incorrect." That was in 1974. But the passage remains in the 1999 revised edition of *TJ*, at p. 154, though the imputation of incorrectness remains too, in the version of "Reply to Alexander and Musgrave," reprinted in *CP* at p. 252n.

[7] See Nozick, *ASU*, Chapter 7.

know that when the veil is lifted, they will be material need-laden beings and they will know that the human animal is not capable of infinite self-motivation or unlimited self-restraint. They know that people sometimes get cold, hungry, hurt, angry, and desperate; they know that this can result from social arrangements; and they know these conditions are connected with what they can bring themselves to do (and forbear). Since they have this knowledge about what Rawls calls "the general facts of human psychology" (*TJR*, p. 405), they must use it in their deliberations about what they are capable of committing themselves to.

None of this is about regret or dissatisfaction. Rawls uses the language of something's being "intolerable"[8] and that should be understood more or less literally. It is possible, I suppose, to use such language to characterize the dissatisfaction of the well off. So, according to Richard Miller, "It might be said that the best-off people will generally find it intolerable to give up great advantages in order to maximize the situation of the worst-off."[9] But I am not sure what "intolerable" is supposed to mean in that context. Miller says it is a claim that Marxists would make: "They would claim that the best-off people in any exploitive society cannot be made to give up their privileges except by force":[10]

> If Marxist social theory is right . . . someone in the original position would foresee that the difference principle may be intolerable for him, if he turns out to be a typical member of a dominant exploitive class. Thus, he could not accept, as grounds for a commitment to help realize the difference principle, an argument that this commitment, unlike its rivals, will be one he can live up to, no matter what social position he turns out to occupy.[11]

But experience also shows us that force may be necessary simply to uphold a principle in the face of strong contrary preferences even when it is far from literally impossible for a class to conform themselves to that principle. The probability that a person will be determined to cling to the extra advantages that a given conception confers until he is forced to give them up is not the same as the literal impossibility of his disgorging those benefits. The person in question may be perfectly aware of his physical or psychological *ability* to give up those advantages even while he is determined to try to keep them if he can. Accordingly he can be aware, in the original position, of the possibility of this very strong regret (and of the determined political attitudes that it may

---

[8] Rawls uses this language in *TJR* at pp. 135 and 153.
[9] Miller, "Rawls and Marxism," p. 175. See also Clark and Gintis, "Rawlsian Justice," p. 318.
[10] Miller, "Rawls and Marxism," p. 175.   [11] Ibid.

generate) without being able to say sincerely that he will be unable to resist acting on that regret. It is a mistake, therefore, to represent the forcefulness of a person's wish that he had done better for himself as, by itself, a matter of the strains of commitment. True, the strains of commitment may be a matter of degree.[12] But the degree is between greater and lesser difficulty in conforming one's conduct to the requirements of a given principle, greater or less tolerability of the burdens the principle imposes. We are not talking here about a spectrum which has intolerability at one end and simply strong preference at the other. The spectrum of preference is quite different.

Having said all that, it is possible that the strains-of-commitment idea is a chimera. Maybe there is no degree of deprivation which is literally insupportable by those who are supposed to bear it.[13] Maybe it is just a matter of preference. I don't believe that, but perhaps some economists do. No doubt their belief to this effect is reinforced by independent methodological commitments that seek to represent all factors of motivation in the light of "preferences." If this position is accepted, then there is reason to abandon the strains-of-commitment idea altogether, not to extend it to a wider range of cases involving the better off. That the outcomes of certain conceptions of justice would be strongly preferred by some people to the outcomes of others is a starting point of analysis; it can't be a decisive factor. A theory of justice is supposed to review, criticize, and evaluate the preferences that we bring to this matter, not pander to them. And the strains-of-commitment idea was supposed to be one way of doing that.

So my answer to the first difficulty is conditional. Either there is something to the strains-of-commitment idea or there is not. If there is, it should not be confused simply with people having strong preferences for one outcome or another. Rawls maintains that "no one is permitted to agree to a principle if they have reason to doubt that they will be *able* to honor the consequences of its consistent application" (*CP*, p. 250). This is quite different from having reason to doubt that they will be *willing* to honor the consequences of the principle's application. So long as this distinction holds up – even if it is a distinction

---

[12] This is what Rawls implies when he says, in Rawls, "Some Reasons" that "in the original position the parties are to favor those principles compliance with which should prove more tolerable, whatever their situation in society turns out to be" (*CP*, p. 229).

[13] I discussed this in Waldron, "John Rawls and the Social Minimum." There I argued that the strains of commitment is more credibly adduced in support of a social minimum approach than a maximin approach: the social minimum would be specified in terms of that level of deprivation – whatever it turns out to be – that is literally unsupportable by those who might be required by social principles to bear it.

between two (different) matters of degree – the strains of commitment remains a powerful tool in the arsenal that Rawls deploys against rival principles. But if the distinction does not hold up, there is no argument here at all.

3.2 The model-theoretic objection

In 1974 Rawls wrote that "[t]he argument from the strains of commitment has an important place in justice as fairness, and the concept of a contract (agreement) is essential to it" (*CP*, p. 249). He said that it is "[t]he notion of a contract [that] implies that one cannot enter into an agreement that one will be unable to keep" (*CP*, p. 229). But is one entitled to use the notion of a contract in this way? I said at the beginning of this chapter that the strains-of-commitment argument seems to involve the importation of features of the original position model into the real-life situation to which that model is being artificially applied. It is natural to see this as a confusion, inasmuch as contractarian choice in the original position is supposed to be thought of as purely hypothetical.

After all, Rawls is careful to tell us that "[n]o society can ... be a scheme of cooperation which men enter voluntarily in a literal sense" (*TJR*, p. 12). So shouldn't we distinguish between (1) the choice of principles in the original position and (2) the real-world application of the principles that are chosen? The fact that (1) is conceived in a contractarian sprit is not supposed to imply that (2) involves the voluntary carrying out of a contract. At level (2), the chosen principles might be applied to people's behaviour and to the basic structure in all sorts of ways – sometimes, for example, by the direct enforcement of legislation. "[O]nce the full set of principles ... is on hand, we can simply forget about the conception of the original position and apply these principles as we would any others" (*TJR*, p. 99). Level (2), then, is not necessarily to be understood as the consummation of a contract. The elements of contract are supposed to be confined to level (1). And the trouble with using the strains of commitment as a level (1) argument against the choice of certain principles is that it blurs this line. That is the difficulty.

It is as though a utilitarian were to insist on special provision being made in his conception of justice for the ideal observer (or impartial spectator), e.g. making sure that enough resources are reserved for the use of the ideal observer so that his epistemic position is truly ideal and so that he has everything he needs to figure out the distribution of utility. That would be an absurd category mistake, for the utilitarian uses the ideal observer model to capture the spirit of his principles: he does not propose it as a political role for which fiscal and institutional provision must be made. Well, similarly with the commitment aspect of choice in the original position: it is part of the hypothetical model that we use to arrive at principles of justice; it is not supposed to be a feature of the principles' application in society.

I believe this objection can be answered, though the answer takes us deep into the overall liberal orientation of Rawls's theory.

The answer is actually suggested by Rawls's discussion of the utilitarian model of the ideal observer. The ideal observer model, he said, was defective inasmuch as it failed "to take seriously the distinction between persons" (*TJR*, p. 163). In the model, the observer is supposed to experience the pleasures and pains of everyone in society and to respond to them in the way that a single rational individual might be imagined to respond to such an array of experiences. "The principle of rational choice for one man is taken as the principle of social choice as well" (*TJR*, p. 163). And Rawls's point is that, although this is just a model, it does seem to involve a serious mismatch between what matters to us in society and the way we are going about addressing the question of justice. Justice presupposes plurality: to adapt a phrase from Hannah Arendt, we face questions of justice because not one man but men in the plural inhabit the world, not a person but people.[14] And the way we approach justice – even the models we use – should reflect or at least not erase this fundamental plurality. So that is a negative point about the theoretical model that certain utilitarians use.

Equally, Rawls might want to emphasize a certain affirmative consonance between the contractarian aspect of his original position model and the way we think about liberal societies in the real world. We do not think of such societies as having liberal principles of justice thrust upon them (as though by a benevolent colonial power or a liberal theocracy), imposed and enforced even against the will of the inhabitants. The liberal vision of society is of a cooperative life together in which individuals understand and appreciate the principles they live by, in which they take ownership of those principles, and offer one another assurances that they are ready to stand by them, so that all of them can benefit reciprocally from one another's acts and forbearances.[15] All societies face the problems defined in what Rawls calls "the circumstances of justice" (*TJR*, pp. 109ff.); the fundamental question for a liberal theorist of justice is "How can these problems be overcome in a life lived freely together?"

---

[14] Arendt, *The Origins*, p. 476.
[15] All this is evident from Rawls's conception of "a well-ordered society" set out in *PL* at pp. 35 and 66.

An understanding of this kind is valid and important quite apart from the contractarian structure of Rawls's original position. In itself this understanding has nothing to do with the original position. It invokes deep and principled liberal perspectives on the problems to which theories of justice are supposed to be a response. And we should expect such a perspective to make a difference to the manner in which we approach such problems and, in political philosophy, to the way we go about building the models that will help us to solve them.

With all this in mind, we can see that it is actually a mistake to think of contractarian ideas as being hermetically confined to the theoretical stage in which the original position model is built. Contractarian ideas answer to and resonate with the basic liberal orientation. And even though it remains true, as Rawls puts it, that the parties who are imagined to face the choice of principles in the original position are simply "artificial creatures inhabiting our device of representation"(*PL*, p. 28), he nevertheless insists that

> [w]e introduce an idea like that of the original position because there seems no better way to elaborate a political conception of justice for the basic structure from the fundamental idea of society as an ongoing and fair system of cooperation between citizens regarded as free and equal. (*PL*, p. 26)

Or, as he put it in a 1980 article, the choice situation of the original position may be seen as a heuristic device helping us to "uncover the fundamental ideas (latent in common sense) of freedom and equality, of ideal social cooperation, and of the person"; that is what we are doing, he says, in "formulating what I shall call 'model-conceptions'" (*CP*, p. 307).

Suppose we were indifferent to this connection. Then we might think of the overall conception as not implying anything about the way the principles of justice chosen in the original position were to be applied to societies in the real world. They might be adopted voluntarily or they might be applied at the point of a bayonet. Though the selection of principles might be conceived as a matter of choice, nothing resembling choice or commitment might be involved in their imposition.

The most striking example of theorizing about justice along these lines is the thought experiment presented in Bruce Ackerman's 1980 book, *Social Justice in the Liberal State*.[16] Ackerman invites us to think about justice using the model of a spaceship full of colonists approaching an uninhabited but

---

[16] Ackerman, *Social Justice*, pp. 19ff.

well-endowed planet. The commander of the spaceship gathers the colonists all together and tells them that they will not be allowed to land on the planet until they settle among themselves the principles that are going to govern their life together down there and the division of the resources that the planet is known to contain.

Various constraints of neutrality, reasonableness, and rationality are to be placed on the conversation that ensues, but, for our purposes, the most striking thing about Ackerman's model is that the spaceship is imagined to have the technological wherewithal to costlessly enforce any principles that we agree upon. There are ray guns and force-fields that will uphold the distribution and sustain and operate the institutions which the application of principles of justice involves. As we orbit the planet, we know that the ship's "ray guns can be costlessly transformed into a perfect police force, giving constant and infallible protection to whatever distribution of manna we think right."[17] The shape of the overall conception is based on the following thought:

> So long as you and I can imagine a power structure, P_i, in which we might defend all our claims to scarce resources through Neutral conversation, the perfect technology of justice will costlessly permit us to shape our relations in the way specified by P_i.[18]

This, says Ackerman, "permits the polity to focus clearly on the question of ultimate objectives ... to define the kind of power structure worthy of collective support."[19] Proceeding on this basis, we do not waste the time allocated to the issue of justice "by talking about important, yet ultimately secondary issues of implementation."[20] As Ackerman reflected in a later article, it was the aim of his "ideal theory" to focus steadfastly upon the choice of principles "by introducing a temporary conversational stop upon all questions involving implementation."[21]

Consider what a difference the assumption of a perfect technology of justice would have made to Rawls's conception. If the people in the original position knew that whatever principles they agreed on could be enforced by ray guns and force-fields, they would not have had to worry about strains of commitment. They could have signed up for any principles that appeared on the whole attractive, and they would not have had to consider their ability or inability to steel themselves to those principles should the worst outcome prove to be the case. They could have succumbed to the

---

[17] Ibid., p. 31.   [18] Ibid., p. 21.   [19] Ibid.   [20] Ibid., p. 34.
[21] Ackerman, "What is Neutral?" p. 377.

arguments for average utility, secure in the knowledge that it was a good bet and that, in the unlikely event they lost, there would be no question but that they would comport themselves as good losers. They would understand that the ray guns and the force-fields would leave them with no other choice.

Now there is nothing wrong with abstraction in political thought. If we have reason to think that the choice of a solution to one problem, A, depends on a prior and independent sense of the solution to another problem, B, then it may be appropriate for us to try and focus on B for a while undistracted by A, not because we think A is unimportant, but because we believe this is the way we can put ourselves in the best position to address it.

Arguably this is what is going on with Rawls's own assumption of strict compliance (*TJR*, pp. 7–8). In ideal theory, which is what we are supposed to be engaged in when we consider the choice between Rawls's principles and principles like average utilitarianism, we are told to imagine that in the society for which we are choosing principles, people will actually play their part – whatever part is assigned to them – on the basis of the principles that are chosen. At this stage of our theorizing, the chosen principles are not imagined to face difficulties of compliance and enforcement. So again, it may be asked, why are we concerned at this stage with the strains of commitment? Of course, non-ideal theory will have to confront these matters – how much money will have to be allocated to law enforcement and barbed wire in circumstances where some people are unwilling to do what justice requires. But Rawls's view is supposed to be that we can and should postpone those calculations until we have already figured out what the true principles of justice are. And we figure out what the true principles of justice are by working through the original position model on the assumption, at least in the first instance, that enforcement of the chosen principles is not expected to be a difficulty. Isn't this just the same as Ackerman's model, although Ackerman's model is imagined more vividly?

Well, not quite. Consider Rawls's own observations on the connection between strict compliance and the strains of commitment:

Once principles are acknowledged the parties can depend on one another to conform to them. In reaching an agreement, then, they know that their undertaking is not in vain: their capacity for a sense of justice insures that the principles chosen will be respected. It is essential to observe, however, that this assumption still permits the consideration of men's capacity to act on the various conceptions of justice. The general facts of human psych-ology are relevant matters for the parties to examine. If a conception of justice is unlikely to generate its own support, or lacks stability, this fact must not be overlooked. (*TJR*, p. 125)

The assumption of strict compliance, Rawls insists, "only says that the parties have a capacity for justice in a purely formal sense: Taking everything relevant into account, including the general facts of moral psychology, the parties will adhere to the principles eventually chosen" (*TJR*, p. 126). And he follows this by repeating that the parties "will not enter into agreements they know they cannot keep, or can do so only with great difficulty. Along with other considerations, they count the strains of commitment" (*TJR*, p. 126). They distinguish in other words between the questions "Can I comply with these principles?" and "Will I comply with these principles (assuming that compliance is possible)?" An affirmative answer to the latter is what is implied by the assumption of strict compliance. But that assumption does not magically provide an affirmative answer to the first question. And the trouble with Ackerman's perfect technology of justice is that it blurs the line between these two questions. Strict compliance is about what people will do when they have a choice, whereas consideration of the strains of commitment establishes the psychological credibility of the strict compliance assumption. In Rawls's conception, strict compliance is not used in the way that Ackerman's perfect technology of justice is used – to establish that people can be *made* to do what they may not be able to bring themselves to do.

There are all sorts of things wrong with Ackerman's perfect technology idea. He does not address the issue of how principles can be administered by a machine – odd, one would have thought, for a professor of American constitutional law.[22] He is asking us to imagine the choice of principles of justice in light of the availability of literally unlimited resources to enforce them[23] – a premise that takes us so far from actuality as to call in question the interest of principles chosen against this assumption. It comes close to repudiating what Rawls calls the circumstances of justice (*TJR*, pp. 109ff.), at least if these are supposed to include our vulnerability to one another.[24] Principles chosen when these circumstances are sidelined are like principles chosen without any assumption of moderate scarcity or limited altruism.

---

[22] Ackerman later suggests that the perfect technology of justice might better have been described as an "ideal legal system": see Ackerman, "What is Neutral?" p. 377.

[23] Ackerman, *Social Justice*, pp. 23 and 235.

[24] Compare Hume, *Treatise*, pp. 487–8, on the easy movability of resources from one person to another ("the instability of their possession"), and Hart, *Concept of Law*, pp. 194–5, on the problem of our mutual vulnerability as a feature of the minimum content of natural law.

Anyway, before designating a perfect technology of justice as an aspect of *ideal* theory, maybe we should ask whether it is actually something to aspire to. Would ours be a better world if barbed wire were so sharp, force-fields so impenetrable, ray guns programmed so perfectly, that no one could ever violate another's rights or deny the claims that justice supports? Is this something we should hope for, as we acquire the means to realize liberal ideals? Is it a matter of regret, that in the real world we have to rely on each other for respect for our rights, not on some perfect technology of justice?

I see three reasons in this tradition for not including a perfect technology among our aspirations for justice. First, much of modern liberalism is prem-ised on a certain sort of apprehension about the political and legal means that we use to uphold our rights. The state is the guarantor of our rights but the state also is one of the largest threats to our rights; and any technology used for the one purpose is usually also available for the other. Maybe there is some magical way of separating the two in a thought-experiment: perhaps it follows from Ackerman's approach that people devoted to justice have nothing to fear from the vast apparatus of enforcement that his fantasy involves. But in the real world, the biggest threat to our rights comes in fact from those empowered to enforce them, those entrusted with whatever rudimentary technology of justice we have. And we have to choose our principles knowing that the means of enforcing them will always be liable to abuse in this way.

Secondly, Ackerman's conception ignores the point that we are accustomed to facing issues of justice on the assumption that, like the laws we are familiar with in modern democracies, principles of justice will work mainly by self-application.[25] True, there will be some policing and some technology like locks and closed-circuit cameras, but the main burden of the application of the laws that a just basic structure comprises will fall on the routine voluntary acts of individuals. And this is how modern societies work. They depend largely on the willingness of their members (or almost all of them) to bear with and work within the basic institutions that purport to structure their lives. This is a truth independent of any social contract hypothesis, though of course it is the foothold in social experience that contractarian theories step up on. So much is the self-application of law taken for granted in society, that we tend not to focus on its significance for political philosophy. But it is a massively important aspect of the presence of a basic structure of laws and institutions in our lives. To imagine away the necessity for widespread

---

[25] For discussion of "self-application" in legal theory, see Hart and Sacks, *The Legal Process*, pp. 120–1 and Waldron, "How Law," pp. 200–22.

voluntary self-application is to imagine a kind of life together that is utterly different from our own.

More than that – and this is the third point – we do not just value the assurance that people will play their part and support one another voluntarily in this matter of justice. We build on it. The reciprocity of mutual respect makes possible other forms of cooperation (and maybe also forbearance) that go beyond justice but that may not easily be predicated on the relations that obtain between persons snarling at one another in aggressive frustration from outside one another's force-fields.

For these reasons, then, we should probably be chary of any move in political philosophy that invites us to sideline the question of people's willingness to act on just principles. Of course, non-compliance is an issue in non-ideal theory. But even there it is envisaged as sporadic rather than endemic, something that can be taken care of by familiar mechanisms of law enforcement rather than by the quite different paradigm that Ackerman's perfect technology involves. Law enforcement in non-ideal theory always has to be imagined against a background of widespread voluntary compliance with just laws. For these reasons, we should always have in front of us the question of whether people can bring themselves to comply with a given set of principles supposing that they are willing to do so (if they can). That point is made vivid to us by the idea of bargaining in good faith in a contractarian original position. But it is not just a feature of the contract model. It poses questions about the real-world societies that we are trying to make just – to make just on the model of willing compliance with just principles rather than their wholesale mechanical enforcement.

The fit between strains of commitment and the real-world issue of self-application is not the only instance of resonance between Rawls's contractarian model and important features of liberal society in the real world. Transparency (or publicity) is another. In considering the principles on their agenda, Rawls says that the parties in the original position "assume that they are choosing principles for a public conception of justice" (*TJR*, p. 115). It is assumed that "everyone will know about these principles all that he would know if their acceptance were the result of an agreement" (*TJR*, p. 115). Now although Rawls says that it is "characteristic of contract theory to stress the public nature of political principles" (*TJR*, p. 15), it makes no sense to suppose that the idea of this publicity is confined to the contract model. On the contrary, principles are to be rejected if it is the case that, though they are understood by the people in the original position, their effectiveness in the real world will have to depend on concealment or popular misapprehension (*TJR*, p. 398). The contractarian apparatus brings into focus a deeper but more direct commitment to the idea of a society whose principles are amenable to explanation and justification in the understanding of those who have to live under them.[26]

Democratic ideas also represent a projection of the contract idea into the society to which it is applied. We see this in Rawls's account of what he calls "political justice" (*TJR*, pp. 194ff.):

> Justice as fairness begins with the idea that where common principles are necessary ... they are to be worked out from the viewpoint of a suitably defined initial situation of equality in which each person is fairly represented. The principle of participation transfers this notion from the original position to the constitution ... If the state is to exercise a final and coercive authority over a certain territory, and if it is in this way to affect permanently men's prospects in life, then the constitutional process should preserve the equal representation of the original position to the degree that this is practicable. (*TJR*, p. 195)

The plenary assembly imagined for the original position resonates with the participatory politics of a free society in which social questions which need to be resolved are actually and not just notionally submitted to the representatives of all the people for decision. There is a lot more to be said about political participation than this, and Rawls addresses the subject extensively in Chapter 4 of *TJ*. But along with the argument about publicity, the argument about self-application, and the argument about strains of commitment, it proceeds on the basis that there is a certain and essential fit between the contractarian model and the free spirit of the society for which principles are to be chosen.

3.3 Some conclusions

Answering these two objections to the strains-of-commitment argument – the model-theoretic objection and the malcontents objection – has enabled us to reflect on the character of the original position argument and the notions of choice and well-being that it embodies. The original position is largely a heuristic device in relation to the principles of justice that Rawls is arguing for. It is a heuristic device in the sense that the principles of justice as fairness

---

[26] This passage is adapted from Waldron, "Theoretical Foundations," pp. 35–62.

could be presented and justified (in reflective equilibrium) without it. But it is not wholly a heuristic device. We know this partly because the device is itself supposed to represent something about fairness and impartiality: it stands itself in reflective equilibrium in relation to our considered judgments about what is the fair way to resolve disagreements (*TJR*, pp. 15–19). And we have seen that it also represents something abstract but important about the envisaged character of the society to which principles of justice are to be applied. They are to be applied to a free society in a spirit of freedom, as though they represented a voluntary commitment. The social contract may be a myth but it captures something important about our reciprocal willingness to respect one another as free and equal participants in the shaping of a social order.

Accordingly, Rawls's idea of the strains of commitment represents something important about the way we regard one another in our common allegiance to just principles. In the original position, all parties have to recognize that there are limits on what they can commit themselves to. This is not just a matter of what they strongly prefer, but a matter of what human agency can reconcile itself to. I argued at the outset that Rawls turns this against any possibility of choosing utilitarian principles. Those in the original position must contemplate the possibility that such principles will turn out to make unbearable demands on them. This argument has its counterpart in our – not the parties' – vision of what would be wrong with a society governed by such principles. Not only do such principles threaten to impose burdens on some that strike us as unpleasant and unfair, but the imposition of such burdens cannot be reconciled with the spirit of a society in which benefits are enjoyed and burdens shouldered in a spirit of willing cooperation. The strains of commitment is a device that links the character of that direct but rather unelaborated criticism to the more indirect and theoretical argument that graces the pages of *TJ*.

4 Our talents, our histories, ourselves: Nozick on the original position argument

John Christman

In considering how society should be structured, in particular how social institutions that fundamentally shape our life prospects should be arranged, what facts about people should we take into account? In drafting the principles governing those basic institutions, should we consider how talented people are, their sex or race, or other variable contingencies about them? If we do, we may well structure those principles in ways that favor certain groups, such as those with more natural talent, or those whose race, gender, or social identity are dominant in the power structure of society. But would that be fair? Rawls's original position procedure is a representational device to construct a negative answer to that question and thereby determine the principles that shape basic social institutions in ways that abstract from those contingencies.

Robert Nozick objected to many aspects of this procedure, and he did so as a defender of libertarian political philosophy. Nozick produced, in fact, the most developed and nuanced defense of that libertarian vision that we have. And for a good while after *TJ* and *ASU* were published, much of the discussion of distributive justice centered on the conflict between these two theories.

And while much of the commentary on this debate critically analyzed the two theories themselves, either separately or together, less attention was paid to Nozick's objections to the original position specifically. Of course, since the original position is so central to Rawls's theory, especially in *TJ*, any discussion of the two thinkers contained implications for the plausibility of the original position argument and, by extension, the questions Nozick raised about it. In that light, I want to discuss some of the representative themes in Nozick's critique and consider how well the original position holds up against them. While libertarianism no longer holds the broad

I am grateful to Timothy Hinton for helpful comments on an earlier draft of this chapter.

appeal in the philosophical world it once did,[1] Nozick's objections are still trenchant and interesting.

In the end, I will suggest that Nozick's critique fails, but not exactly for the reasons discussed by the commentators I mention (though for closely related reasons). Indeed, I want to argue that Rawls's claims motivating the design of the original position can be seen as consistent with Nozick's own view when we look at the principle of rectification he offers as a palliative to the ubiquitous injustices that we know mark the history and current practices of most (all?) societies. In our own non-ideal world, I think Nozick should agree that a fair solution to the problem of distributive justice would entail abstracting from the largely arbitrary inequalities that structure the social world in which people must live their lives, given that they are born and grow up under non-ideal conditions not of their own choosing.

Rawls begins with the idea that social institutions must be shaped by principles that reflect the perspective of free and equal moral persons, ones with the capacity to pursue a conception of the good within the constraints of justice. As Nozick puts a similar idea, justice is based on respect for a "person's shaping his life in accordance with some overall plan" (*ASU*, p. 50). Nothing in the original position procedure or the egalitarian economic principles that flow from it should be seen to conflict with this basic value commitment.

Before laying out Nozick's objections, which I do in section 4.2, I first sketch the relevant parts of Rawls's original position argument so as to be clear on the terms of this debate, as I understand them. After critically discussing Nozick's lines of critique, I conclude by noting what I take to be the crux of the disagreement as well as what might indeed turn out to be a point of convergence.

4.1 Background: relevant aspects of the original position procedure

The original position procedure requires that principles of justice be determined under conditions which are themselves fair, in particular that they model the conditions of rational choice for (and by) persons who consider

---

[1] This is relatively speaking of course, as there is still much interesting discussion of libertarianism in various forms (see e.g. Narveson and Sterba, "Are Liberty?"), and of course a particularly unphilosophical form of libertarianism in the form of neo-liberalism is quite prominent in various current political debates.

themselves as free and equal rational beings. Specifically, the procedure bars knowledge of those aspects of the representative person's condition that would, if they were part of the process, undercut its fairness.[2] Picturing this as a hypothetical choice among representative persons, we imagine that those in the original position are barred from knowing aspects of themselves that are "arbitrary from a moral point of view," that is, they are barred by the veil of ignorance from knowledge of factors that would conflict with the fairness of the choice procedure. Among those factors that Rawls claimed were arbitrary are a person's natural talents as well as other accidents of birth and upbringing that may largely determine her success in a market economy but which would skew the choice of principles if known behind the veil (*TJ*, pp. 16–17).

Prior to the invocation of the original position procedure, however, is the fundamental problem of distributive justice, as Rawls understands it, as determining how to direct the distribution of the benefits of social cooperation itself. Both those who are comparatively more fortunate, as measured by their natural assets and the contingencies of their social location, and those who are less so by the same measures, gain from the benefits of social cooperation. Without a general scheme of coordinated social interaction, economic production, family life, social practices, and so on, life would be relatively unlivable.[3] So everyone gains from living in a well-ordered society. Now some are born with and in conditions that allow them to be better off generally, say by having certain talents that their society happens to favor (and might pay them to exercise if given the chance).[4] But since having those advantages is "arbitrary from a moral point of view" institutions of distributive justice cannot be arranged to benefit such groups "twice over" (*TJ*, p. 88). This "ensures that no one is advantaged or disadvantaged in the choice of

---

[2] This initial discussion of the original position will reflect the formulation found in *TJ*, primarily because that is the version that Nozick is criticizing. However, I will note where emendations and clarifications in Rawls's later work, specifically in *PL*, bear specifically on the structure and plausibility of Nozick's critique.

[3] Indeed, in *PL*, Rawls makes clear that for the purposes of his version of social contract theory, life outside of societies is inconceivable. See *PL*, p. 270.

[4] In what follows I will use the phrases "natural talents" and "natural assets" to follow Rawls and Nozick. But it should be noted that the full specification should be "natural skills and background conditions that significantly shape one's relative social position." That longer phrase is needed because "natural" skills and talents are only beneficial to the person in social settings where they can be used to advantage, specifically in ways that others value and may want to pay for. As we will see, this *interaction* between the contingencies of one's birth and background and systems of (market) exchange that affect a person due to those contingencies will be the crucial focus in this debate.

principles by the outcome of natural chance or the contingency of social circumstances" (*TJ*, p. 11).

For these reasons, Rawls's theory utilizes the original position procedure, from which are derived the two principles of justice, the second of which has two parts. We can simplify and describe them as three principles: the basic liberties principle (persons have an equal right to the most adequate scheme of basic liberties); the fair equality of opportunity principle (inequalities must be attached to positions open to all); and the difference principle (inequalities are allowed only insofar as they benefit the worst off group). The difference principle will be our main focus here, as it is for Nozick. But we should add that the principles are to be imposed in lexical order, the first being prior to the second and the second to the third.[5] No infringement of a prior principle can be justified by advances in one lower on the list. As we will see, this is a significant claim regarding the acceptability of the difference principle and, by extension, the original position procedure that produces it.

Also, the most salient alternative to the difference principle for the purposes of discussing Nozick's views is what Rawls calls the "system of natural liberty," a system which roughly conforms to what Nozick calls his historical "entitlement" theory of justice (*ASU*, Chapter 7, Part I). Under such a theory, individuals acquire entitlements to goods by way of appropriation and exchange. Justice in appropriation is secured when persons acquire goods in ways that do not violate the Lockean rights of others in the process, specifically leaving "enough and as good" for them after appropriation. This is the Lockean proviso, which Nozick operationalizes as requiring that appropriators not make others worse off through not being able to appropriate or use resources (both the specific ones appropriated and all others that are available), including those made available by a productive system of private property. Such a system, Nozick suggests, has created unfathomably more goods than would have been available in a state of nature prior to all appropriation (*ASU*, pp. 176–7), so even after all goods are acquired, those left with no further opportunity to appropriate still have no complaint on the ground of their Lockean rights. This proviso, and Nozick's view in general, has been much discussed, and many criticisms have been leveled against it on its own terms.[6]

---

[5] I have simplified Rawls's presentation by referring to three principles rather than two; the lexical ordering of the principles I describe is the same as Rawls's (see *TJ*, pp. 53–4 and *PL*, pp. 310–23).

[6] This literature is vast, though examples of the critique of Nozick's view are Ryan, "Yours, mine," Gibbard, "Natural Property," Cohen, "Robert Nozick," and Christman, *The Myth*,

I mention it here only to specify the system Nozick envisions as the relevant alternative to life under the difference principle. For our purposes, it amounts to a market system of exchange without regulation or redistribution except for those needed to enforce the property rights involved in those exchanges.[7]

In contrast to the difference principle as well as other welfare state or egalitarian elements of economic justice, this structure allows people's lot in life to be largely determined by their ability to sell their labor or justly acquired (or created) goods with others in a market of voluntary exchange. No *re*distribution is allowed, and the result is what we would recognize as free market capitalism with a minimal state. Against this background, then, let us consider Nozick's major objections to both the difference principle in particular and the original position procedure which generates it.

4.2 Nozick's criticisms

Nozick develops several overlapping lines of criticism of the Rawlsian view. These criticisms are mutually dependent but can be separately labeled for now. They are: the social benefits argument; the bias against historical principles argument; the slavery of the talented argument; and the critique of arbitrariness. Let us begin by looking at these in turn, though explicating them will reveal their mutual dependence (and indeed how they all rely on the fourth). Some of these lines of argument are aimed specifically at the principles that form the core of justice as fairness, the difference principle in particular, but as I will explain, the shape of the criticisms is such that the design of the original position itself is always included in their scope.

Moreover, as originally formulated, the criticisms rely on an interpretation of the original position and of the principles of justice that differs sharply from what Rawls later took to be his considered view. Specifically, Nozick views the problem of distributive justice as structured by the question of what people (with certain rights) can be expected to agree to, while Rawls makes clear that this misunderstands why we must focus on the basic structure as the primary locus of principles of justice (*PL*, Lecture VII). As I will explain below, Rawls argues that agreements among persons are not justified in isolation unless they are made against a background of (already established)

Chapter 3. For recent discussions, see Otsuka, "Self-ownership" and Meadowcroft, "Nozick's Critique."

[7] There is also, as we will discuss below, a principle of rectification, which provides the third prong of Nozick's theory of distributive justice.

just practices and institutions (*PL*, pp. 266–7). Moreover, the question of the "surplus" from social cooperation should not be understood as over and above what people could expect if they lived *outside of society*, as Nozick frames it.[8] Nevertheless, I proceed initially here with Nozick's approach.

4.2.1 Sharing the benefits of social cooperation

As we noted, Rawls sets up the problem of distributive justice as the problem of dividing the "social surplus," namely the benefits of social cooperation that come from living together in a relatively stable manner in a well-ordered society. As we saw, Rawls thinks all citizens benefit from this arrangement, and indeed life without it would be impossible to envision, or if conceivable, hardly worth living. Rawls argues in particular that those worst off in terms of social benefits have a special claim on the fairness of the distribution of those benefits.[9] Nozick argues, however, that this focus on the less favored is unmotivated, and that both the richly and poorly endowed are owed a fair share of the social surplus. Rawls illegitimately focuses on the latter, he claims, but the skilled can always complain that they would fare much better without a system of social cooperation as compared to Rawls's system of redistribution, in particular one obeying the difference principle. So it must be shown that their cooperation in social life is worth the cost to them as well (*ASU*, pp. 183–97).

Further, the better favored can *calculate* their share in the social benefit in two ways, both of which militate against Rawls's manner of viewing the social surplus. The first considers life outside society, where the well off live as separate Robinson Crusoes on different islands, for example. Why would such individuals have any obligation to share in the benefits of coordinating production across the island chain? Certainly each Crusoe would have to consider her lot in isolation and then ask what the benefits are for her from joining with others in a society. Unless both the less- and the *more*-talented could be convinced to join, a distributive scheme that divides the social surplus only with regard to the gains for the least favored is unfair. Nozick writes, "The better endowed gain by cooperating with the worse endowed,

---

[8] As do David Gauthier, *Morals*, and other libertarian theorists (Narveson, *Libertarian Idea*). For Rawls's response to Gauthier specifically, see Rawls, *PL*, p. 278. I am grateful to Timothy Hinton for helpful suggestions for clarifying these points.

[9] This explication utilizes the relatively simplified notion of the institutions of the basic structure, along the lines Rawls originally presented it (*TJ*, p. 6). For a detailed discussion of the ambiguities in Rawls's notion of the basic structure, see Pogge, *Realizing*, pp. 15–28.

and the worse endowed gain by cooperating with the better endowed. Yet the difference principle is not neutral between the better and the worse endowed. Whence the asymmetry?" (*ASU*, p. 193).

As Thomas Pogge points out, however, this argument is relatively unconvincing, if only because the benefits of living as a Robinson Crusoe are so entirely indeterminate.[10] A person currently favored in her social standing might well *imagine* that she could do quite well on her own in a *Survivor* type setting where she produces all she needs for a satisfying life, but this is mere fantasy. No one has *any idea* what life would be like in such a setting, especially since there are virtually no islands of this sort left to inhabit (and who would flourish on an *island* anyway?). And does such a person have no parents? Or children? If so, then we are talking about mini-societies already, so what would be the fair principles for *those* arrangements?[11]

Indeed, Rawls later emphasized that in justifying principles of distributive justice, we cannot *envision* life outside of society and make comparisons with the level of advantages we enjoy in our particular social space. Partly, this is because the history, culture, and institutional structure of our society has shaped the value perspective we come to embody. As Rawls says, "the institutional form of society affects its members and determines in large part the kind of persons they want to be as well as the kind of persons they are" (*PL*, p. 269). And as we will see, this observation affects the dispute about natural talents that Nozick also raises.

A seemingly more promising version of Nozick's argument concerns the *marginal* contribution to the social product made by the (currently) most favored people in a society. Indeed, Nozick points out that Rawls asks how to divide the *entire* social product resulting from cooperative behavior, but he goes on to ask why should we not focus on the net *increase* from cooperation over non-cooperation? In particular, Nozick argues that standard marginal productivity theory can help us calculate the difference that each person's participation makes in the overall social product (and hence the benefits flowing therefrom). And in fact Rawls himself must accept that this marginal contribution can be calculated, for the difference principle depends on being

---

[10] *John Rawls*, pp. 178–84.

[11] As with other traditional social contract theories, abstracting away from families, and in particular women and children, allow for a simplification that covers significant bias in the approach to the rationality of the choice to "enter" society. See e.g. Pateman, *Sexual Contract* and Okin, *Justice*.

able to identify those whose contributions benefit the worst off group the most in order to incentivize their continuing to do so (*ASU*, pp. 183–9).

If we can calculate marginal product in this way, we must then frame the question of social benefit differently. Insofar as the worst off need to be convinced that the distribution of the social product is fair to them, the better off need the same kind of assurance, but under the difference principle they will not receive it since they will calculate that the returns to their marginal contribution under the difference principle will be less than under a system of natural liberty (a free market). Moreover, egalitarian theories like Rawls's treat the goods available in society like "manna from heaven," dropped down unattached to any producer. But of course goods are produced largely (Nozick thinks) through the efforts and talents of people, and if we can calculate the marginal increase in total product value that comes from the efforts of a single (representative) person we can calculate her contribution to the social surplus (*ASU*, p. 198).

More pointedly, the argument from the existence of a social surplus fails to motivate the need for a veil of ignorance which, in turn, justifies the difference principle. The argument that *since* there is a problem of dividing the social surplus, *then* we should adopt the original position and hence the difference principle is invalid. Any otherwise acceptable principles of distribution will also divide the surplus adequately. Moreover, Nozick thinks, the entitlement theory he favors has the added bonus of giving people what they are entitled to by way of (non-rights-violating) acquisition and production and free exchange (*ASU*, pp. 196–7).

I won't address the latter point, as others have discussed criticisms of Nozick's own view in detail.[12] But does this pose a challenge to the use of the original position, since the latter rests on the assumption that a person's natural assets should be ignored in deriving principles of justice? First, Rawls claims that the worst off have a special claim to justification for their social position because of the deviation from *equality* that this embodies, and that all deviations from equality of treatment must be justified, specifically in a way that satisfies those who suffer from that inequality. Nozick maintains that this presumption of equality itself needs to be justified, as must Rawls's particular interpretation of what it means for people to be "treated" equally (by whom?). I discuss this response further below.

---

[12] See e.g. the essays in Paul, *Reading Nozick*. I develop criticisms myself in Christman, *The Myth*, Chapter 3.

Before doing so, I should note that in Rawls's later political view he made an appeal to the commitment to equality implicit in the public culture of modern democracies (*PL*, pp. 154–72). But for this to be an adequate response, he has to claim, further, that the *particular* conception of equality to which people are so committed implies that people enjoy equality only if their lot in life is not solely or largely determined by the "natural lottery" of skills and talents (and background social circumstance). But in many actual modern democracies there are numerous persons and groups who claim a nominal commitment to equality but believe that the free market should determine our position in society. So on sheer sociological grounds it is doubtful that people are already committed to a principle of equality that requires the original position for its operationalization.

But this leads us to the argument from "arbitrariness," that people's natural advantages are "arbitrary from a moral point of view" and hence distributions in which people's natural assets largely determine their position are unjusti- fied. However, before turning our attention to that point, which we consider in section 4.2.4 below, let us look at two other intervening critiques of the original position that Nozick advances.

4.2.2 Bias against historical principles

Recall that Nozick's own theory of justice claims that a distribution is just if it is the result of proper acquisition and transfer of goods, namely if that distribution has the right *history*. People in the original position will never choose such a principle because they lack the knowledge of their own history that would be needed to support such a choice, on the assumption that they are choosing rationally (advancing their own determinate ends, though without specific knowledge of what those ends are). Therefore, Nozick points out, people in the original position will always opt for "end-state" or "patterned" principles of distribution, namely ones that ignore the particular history of acquisition and exchange and aim for future patterns of holdings for the citizens involved. Nozick claims that this is a defect in Rawls's view, in that historical principles such as his own are ruled out of court by the decision procedure itself, a procedure that was meant to be neutral regarding the particular principles of justice that would emerge from it (*ASU*, pp. 198–204). But libertarian views like Nozick's are ruled out from the outset. How is this a fair procedure?

It might seem as though Rawls has set up his procedure to surreptitiously rule out theories he doesn't like, such as Nozick's libertarianism. But this complaint rests on a misunderstanding of the purpose and motivating ideas behind the original position. The original position rules out historical principles in the sense that those behind the veil are barred from choosing principles based on *their own* prior claims and natural assets. And the main reason Rawls adopts the original position in the first place is that such a choice would be biased in favor of those who are arbitrarily placed in a position of advantage. Moreover, as Kukathas and Pettit point out, the difference principle does not prevent the operation of the process of exchange of entitlement playing a role in the shaping of the distribution governed by it, for as long as the inequalities generated by people producing and selling their goods work to the benefit of the worst off group, such favored individuals are free to produce, buy, and sell in ways sanctioned by the entitlement theory.[13] As we will see below, this controversy turns on contested conceptions of "entitlement" (property rights), in that Nozick thinks that only if a person can use, exchange, and keep all proceeds from her goods can she be said to have an entitlement to them.

To clarify his point, Nozick considers an example of students taking tests they have studied for throughout the year. When it comes to finding out their individual grades, students are allowed to choose a "distribution" of grades, even though they have each been assigned an instructor's numerical grade based on the test itself. Nozick argues that given such a choice, students who were ignorant of their assigned grade would not choose the "historical" principle that people should be given their grades based on their individual performance, since some of them will come up short under such a scheme. But this illustrates the bias against (in this case clearly correct) historical principles of entitlement (*ASU*, pp. 199–201).

But again, we should not ask what any person should receive in the application of the principles we are considering; rather, we should ask what *system* of grades should be adopted in general. In other words, we're asking about which *institutions* should be developed to govern people's lives. At that level, there actually are many grading schemes to choose from that would deviate from the strict entitlement idea that guides Nozick's example – such as curves that assign grades relative to a class median, grades assigned to groups rather than individuals to prompt cooperative learning, and so on – and the question of what system is fair is not so easily answered. At that level, it would be quite unfair for the students who will predictably benefit from one of those schemes to choose that one simply because of that prospective benefit.[14]

---

[13] *Rawls*, pp. 74–91.

[14] For a different but compatible response to the grading example, see Sterba, "In Defense."

This controversy exemplifies Nozick's use of "micro" examples to try to draw out what he takes as unacceptable implications of the difference principle, which leads naturally to our next objection.

4.2.3 Slavery of the talented and the priority of liberty

Nozick claims that Rawls's repeated description of natural talents as "social assets" as well as the operation of the original position itself, open the way for the justification of not only the redistribution of the economic *proceeds* from one's natural assets but an intrusive redistribution of those assets themselves. If I have two perfectly healthy kidneys, and the worst off (representative) person suffers from kidney disease, then clearly she would be made better off if one of my healthy organs were removed and given to her, and it appears that the difference principle would mandate such a removal (*ASU*, pp. 206–7).[15]

As several commentators have noted, however, this implication will be blocked by the very conception of the person that underlies the original position and, in turn, motivates the priority of the basic liberties.[16] As we pointed out in section 4.1 above, the parties in the original position will choose a principle of basic liberties which will protect people from intrusions of this sort, and the lexical priority of such liberty ensures that these rights may not be infringed for the purposes of satisfying the difference principle, which is lower down on the lexically ordered list. Now Nozick expresses (but does not fully explain) a level of skepticism about the stringency of this priority (*ASU*, p. 346 n. 29), but the insistence that personal liberty of this kind is protected from the demands of economic justice is fairly explicitly stated in Rawls's theory.[17]

However, even if the actual appropriation of one's organs or talents is forbidden, distributive justice (the difference principle) might require curtailing one's *economic* activity *vis-à-vis* those factors in order to balance the overall enjoyment of social advantage in favor of the worst off group.

---

[15] As Pogge points out, these examples confuse abstract principles that define the rights we have in our goods (the topic of Rawls's and Nozick's theories) with first order actions by a government executing those principles (*Realizing*, p. 17). But Nozick discusses this point in claiming that the use of "micro" examples is relevant to the overall appraisal of the abstract principles themselves (*ASU*, pp. 204–13).

[16] See especially Pogge, *Realizing* and Metz, "Arbitrariness."

[17] As Rawls puts it, "[t]o be sure, the more advantaged have a right to their natural assets, as does everyone else; the right is covered under the first principle protecting the integrity of the person" (*TJ*, p. 89). He also elaborates on this in *PL*, Lecture VIII.

The question comes down, then, to whether being able to reap benefits from one's natural advantages, benefits that would run afoul of the limits of the difference principle, is necessary to express one's identity in pursuit of the good. The original position is designed so that one knows that one has a capacity for a conception of the good and a motivation to pursue it; for this reason, one would favor the lexical priority of rights to be allowed to engage in such a pursuit. One does not know, however, that one has any talents the demand for which would allow one to reap disproportionate economic benefits from trade in a market for such talents. So one favors the lexical priority of the protection of liberty over any rights to profit economically from the contingencies of one's social situation.

The argument for this is straightforward: the conception of the person fundamental to political thought in the liberal tradition includes the capacity to reflectively develop and pursue, and if needed revise, one's conception of value within the bounds of fairness to others with whom one must share social space. In Rawlsian language, justice is based on the model of the person with higher order interests in pursuing the good and conforming to the principles of justice. For Nozick, as I noted earlier, this idea is that of a "person's shaping his life in accordance with some overall plan." In either case, the ability to reap benefits from the trade of one's advantageous social position is not included in the central model of the person whose value lies at the root of liberal thought. Clearly Nozick doesn't think that people's differences in natural talents should issue in differences in their enjoyment of basic Lockean rights (where the beautiful and the talented get more *freedom* than the rest of us!).[18]

This is the crux of the debate of the famous "Wilt Chamberlain" argument that Nozick develops elsewhere in his discussion. With the example of a talented basketball player being paid by willing fans to watch him play, Nozick develops his general claim that enforcing "patterned" theories of distributive justice like the difference principle will always interfere with liberty. Several commentators have pointed out, however, that it is not at all counterintuitive to say that limitations on the amount one can profit from the use of one's talents are not a fundamental limitation on liberty, much less the equivalent of "forced labor," as Nozick claims.[19]

---

[18] This point is made by several commentators; see e.g. Metz, "Arbitrariness," pp. 37–8.

[19] See e.g. Cohen, "Robert Nozick." Rawls also claims that under the difference principle, "[t]here are no unannounced and unpredictable interferences with citizens' expectations

What this means is that the enjoyment of one's embodied skills, talents, organs, and so on are not the subject of distributive justice, for these are, at best, natural (not social) primary goods and so not factors to which the measurement of relative advantage will be sensitive, unless, that is, their use (in exchange, for example) places one in an advantaged position as measured by the social primary goods, specifically income and wealth.[20] The idea is simply that the measures of social advantage we use lead us to adopt policies that allow people to express and act upon their personal characteristics (within the constraints of the fundamental principles) even if those policies prevent them from getting unduly rich from doing so.

4.2.4 Arbitrariness

Clearly, however, the criticism that Nozick raises against the original position procedure that supports all the others is its treatment of what Rawls calls "arbitrary" facts about the person, abstraction from which defines the essence of the choice situation. Nozick advances what he calls both "positive" and "negative" arguments against Rawls's position, the latter being a rebuttal of an argument *for* the Rawlsian view.[21] The positive argument, in its several variations, points directly to Rawls's view that various contingencies of a person's personal profile should not be taken into account in the derivation of the principles governing the design of the basic institutions of society. Nozick questions why this should be so (see *ASU*, pp. 216–24).

Recall that the contingencies we are dealing with here are those that tend to figure prominently in determining a person's position in the scheme of social advantage, such as talents, family and educational background, gender and race, and so on. But Nozick claims that merely because a distribution of goods results from factors which are themselves arbitrary in some sense does not make those distributions illegitimate. Indeed, he claims that Rawls is actually inconsistent on this point, in that the application of his two principles of justice fails to eliminate arbitrariness itself. For the claim that arbitrariness undercuts the legitimacy of a distributive pattern infects the difference principle itself. Under the difference principle, it is acceptable to structure

and acquisitions" (*PL*, p. 283). The claim that taxation amounts to forced labor is made in *ASU*, pp. 169–72.

[20] See Pogge, *Realizing*, pp. 36–47.

[21] I skip over the negative argument here; it involves an argument based on moral desert which neither Rawls nor Nozick would accept.

policy so as to allow the better off to reap rewards for their greater contributions to the production of social goods (contributions measured by their success in the market), as long as doing so benefits the worst off group. As we discussed earlier (concerning the marginal productive contribution), those with more to offer may be given incentives to produce more so that it trickles down to the worse off, making the latter better off than under equality. But doing so, Nozick notes, legitimizes a distributive pattern based on arbitrary factors, namely the arbitrary fact that the better off were born with whatever socially beneficial proclivities and talents allow them (at least in part) to produce those beneficial trickles (*ASU*, pp. 219–20).

These objections are interesting, to be sure, but they rest again on a misunderstanding of the way the original position is designed to operate in the development of principles. Rawls does not claim that arbitrary contingencies cannot play a role in how people end up in their relative position of social advantage – that would be absurd, as contingencies and happenstance infect every aspect of our social existence. Rather, the claim is that at the level of *institutions* – the broad structure of economic and property law – policies should be chosen that operate so that the effects of the accidents of birth and background social circumstances are mitigated, and that those with less of those natural traits that tend to be valued by others are not victimized twice over by an institutional structure that allows those losses to multiply. As Sterba puts it, the original position "leads to a conception of justice which only nullifies these factors as *partial* counters in the quest for political and economic advantage."[22] Nothing about this implies that all traces of those accidents of birth (and so on) are to be erased from view in the day-to-day life of a functioning just society.

Nozick goes on to speculate, however, that the driving force behind the arbitrariness claim, for Rawls, is the idea that all deviations from *equality* are inherently suspect and so must be justified, so that any inequality in natural talents must withstand evaluative scrutiny. Hence, since the inequality of natural skills is random and accidental, an unequal distribution flowing from them fails that test. But as we noted earlier, Nozick questions this presumption against inequality, pointing out that at the interpersonal level we have no hesitation in accepting the "inequalities" inherent in people's relations

---

[22] See Sterba, "In Defense," p. 301. He adds that being entitled to natural assets (as Nozick insists we are) justifies a place in the distribution of goods no more than being inclined to criminality justifies taking that into account in the determination of whether one's basic liberties ought to be protected (Sterba, "In Defense," p. 302).

with each other, the effects of their choices, and so on (*ASU*, pp. 222–4). The beautiful people tend to attract other beautiful people, but barring sheer envy, we don't claim injustice because Brad and Angelina get to live lives of personal bliss compared to us frumpy sorts. So why should we demand that the effects of government policy correct for every other inequality?

Here again we should follow Pogge and reframe this question at the level of institutions. The question is what rules of the game should we choose (or judge to be just), not what particular action or social phenomenon we deem acceptable or worthy of complaint.[23] So it does seem unfair to arrange social *rules* so that "beautiful people" (whatever that means) not only attract other stunning types but also, by virtue of their good looks alone, enjoy higher social status, pay fewer taxes, enjoy more political liberties, and so on. It is one thing to notice that certain people fare better than us in life's strange lottery, but it is quite another to look at the rules of that social lottery and realize that there is a provision that says the lucky folks get extra chances to win![24]

Now it is true that the conception of equality that guides the shape of the original position is part of what Dworkin calls Rawls's "deeper theory," namely the prior commitment to a certain view of equality.[25] In his earlier view (to which Nozick was replying), Rawls grounded this commitment in a comprehensive liberalism in a Kantian moral framework. In his later political phase, Rawls makes clear that the commitment to freedom and equality used to shape the derivation of principles should be seen as part of the background culture of modern constitutional democracies (*PL*, pp. 24–5). In addition, the apparatus of the original position is used as part of a free-standing political conception of justice that is posited as the object of an overlapping consensus among citizens who regard themselves as free and equal and who hold differing reasonable comprehensive (philosophical, moral, or religious) views.

As Gorr points out, the basic idea behind the original position is that bracketing these personal contingencies allows the principles to reflect the nature of (political) personhood, whereby citizens are rational, moral, free, and equal.[26] Nozick is certainly free to object here that this is hardly the only construal of equality (or indeed of freedom) available in the landscape

---

[23] Pogge, *Realizing*, pp. 15–62. Rawls also makes this point in *PL* where he stresses the need to focus on the basic structure. See *PL*, Lecture VII.

[24] As Rawls puts it, the veil of ignorance "must nullify the effects of specific contingencies which put [people] at odds and tempt them to exploit social and natural circumstances to their own advantage" (*TJ*, p. 118).

[25] See Dworkin, "Original Position." For discussion of this point, see Gorr, "Rawls."

[26] Ibid., pp. 22–3.

of modern democratic sensibilities. And his idea of equality as consisting of equal Lockean rights to non-interference, and the entitlement theory of distributive justice to which it gives rise, is at least one alternative.[27] However, as the later Rawls makes clear, what is "essential" to persons *as citizens* is what is captured by the model of the person used in constructing the (political) theory that both expresses our prior commitment to equality, vague though that is, and could be the object of an overlapping consensus. The original position is used to derive principles that are invariant across the range of personal characteristics we know ourselves to have because being able to pursue a (reasonable) conception of the good is not contingent upon having any *one* of those traits.

Seeing things this way raises questions about the relation between social identities – the way people regard themselves and wish to be regarded in political institutions – and the fair rules of social cooperation governing the basic structure that theories like Rawls's are meant to produce. In the final section, then, let us reflect more generally on the function of the original position in ways that bring into sharper focus the depths of disagreement between Nozick and Rawls on this point and, surprisingly perhaps, point to a level of potential convergence between them.

4.3 General reflections: the complexity of entitlements and the marks of historical injustice

As we saw, one of the fundamental points of contention between Nozick and Rawls concerns the connection between our rights and various facts about ourselves that political institutions allegedly ought to recognize, in particular what facts those are and what array of rights, liberties, and opportunities ought to be afforded us because of them. There are, I think, two fundamental conflict points in this confrontation. The first involves disagreement over what it means to have a "right" to one's own person – the pre-political right to one's talents (and so on) the use of which should be recognized and protected by just institutions. The second concerns the very function of political philosophy, involving the proper response to not only the contingencies of our personal circumstance but the thoroughly non-ideal conditions that mark the history and current structure of modern democratic life. Let us consider these foci in turn.

---

[27] Gorr goes on to argue that Rawls fails to justify equal treatment based on people's nature as rational, moral, free, and equal persons when people also have (and identify themselves as having) talents and traits to different degrees (Gorr, "Rawls," p. 33).

4.3.1 The complexity of personal entitlements

As we saw, the original position functions to bracket consideration of arbitrary factors about one's identity and Nozick insists that this is unmotivated; indeed, he claims that his entitlement view of justice better captures our fundamental interests in expressing our essential nature as persons (and hence our pursuit of "the meaning of life" as he puts it – *ASU*, p. 50). For Nozick, recognizing personal and property rights as absolute side constraints on the way others can treat us is the only way to show respect for persons understood in this way. For Rawls, this basic respect, which he expresses as recognizing the "separateness of persons," involves the protection of basic liberties and opportunities equally but does not extend to allowing citizens to use their talents in exchange with others in order to reap all benefits from such exchanges no matter what the outcome, even if we accept that people *own* their talents as an expression of their basic liberty.[28]

What this disagreement shows, I think, is that the notion of entitlement here, more particularly the idea of *ownership*, is complex and subject to a variety of interpretations and modes of disaggregation. Nozick's libertarian view assumes that conventional (that is, state) structuring of property rights in ways that deviate from full rights to exchange and gain income from those exchanges in a market counts as *interference* with the liberty of agents in the deep sense that justice forbids. This implies, of course, that taxation is a restriction on liberty. The question that must be addressed, however, concerns the plausibility of the claim that all such state "restrictions" of ownership rights have the same status as an interference as any other. Clearly complete and direct *expropriation* of holdings carries with it the air of intrusion, restriction, and coercive interference that conflicts with our idea of personal liberty (even if such an action is ultimately justified because the concern with liberty is somehow overridden). But do we really want to say the same about the other elements associated with taxation and property law?

These sorts of considerations have also led writers such as Nagel and Murphy to simply brush aside the idea that property rights are pre-political. They write "[p]rivate property is a legal convention, defined in part by the tax system; therefore, the tax system cannot be evaluated by looking at its impact

---

[28] G. A. Cohen argued that this disagreement comes down to differing conceptions of *self-ownership*, where Nozick recognizes full rights to oneself and one's talents and Rawls and other egalitarians do not (Cohen, *Self-Ownership*, Chapters 3–4). This criticism has spawned a rich and complex debate over the relation between self-ownership and distributive justice. See e.g. the essays in Vallentyne and Steiner (eds.), *Left-Libertarianism*, Part II.

on private property, conceived as something that has independent existence and validity" – the "conventional nature of property is both perfectly obvious and remarkably easy to forget."[29]

Even if one accepts that current owners of goods have some pre-political title that government policy must respect, the kinds of property interests that such a title protects are quite variable. It is far from clear that the interests that would be curtailed by state policies aimed at correcting emergent distributive inequalities are those that are central to what it means to have such a title. That is, it is unclear that the interests that would be frustrated, say, by redistributive tax policies are central to people's essential nature as free persons able to pursue conceptions of the good, a consideration that allegedly grounds the pre-political title in the first place.[30] The original position merely invokes a conception of freedom and equality that puts primary emphasis on people's ability to form and pursue a valued life, given their personal characteristics and situation, without corresponding rights to market returns from exchanging the exercise of those characteristics or things they can produce with them.

4.3.2 Justice in the non-ideal world

The second point of contention between Nozick and Rawls cuts even deeper, for it touches on the very role of political philosophy in the modern world. Although not stated in this way, Rawls's claims about the "arbitrariness" of one's starting point in life can be understood as an acknowledgment that in developing theories of justice we are not formulating principles for an ideal world conjured up in philosophers' thought experiments, but rather for well-ordered societies characterized by the circumstances of justice, which include moderate scarcity and conflicts of interest. This may seem to be a surprising way to put this, given Rawls's insistence that he is engaging in "ideal theory,"[31] but my point is consistent with seeing both Rawls and Nozick as producing ideal normative theories that are meant to apply to our current, non-ideal world. Rawls quotes Rousseau in viewing political philosophy as an

---

[29] Murphy and Nagel, *The Myth*, p. 8. They also argue that "[i]t is now widely believed that the function of government extends far beyond the provision of internal and external security through the prevention of interpersonal violence, the protection of private property, and defense against foreign attack. The question is how far" (*The Myth*, p. 6).

[30] For a general argument for this and related claims, see Christman, *The Myth*. For skepticism about this sort of disaggregation of the elements of ownership, see Attas, "Fragmenting."

[31] On the role of ideal theory see Rawls, *TJ*, pp. 7–8.

enterprise in which we "take men as they are and laws as they might be"[32] which can be understood to take "men" as living in societies marked by past and ongoing deficiencies, arbitrary concentrations of power, and established patterns of social life in light of which principles of justice must be developed.

Moreover, Rousseau's approach to political philosophy generally involves accepting the arbitrariness that riddles the actual histories of societies, full of various concentrations of power that have nothing to do with the equal moral worth of persons but everything to do with the happenstance of geography and sociology, not to mention avarice and human folly.[33] When we consider ideal principles of justice for currently functioning societies, then, we need to acknowledge that events leading to these current conditions are rife with such arbitrary contingencies. Of course, Rawls mentions the happenstance of personal assets and individual upbringing, but these acknowledgments could be extended to include reference to broader social forces, patterns that have included (and still include) domination, slavery, murder, imperialism, conquest, and so on. This is not to slip into the realm of non-ideal theory, which involves developing rules for practices that respond to non-compliance, but rather shoring up the case for treating people's starting point in society as arbitrary in Rawls's sense.[34]

Rawls makes essentially this point in articulating his departure from Lockean social contract theory in ways that apply directly to Nozick's entitlement view: "Locke's doctrine improperly subjects the social relationships of moral persons to historical and social contingencies that are external to, and eventually undermine, their freedom and equality" (*PL*, p. 287). That is to say, viewing justice as the exercise of entitlements over talents and goods whose possessions emanate from contingent historical processes ensconces the effects of those processes in an "as-if just" history; but history is not just, either on libertarian grounds or egalitarian ones. So the system of natural liberty Locke and Nozick recommend as the alternative to justice as fairness is unacceptable.

Acknowledging this checkered history, we need to abstract from those characteristics of ourselves that would afford us unchecked advantages or

---

[32] Rousseau, *The Social Contract*, Book I in Rousseau, *Basic Political Writings*; see also Rawls, *LP*, p. 7.

[33] See e.g. *Discourse on the Origin of Inequality* in Rousseau, *Basic Political Writings*.

[34] That is, non-ideal theory, for Rawls, includes theories of punishment and just war which are designed specifically to respond to non-compliance with just principles. My observation here is a way to more fully motivate the need for fair principles to abstract from the happenstance of people's actual social starting point, which the original position is meant to do.

more deeply entrench our disadvantages. The original position is a mechanism that forces us to acknowledge the non-ideal characteristics of the social world and to insist that just institutions avoid multiplying the unfairness of the relative positions these factors have put people in. Even free-market economist Ludwig von Mises said: "Nowhere and at no time has the large-scale ownership of land come into being through the working of economic forces in the market. It is the result of military and political effort. Founded by violence, it has been upheld by violence and by that alone."[35]

Surprisingly, this is a point with which Nozick should readily agree, and in a notorious passing comment he expresses a degree of sympathy with it (albeit in different terms). That is, Nozick includes in his theory of distributive justice a principle of rectification, according to which resources should be redistributed from their current possessors to compensate the victims of those acts which deviate from the strict procedures of historical entitlement his theory otherwise lays out (*ASU*, pp. 152–3). He even mentions the difference principle as a possible "*rough* rule of thumb" for rectifying these injustices.[36]

The original position can be seen, then, as a mechanism needed to abstract away from the legacy of inequality, violence, discrimination, and domination that marks the contemporary world. Nozick's treatment of this mechanism shows the contentious manner in which theorists are forced to confront that legacy. Rawls's egalitarianism is merely one way in which to attempt such a confrontation, and whatever else one can say in its favor, the attempt to prevent further victimization and domination in this way is a noble one.

---

[35] Von Mises, *Socialism*, p. 375.

[36] *ASU*, p. 231 (emphasis in original). Admittedly, however, he expresses great ambivalence about this suggestion given the dearth of information about who are the precise victims of what acts of injustice that pepper the history of any society.

5   Rawls and Dworkin on hypothetical reasoning

Matthew Clayton

It is a striking fact that the two leading egalitarian liberals of recent times, John Rawls and Ronald Dworkin, deploy hypothetical reasoning in their somewhat different conceptions of justice. As is well known, Rawls uses the device of the original position in which representatives must choose between candidate principles of social justice – in the first instance, between the principles Rawls favors, the two principles of justice, and utilitarianism. Principles of justice, he argues, are those that would be chosen by representatives charged with the duty of securing their clients' enjoyment of primary social goods while lacking particular information about their clients' characteristics, including their socioeconomic class, natural talent, sex, race, and conception of what it means to live well. True, Rawls nests what I shall call the *original position argument* within a more general moral methodology of "reflective equilibrium" in which we reason about political morality by seeking consistency between our abstract and concrete considered judgments about justice in the light of the leading alternative moral theories available to us. However, the original position argument plays a central role in Rawls's distinctive conception of justice, *justice as fairness*. He recommends the original position as a thought experiment to be used when theorizing the demands of justice. Just terms of cooperation should be viewed as if they stemmed from an agreement between citizens, but the agreement must be one not reached out of fear or because of one's poor bargaining position. The agreement we are after is a *hypothetical* agreement: an agreement that would be made by representatives in the original position who were deprived of certain kinds of information the use of which would tend to render the agreement unfair.[1]

Dworkin also uses hypothetical reasoning in his account of justice, *equality of resources*, in the device of the hypothetical insurance scheme. Resources

For their help with this chapter, I am grateful to Timothy Hinton, Tom Parr, and Andrew Williams.

[1] See *TJR*, especially §§3–4, 20–5, 87; *JFR*, §§6, 23–6.

should be distributed equally between citizens, he insists, and once we have an egalitarian distribution of external resources – land and the goods produced from it – we are faced with the question of how we ought to compensate individuals who suffer misfortune in the distribution of internal resources – disability, ill health, or a lack of marketable skills, for example. Dworkin proposes that we ought to transfer external resources from the lucky to the unlucky so that individuals get what they would have insured for under conditions that ensure that everyone is equally placed with respect to the insurance decision. Everyone has perfect information about the costs and benefits of different insurance policies, an equal share of external resources with which to purchase insurance, and although everyone knows the general facts about the incidence of good and bad luck in society, no one knows whether she herself is on the up- or down-side of that distribution. Dworkin's suggestion is that justice demands that the social policies we put in place to compensate people for their bad luck with respect to internal resources must mimic the outcome produced by the package that the average individual would buy in the equal insurance market. So, like Rawls's conception, hypothetical choices play an important role in equality of resources.[2]

Notwithstanding their similarities, there are important differences between Rawls and Dworkin in their understanding of what kind of hypothetical agreement is relevant to justice. First, Rawls's representatives lack knowledge of the society-wide distribution of good and bad luck as well as information about the probability of their clients being the recipients of good or bad luck; Dworkin's individuals lack information about the likelihood of themselves being a victim of bad luck but they have general probabilistic information about the incidence of bad luck in society. Second, whereas representatives in the original position do not know their clients' conceptions of the good life, Dworkin allows his hypothetical individuals to choose insurance policies on the basis of their ambitions – their conceptions of what it means to live well and their attitudes to risk.

The differences between Rawls and Dworkin about the knowledge available within their respective hypothetical agreements reveal important differences in their conceptions of justice. It is those differences that I want to explore in this chapter. Before undertaking that exercise, however, I assess the question of the proper role of hypothetical reasoning within an account of justice. I begin the chapter with a brief discussion of Dworkin's early review of *TJ* and

---

[2] Dworkin, *Sovereign Virtue*, Chapters 2, 8, and 9; *Justice*, Chapter 16.

of Rawls's reply to it. Having established that both Rawls and Dworkin believe that hypothetical reasoning is relevant to justice, I turn to explore the differences between their descriptions of the proper role of hypothetical choice. I also examine their different views of the appropriate hypothetical context of choice for the purposes of identifying the demands of justice.

5.1 Dworkin on the original position

Some mistakenly read Dworkin's review of *TJ* as a wholesale rejection of Rawls's use of the original position by arguing that hypothetical agreements are irrelevant for theorizing the demands of justice.[3] Rather, Dworkin's aim is to show that Rawls's argument for his two principles by appeal to the agreement that would be made by parties in the original position might be sound; but, if it is sound, the argument's force relies on a deeper moral theory that posits every citizen's right to equal concern and respect.

In the first part of his article Dworkin argues that the mere fact of a hypothetical agreement on particular principles of justice does not *itself* give us a sufficient reason to enforce those principles. "A hypothetical contract is not simply a pale form of an actual contract," Dworkin famously observes, "it is no contract at all."[4] He notes that *actual* contracts are often binding. Although he does not explain why they bind, Dworkin is surely right. The bindingness of contracts – at least contracts that are freely and fairly entered into – is commonly accepted, because we have reason to value normative devices, such as agreements and contracts, that facilitate cooperation and voluntarily accepted amendments to the rights and duties we enjoy. Moreover, in the case of actual contracts, Dworkin argues that the fact of agreement is "an argument in itself, independent of the force of the reasons that might have led people to enter the contract."[5] Here he is appealing to our moral intuitions: if an individual voluntarily enters into an agreement then it is fair to hold her to that agreement, at least if the agreement was made under fair background conditions and doesn't violate relevant moral standards.

---

[3] G. A. Cohen seems to interpret Dworkin in this way. See his *Lectures*, p. 89. There, Cohen refers to Dworkin's objection "in his critique of Rawlsian contractarianism ... that a hypothetical contract can't bind ... [a] hypothetical contract, one might say, isn't worth the paper it's not written on." As I suggest in the text, Dworkin regards his observation that hypothetical agreement do not themselves bind as neither a critique of Rawls nor an argument for the conclusion that hypothetical agreements have no relevance for justice.

[4] Dworkin, "Original Position," p. 501.   [5] Ibid.

Unlike actual contracts, hypothetical contracts do not supply an independent reason of fairness to enforce a particular solution to, say, a dispute, because the person on whom the solution is imposed can reasonably claim that she didn't in fact agree to the terms that are now being imposed upon her. In his example, the fact that I would have sold you a painting for a pittance yesterday does not make it the case that a court of law can fairly require me to sell you the painting for that amount today now I know that it is a masterpiece.[6]

To be sure, Dworkin notes that hypothetical agreements can sometimes have force in their own right. If an individual is in a coma following an accident, and has not given the surgeon prior instructions as to how to treat him in that condition, it is right for the surgeon to treat him according to the best evidence of how he would want to be treated. If the unconscious patient were known to be a devout Jehovah's Witness, for example, it would be right not to give him a blood transfusion in the course of his operation. However, the relevance of hypothetical agreements in such cases rests on the fact that the individual has a preference for such treatment here and now – it is his settled wish – even though he cannot presently express it.[7] And the relevance of hypothetical agreements in those cases does not extend to cases in which a particular treatment is imposed on an individual without his consent on the grounds that he would have consented to the treatment if he didn't know his religious affiliation. Thus, without further justification, the mere fact that an individual would agree to Rawls's two principles if placed in the original position is not itself a reason for her to be governed by those principles here and now if she presently rejects those principles as unjust.

Suppose that we accept Dworkin's argument that hypothetical agreements do not themselves give reasons for particular principles. Are there other ways in which such agreements might be relevant to identifying the demands of justice? One possibility is that the decisions taken by individuals in the original position would be made on grounds that were relevant to justice. In other words, the derivation of principles from the original position could supply *evidence* of there being reasons that support those principles. Suppose that I know that Annie's taste for ice cream is similar to mine. Annie has lived in Florence for years and I am visiting for a week. I want the best ice cream the city has to offer. Accordingly, I have a reason to buy my ice cream from the parlor that Annie would choose. Here, Annie's hypothetical choice of

---

[6] Ibid., p. 502.   [7] Ibid.

a particular parlor is evidence that that parlor will supply me with the best ice cream. Similarly, we might think that the decisions made by representatives in the original position are relevant for justice because the representatives choose what is best for their clients under conditions that eliminate factors that would corrupt the fairness of the agreement. Given the way the original position is set up, the representatives' adoption of the two principles is evidence that those principles are just. But, like the ice cream example, the choice is not what makes the principles just; they are just in virtue of the fact that they embody the choice-independent requirements of fairness.

A different possibility is that, although the original position argument does not stand alone, it is a constitutive part of more complex argument for the two principles. Dworkin appears to endorse this suggestion as an interpretation of Rawls's position. The original position, he says, is:

> the product of a deeper political theory that argues for the two principles *through* rather than *from* the contract. We must therefore try to identify the feature of a deeper theory that would recommend the device of a contract as the engine for a theory of justice ...[8]

Dworkin's considered position, then, appears to be that the decisions that would be taken by parties in the original position might give us reason to govern society by the two principles. But if they do, then that is because the original position is designed in the light of a deeper normative ideal that is appropriate for identifying the demands of social justice.

Consider the analogous case of a fair lottery to distribute a scarce indivisible good. Suppose that no one's claim to the good is weightier than anyone else's. If so, then it is fair to give everyone an equal chance of obtaining the good. That ideal might motivate us to run a lottery in which everyone had an equal chance of winning. We have reason to give the good to the winner of the lottery because we are committed to a deeper moral ideal, that of giving everyone an equal chance of obtaining a scarce indivisible good. However, the lottery plays a constitutive role in determining a just outcome – it is the "engine," as Dworkin calls it, that gives us a determinate result. It does not supply us merely with evidence of who is entitled to the good (where entitlement to the good is conferred by properties making no essential reference to the lottery's outcome). The lottery makes it the case that some particular person is entitled to it; it plays an essential role in determining who is entitled to what.

---

[8] Ibid., p. 519.

So Dworkin is not arguing that hypothetical choices play no role in determining justice, merely that, if they have a role to play, their role derives from a more fundamental political ideal. He characterizes that fundamental ideal as the "right-based" ideal that government should treat its citizens with equal concern and respect. According to this, each citizen has a claim to a certain kind of treatment – to non-interference when performing certain kinds of action and to the provision of certain goods.[9]

But why does Dworkin believe that the original position relies on the right to equal concern and respect? He does so because he understands the original position as a way of evaluating different candidate principles of justice. The veil of ignorance ensures that political institutions cannot intentionally or unwittingly be designed to favor a particular class or religion, for example; and the view that it is unjust for particular citizens to press for political institutions that favor their own class, or those with the same natural talent or religion, presupposes the right to equal concern and respect.

5.2 Rawls's reply

Rawls rejects Dworkin's suggestion that the original position is grounded on any right-based theory, and hence on an alleged right to equal concern and respect.[10] Instead Rawls describes his view as "conception-based." It begins with the organizing ideal of "society as a fair system of social cooperation," which he elaborates with the use of several further ideas that are derived from the tradition of liberal democratic theory: the idea of "free and equal" citizens who have important interests in developing and deploying a sense of justice and in rationally reflecting on and pursuing a particular conception of the good life; and the ideal of a "well-ordered" society, including the "publicity requirement," under which citizens accept the principles of justice together with their justification and they are in a position to know that those principles are realized in their society.

Notwithstanding their disagreement over whether justice as fairness is right or conception based, it is important to note that Rawls does not resist Dworkin's interpretation of the original position argument as nested within a larger argument whose fundamental moral premises are given independently of people's choices. From the outset, Rawls defended the hypothetical reasoning of the original position argument as relevant because "[e]ach aspect

---

[9] Ibid., pp. 519–33.
[10] See Rawls, "Justice as Fairness: Political," reprinted in *CP*, pp. 400–1, n. 19.

of the original position can be given a supporting explanation."[11] He describes
it as a "device of representation or, alternatively, a thought-experiment for the
purposes of public- and self-clarification" that models fair conditions for
choosing principles to govern the basic structure and "acceptable restrictions
on the reasons" that might be advanced for political principles.[12] With respect
to the latter, for example, it does not follow from the fact that an individual is
rich that it is just for her to impose on everyone else an economic system that
favors the wealthy. Thus, the veil of ignorance, which deprives representatives
of any knowledge of their clients' marketable skills or wealth, is supported by
the choice-independent moral claim that justice should not be equated with
"to each according to their bargaining power." Thus, although he disagrees
with Dworkin about the character of the moral ideals that frame the original
position argument, Rawls agrees that the power of the argument relies on its
integration within a conception of justice that is given without reference to
the choices people do or might make.

5.3 Headway without hypothetical reasoning

In section 5.1, I reported that in his early review of *TJ*, Dworkin was open to
the view that the original position argument might be right; his aim was to
explain the way in which it would be right if it were right. However, Dworkin
subsequently argued that the original position argument is mistaken. His
principal complaint is that justice as fairness is insufficiently sensitive to
individuals' distinctive ambitions. Before taking up that issue, I should note
that Dworkin believes that considerable headway can be made in identifying
the demands of justice without deploying the thought experiment of a
hypothetical agreement under conditions of equality. We can, he insists,
identify certain elements of justice by reference to a different kind of thought
experiment, an auction of resources between equally placed bidders.

In Dworkin's imaginary scenario, the survivors of a shipwreck wash up
on a deserted island and decide to divide the available resources between
themselves equally. Aware that several different conceptions of equality are
available, Dworkin elaborates what he takes to be the most attractive
conception. In that conception, equality of resources, an equal distribution
is secured only if it satisfies the so-called "envy test," which demands that the
distribution of land and items on the island be such that no individual prefers
to have the set of resources enjoyed by another. To model that requirement,

---

[11] *TJR*, p. 514.   [12] *JFR*, p. 17.

Dworkin asks us to imagine an auction in which each individual is given equal bidding power and an impartial auctioneer is appointed to subdivide any lot – an item or piece of land, for example – should a bidder request such a division. Dworkin argues that the outcome of that auction is equal because it guarantees an outcome in which no one can point to anyone else and claim in good faith that she would prefer to have the resources enjoyed by the other.[13] To be sure, that distribution is not one that satisfies equality of welfare – equality of pleasure, or equality of preference-satisfaction, or lives that go equally well. But Dworkin offers several arguments, which have generated a considerable literature, to explain why his resourcist conception is superior to welfare egalitarianism.[14]

After the auction individuals use their resources in different ways, making different choices with respect to consumption, trade, and investment; this will result in a different distribution of external resources. If we assume, contrary to fact, that individuals enjoy equal internal resources, such as equally valuable health, abilities/disabilities, and marketable skills, and they operate in an environment that is free from prejudice, then the distribution that obtains at that later time might also be egalitarian, because, like the initial distribution, it satisfies the envy test: no one would prefer to live the lifestyle pursued by another, where lifestyles are characterized as including both decisions with respect to consumption/investment and the monetary resources that are at one's disposal.[15] The upshot of this scenario is that we can describe an equal distribution by reference to a history in which symmetrically situated individuals acquire and use the available resources as directed by their ambitions. The fact that they will come to have different levels of income because of their different attitudes to risk, consumption or saving, for example, is not problematic from the point of view of equality. But, plainly, hypothetical agreements do not figure in this account of justice in the distribution of external resources.

Nevertheless, hypothetical reasoning does figure in Dworkin's account of equality with respect to internal resources. After dealing with consumption, production, and trade, Dworkin turns to the question of how to deal with inequalities with respect to morbidity, mortality, abilities/disabilities, and marketable skills. Plainly, such inequalities violate the envy test. If I am born with a disability or ill health then it is likely that I would prefer to have the abilities or health enjoyed by others. Consequently, we need to figure out how to

---

[13] Dworkin, *Sovereign Virtue*, pp. 65–71.   [14] Ibid., Chapter 1.   [15] Ibid., pp. 83–5.

compensate individuals for their relative disadvantage with respect to internal resources. Dworkin's solution invokes his hypothetical insurance scheme. The compensation owed to individuals with disadvantageous internal resources, and how that should be financed, should, he argues, mimic the insurance decisions that would be taken by equally situated and informed individuals.[16]

To answer questions about the distribution of health care, for example, Dworkin suggests that we ask what medical insurance policies would be bought by equally situated individuals if they had perfect information about the costs and benefits of different kinds of care, enjoyed an equal share of external resources including wealth and income, but lacked knowledge of their individual susceptibility to having or developing various medical conditions. Individuals in Dworkin's hypothetical choice situation have information about the society-wide incidence of the various medical conditions, but they are behind a "thin" veil of ignorance so that no one knows whether she is more or less likely than the average person to suffer the kind of ill health in question.

Dworkin argues that his scheme is a suitable basis for identifying justice in health care because individuals are well informed and equally situated with respect to both the risks they face and their means of buying insurance. If we can identify what the majority or the average insurance package is, that, Dworkin insists, is what justice demands. His solution is responsive to people's ambitions in the sense that individuals consult their own goals and preferences, asking themselves how much they value various dimensions of good health compared to other goods, like income and education. In addition, they consider whether they are willing to take risks with their health and whether they prioritize health care in their youth and middle age over health care in their old age.

From this brief summary of Dworkin's conception of equality of resources, it is clear that Dworkin believes that we can make considerable headway in identifying the demands of justice without reference to the hypothetical choices of suitably situated individuals. True, to identify just levels of provision or compensation for bad brute luck with respect to internal resources, Dworkin relies on people's hypothetical choices. But that thought experiment is nested within a more general account of justice, animated by the envy test, which identifies the just distribution of other (external) goods by reference to the actual choices of equally placed individuals.

---

[16] Ibid., pp. 73–83, 92–109, 307–19, 320–46. Dworkin also uses the hypothetical insurance scheme to deal with the intergenerational transmission of unequal advantage via gifts or bequests. See ibid., pp. 346–9.

It is not obvious, however, that the observation that progress can be made in theorizing justice without invoking hypothetical choices amounts to a criticism of Rawls. Rawls proposes the original position argument as *one way* of identifying the right principles of justice; he does not claim that it is uniquely capable of identifying justice. One of the features of Rawls's political thought in general is that he usually offers sufficient conditions for the claims he defends. To be sure, some of the positions he defends – the principles of justice, his political conception of justice and legitimacy, and his methodological claims about moral theorizing – are deeply controversial. Nevertheless, he generally resists portraying his arguments as the only ones available for the conclusions he favors. He is open to the possibility that there might be more than one kind of defense of the political principles he advocates.

Consider how Rawls defends his use of the original position as a "device of representation." The original position models what count as relevant reasons from the point of view of justice. The way in which it is constructed – including the veil of ignorance eliminating the possibility of an agreement that wrongly reflects unequal bargaining power, and the list of primary social goods providing an account of citizens' interests – is designed according to what Rawls takes to be reasons relevant to justice: fair cooperation between free and equal citizens. If, after due reflection, the veil of ignorance successfully ensures that the principles that are chosen do not reflect morally arbitrary differences between individuals in the wrong way, and the account of primary goods is a suitable metric for gauging individuals' advantage from the point of view of justice, then the original position serves its purpose as a way of identifying the principles of justice.[17] But that does not rule out the possibility that we might identify the right principles in a more direct way, without recourse to hypothetical reasoning. Rawls does not rule that possibility out. The central question, then, is whether the construction of the original position does indeed accurately model the reasons that are relevant to justice. Dworkin doubts that it does.

5.4 The relevance of ambitions

Dworkin's principal complaint is that justice as fairness is insufficiently sensitive to individuals' distinctive ambitions: that problem is evident, he argues, in Rawls's two principles of justice, particularly the difference

---

[17] *JFR*, pp. 17–18.

principle, but the criticism also applies to the way in which Rawls constructs the original position.

Let's start with the difference principle, which asserts, roughly, that economic inequalities are just if they maximally serve the economic interests of the economically least advantaged group. Rawls imagines society as divided into several economic classes and argues for tax and transfer arrangements that allow skilled and professional workers to benefit economically only on terms that maximize the average income and wealth of the least advantaged group – unskilled workers.

Dworkin's objection is that Rawls's group-based conception of economic justice is "not sufficiently fine-tuned" and, accordingly, fails to respond to morally relevant differences between individuals: differences with respect to (i) their opportunity to acquire marketable skills and (ii) the lifestyle choices that they make. An individual, Alice, might be a member of the least advantaged group because she has been born with cognitive impairments that prevent her from developing skills that are valued in the market. Another, Bert, might find himself in that group because, notwithstanding his opportunities for enhancing his marketable skills, he chose a different lifestyle in which well-remunerated work is not central. Alice and Bert might both be in the class of unskilled workers and earn the average income within that economic class. But it seems that those facts are insufficient for justice; questions arise as to whether Alice's share of income should be as low as Bert's given that Alice lacked opportunities that Bert enjoyed.[18]

Now consider Dworkin's principal concern about the original position directly. He notes that his own conception of justice makes reference to how people would choose in certain hypothetical circumstances – in his hypothetical insurance scheme to identify justice in the distribution of health care, compensation for disability and lack of marketable talent – in which fairness is achieved by depriving individuals (and insurance companies) of information that is likely to affect the fairness of the resulting choice. Nevertheless, that deployment of a veil of ignorance is importantly different from Rawls's veil. Dworkin describes the contrast in this way:

> [M]y arguments have been designed to permit people as much knowledge as it is possible to allow them without defeating the point of the exercise entirely. In particular, they allow people enough self-knowledge, as

---

[18] Dworkin, *Sovereign Virtue*, pp. 113–17.

individuals, to keep relatively intact their sense of their own personality, and especially their theory of what is valuable in life, whereas it is
central to the original position that this is exactly the knowledge people
lack.[19]

Dworkin means to accept Rawls's thought that, sometimes, the agreements
individuals make in the light of full information are not fair agreements,
because they reflect unequal bargaining power among the parties. Nevertheless, Dworkin highlights a significant difference between his own hypothetical
choice situation and Rawls's. In Rawls's original position, the parties are
deprived of information about conceptions of the good: conceptions of the
goals, occupations, and relationships that are worth pursuing in one's
non-political life, including views about the truth or falsity of different religious doctrines. In Dworkin's hypothetical insurance scheme, those buying
insurance from an equal baseline choose knowing their own personalities and
their own views about what makes their lives go well or badly.

5.5 The exclusion of conceptions of the good

Before addressing the significance of this difference between Rawls and
Dworkin, it is worth reviewing Rawls's reasons for making the parties
ignorant about conceptions of the good. Rawls's move struck commentators
as somewhat perplexing from the outset. In his early review of *TJ*, Thomas
Nagel expressed his puzzlement as follows:

> Let us grant that the parties should be equal and should not be
> in possession of information which would lead them to seek advantages
> on morally irrelevant grounds like race, sex, parentage, or natural endow-
> ments. But they are deprived also of knowledge of their particular concep-
> tion of the good. It seems odd to regard that as morally irrelevant from the
> standpoint of justice. If someone favors certain principles because of his
> conception of the good, he will not be seeking special advantages for
> himself so long as he does not know who in society he is. Rather he will
> be opting for principles that advance the good for everyone, as defined by
> that conception.[20]

Nagel suggests that having knowledge of one's conception of the good is not
unfair, that it does not give an individual an advantage so that she gets more

---

[19] Ibid., p. 118.   [20] Nagel, "Rawls on Justice," p. 226.

than others, because if the conception of the good were correct then everyone would benefit from principles of justice that were chosen to promote that conception. If Rawls's concern is to eliminate information the possession of which would tend to produce inequalities on the basis of morally irrelevant factors, it is not obvious that the parties in the original position should be ignorant of all information about conceptions of the good.

Nagel's challenge is not quite right, because choosing principles of justice on the basis of one's own conception of the good does raise questions of fairness, at least on the plausible assumption that there are several conceptions of the good that are worth pursuing. Suppose that a religious life is valuable and that such a life may take many forms: one can lead a valuable life as a Christian, Jew, Muslim, Hindu, and so on. Someone with Christian convictions might choose political principles favoring Christian practice. These might well benefit her, but not those who hold different, but equally or incommensurably valuable, religious convictions. Choosing principles on the basis of one's conception of the good, then, might not "advance the good of everyone," at least if value pluralism holds.

Nevertheless, there is an important kernel of truth in Nagel's argument. Were parties in the original position given information about the truth about ethics – that several conceptions of the good are sound while certain conceptions of the good are mistaken – but denied knowledge of which conception of the good they hold in particular, the principles selected on the basis of that knowledge would seem likely to advance the good of individuals in society. Such principles need not promote any *particular* worthwhile conception but, rather, support and promote various conceptions worthy of endorsement. But they would also advocate legal and social arrangements that are successful in steering citizens away from conceptions of the good that rest on false ethical ideals or whose pursuit does not make people's lives go well. Allowing parties in the original position knowledge of the truth about the good would lead to a perfectionist account of justice in which questions of fairness need not arise, because, by hypothesis, everyone benefits from being subject to political principles that advance his good.

As is well known, Rawls has other reasons, apart from reasons of fairness, to exclude information about conceptions of the good – what he later called "comprehensive doctrines" – which are elaborated most fully in PL. A well-ordered society, he claims, is one in which there is public acceptance by free and equal citizens of the governing principles of justice and the ideals of political morality that support them. If the familiar civil and political liberties of liberal democracy – including freedom of conscience, expression, and association – are guaranteed, a plurality of conceptions of the good is an inevitable consequence. Within this plurality it is also true that some conceptions of the good are mistaken. Nevertheless, the ideal of public acceptance of the political morality that governs society requires that the principles of justice and the ideals on which they rest be capable of endorsement by individuals irrespective of the particular conceptions of the good they affirm, and irrespective of whether their conceptions describe sound or unsound views about the best way to live our non-political lives. For this reason, principles of justice must be elaborated and defended without invoking the truth or falsity of particular conceptions of the good. Justice as fairness achieves this result by rendering parties in the original position ignorant both of the particular comprehensive doctrine that guides their clients and the truth about which conceptions of the good are worth pursuing.[21]

5.6 Dworkin on continuity between justice and individuals' values

With these ideas in mind, let us return to the dispute between Rawls and Dworkin on whether knowledge of one's own conception of the good is appropriate when choosing principles of justice to deal with the inequalities arising from brute luck in the distribution of internal endowments.

It is important to stress that Dworkin agrees with Rawls that principles of justice should not be selected so as to serve or promote any particular view of the good life. Even if irreligious doctrines rest on radically mistaken views about the universe or ethics, it is not the business of the state to try to educate its citizens to that truth or to try to persuade the impious to abandon their convictions. Political morality should, Dworkin claims, recognize individuals' "ethical independence," that it is their right to decide for themselves without political interference which conception of the good is worthy of adoption and pursuit. True, Dworkin develops a different, ethical, argument for this claim that rests on controversial claims about dignity and what it means to live well. That argument is importantly different from Rawls's defense of ethical independence, which relies on claims about political autonomy, including citizens' endorsement of the laws that constrain them. While fascinating and important, however, we need not delve into these disagreements here. What is significant is that Dworkin and Rawls are of one mind in thinking that the

---

[21] *PL*, especially Lectures I and II.

fact that a particular conception of the good is true or false has no relevance in deciding which principles of justice ought to govern society.

Why, then, does Dworkin insist on individuals having knowledge of their personalities and conceptions of the good in his hypothetical insurance scheme? The answer lies in his conception of what it means to treat citizens as equals, which goes to the heart of his dispute with Rawls and, indeed, other egalitarians. Dworkin's use of the envy test reveals a liberal conception of equality that is responsive to individuals' distinctive ambitions and ethical convictions. Suppose that on Dworkin's imaginary island, while Puja acquires a piece of prime agricultural land with the intention of farming it, Quentin acquires a sandy beach to top up his tan. The envy test is satisfied, let us suppose, because neither would prefer to have the land acquired by the other. There is, accordingly, no unjust inequality between them, and that remains the case even if Quentin would rather have a bigger beach than the one he has: given what he cares about, he would not trade his small beach for Puja's farmland.

Dworkin explains that equality of resources is a "continuous" account of economic justice, which allows "us to cite, as disadvantages and handicaps, only what we treat in the same way in our own ethical life."[22] Each individual, in the light of her distinctive convictions and ambitions for her own life, asks herself whether she prefers to have what someone else has. With certain qualifications, if no one does then the distribution of resources is equal.

This differs from various "discontinuous" accounts of justice in which the individual's considered judgment about whether she is worse off than someone else does not settle the issue of whether she suffers a comparative disadvantage that entitles her to compensation. To illustrate this approach, consider the case of Fred and Paul, which G. A. Cohen uses to argue in support of "equal access to advantage." Although they have equal income, Fred's preference for cheap fishing is more easily satisfied than Paul's more expensive preference for photography. Cohen claims that Paul is beset by bad "price luck," the bad luck of living in an environment in which his photographic preferences are more costly to satisfy than Fred's preference. Accordingly, Cohen believes that Paul ought to be compensated by a transfer of wealth from those, like Fred, who have tastes that are cheaper to fulfill.[23]

Dworkin argues that discontinuous accounts of egalitarian interpersonal comparison are counterintuitive. For example, Cohen's conception is

---

[22] Dworkin, *Sovereign Virtue*, p. 294.
[23] See Cohen, *On the Currency*, p. 923; see, in addition, "Expensive Taste," pp. 3–29.

committed to claiming that there is an unjust inequality between Paul and Fred even when Paul regards his lifestyle as a somewhat frustrated photographer to be a far superior life to Fred's pursuit of fish. How can it be just for Paul to receive a transfer of resources from Fred to finance his lifestyle when he believes that his lifestyle is already more fulfilling than Fred's?[24] In addition, Dworkin suggests that discontinuous accounts are unsound because they impose a particular conception of what matters on the community, even when certain citizens reject that conception, as Paul does with respect to preference satisfaction.[25]

Dworkin's insistence on continuity between an individual's ethical judgments and her claims at the bar of economic justice can be generalized to include a critique of the metric that Rawls uses in the original position for comparing individuals' lives from the point of view of justice, primary social goods. To illustrate this consider Puja and Quentin again. Having acquired her fertile land, Puja cultivates her plot and reaps a harvest that gives her a sizable income. By contrast, Quentin works in the local bar to provide himself with a low but sufficient income to continue to enjoy his beach lifestyle. With respect to the primary good of wealth and income, Puja and Quentin are unequal: while Puja is in the top half of the income distribution, Quentin finds himself in the least advantaged group. The question is whether this inequality of income is unjust. To be sure, Rawls might agree that there is no injustice, but that judgment would depend on establishing whether the inequality stems from socioeconomic arrangements governed by his two principles. An important part of doing so would be to ensure that inequalities in wealth and income are not detrimental to those with least income. On Rawls's view, Quentin may have a valid complaint about the inequality if the level of income of those with least is not as high as it can be. For Dworkin, by contrast, these further questions are immaterial. There is no unjust inequality between Puja and Quentin because the envy test is satisfied, and that remains the case even when the level of income of those with least is not as high as it could be.

Dworkin's continuous approach to justice also explains his preference for a thin, rather than thick, veil of ignorance in his hypothetical insurance scheme. When Dworkin turns to hypothetical reasoning to deal with inequalities in internal resources – ill health, disability, and marketable talents – he argues

---

[24] Dworkin, *Sovereign Virtue*, pp. 287–96; "Ronald Dworkin Replies," in Burley (ed.), *Dworkin and His Critics*, pp. 339–50, especially pp. 344–6. For discussion, see Williams, "Equality"; Clayton, "The Resources."

[25] Dworkin, *Justice*, p. 355.

that we should ask what insurance decisions equally placed individuals would take considering the possibility that they might be burdened by brute bad luck. Recall that individuals and insurers are denied knowledge of certain particular facts about themselves, such as their own individual probability of being burdened by bad luck with respect to health, disability, or marketable skills. They do have general information about these matters, such as the society-wide incidence of disability, and they also know their own conception of the good, including their attitude towards risk taking. Individuals are asked to buy an insurance package given the possibility that they will suffer disability. In making their decisions they are invited to consider how much they disvalue the disability in question and how much they are prepared to gamble with their own health. In this way, equality of resources seeks to compensate individuals for their brute bad luck in a manner that is responsive to their own values and ambitions.

Dworkin describes his account as *ex ante*, rather than *ex post*, egalitarianism. If, as seems likely, people would not take out insurance policies that completely nullified the bad luck that they suffer, then, after differential luck has struck us in the form of ill health for some but not others, some would prefer to have what others have. After receiving the compensation that they insured to provide they would still prefer to be in the shoes of those unaffected by the illness. An *ex post* envy test would be violated. But Dworkin argues that we should adopt an *ex ante* version of the test, so that no one would prefer to swap places with another *before* the effects of differential luck have rendered some ill and others not. He asks us to imagine a simple case in which a disabling disease will randomly beset some, but not all of us, in the future. It is open to us to ensure that no one who suffers the disease is, all things considered, worse off than those who escape its grasp. However, that policy might be expensive to purchase. Perhaps no one would purchase that policy, and everyone would opt for a policy that provides less compensation than that needed to make them no worse off than those lucky enough to be unaffected. Still, if individuals enjoyed equal external resources and were well informed about the costs and benefits of the different choices available to them in an insurance market, Dworkin claims that just compensation for the disease could be left to that market.[26]

The simple case just described involves an *actual* insurance market in which equally placed individuals choose their preferred levels of

---

[26] Dworkin, *Sovereign Virtue*, pp. 342–3.

compensation given the possibility of their being the victim of randomly distributed bad luck. Why then does Dworkin propose the thought experiment of his hypothetical insurance market to identify just levels of compensation for those beset by disability, ill health, or the lack of marketable talent? The answer is that in the simple case bad luck is distributed randomly at some point in the future and, therefore, compensation can be determined in the light of each individual's distinctive preferences in the knowledge that everyone's opportunity to insure is equal. In the real world, however, individuals and insurers sometimes know that a particular individual has a particular disability or is prone to ill health, and this knowledge affects the fairness of any resulting insurance contract. Dworkin thinks that charging more for insurance to the victims of bad brute luck is a paradigm case of unfairness: it is an unjust "double disadvantage," because not only are the unlucky burdened by ill health, they are also charged more in insurance premiums to alleviate the symptoms. Thus, if compensation is to be identified by reference to an insurance market, then it must be a market that eliminates information that is likely to render the outcome unfair, which is what the hypothetical insurance market accomplishes. We are asked to consider what insurance choices would be made by individuals who: (i) have an equal share of wealth and income; (ii) have information about the general probability of being the victim of bad luck, the burdens the bad luck imposes if left unchecked, and information about the costs and benefits of the available insurance packages; but (iii) are behind a thin veil of ignorance so that they lack information about their own particular probability of being the victim of the bad luck in question.

Thus, Dworkin's argument is that a just response to inequality with respect to disability, ill health, and the lack of marketable talent is determined by a hypothetical choice, as described in his egalitarian insurance market, in which individuals choose on the basis of their conceptions of the good and their attitudes towards risk-taking, but in the absence of information that would place them at an advantage or disadvantage in the market. As he observes, the hypothetical insurance scheme is embedded within, and justified by reference to, an account of equality that is responsive to people's ambitions for their lives.

To be sure, Dworkin qualifies this observation with the concession that the hypothetical insurance scheme is responsive only to the *average* insurance decision that would be made. In the hypothetical scheme, unlike the simple case, it is impossible to tailor individuals' compensation to what they individually would have chosen to insure for, because individualized knowledge is unavailable – it is impossible to know how much an individual born with cystic fibrosis would insure to provide by way of medical treatment and other kinds of support if she did not know whether or not she had the disease.[27]

5.7 The veil of ignorance: thick or thin?

Like Rawls, then, Dworkin makes use of hypothetical choice to model a fair choice. But his veil of ignorance is thinner than Rawls's, because Dworkin aims to preserve some responsiveness to people's ambitions as demanded by his interpretation of equal concern and respect. In this final section, I consider what I take to be the central Rawlsian objection to Dworkin's argument that we ought to theorize justice with respect to internal resources by reference to a hypothetical insurance market with a thin, rather than thick, veil of ignorance.

Recall Rawls's argument for a thick veil:

> [T]he fact that we affirm a particular religious, philosophical, or moral comprehensive doctrine with its associated conception of the good is not a reason for us to propose, or to expect others to accept, a conception of justice that favors those of that persuasion. To model this conviction in the original position, the parties are not allowed to know the social position of those they represent, or the particular comprehensive doctrine of the person each represents.[28]

Rawls's ideal of social cooperation requires free and equal citizens to endorse the political principles to which they are subject and the ideals on the basis of which those principles are adopted. If political principles are adopted because they are supported by, or promote, controversial conceptions of the good then universal endorsement would be jeopardized. Accordingly, representatives in the original position are denied knowledge of their clients' conceptions of the good to model the fact that it is not legitimate for citizens to use the state to impose their conceptions on others.

In response, Dworkin argues that Rawls's political conception with its exclusion of comprehensive doctrines from political morality is neither plausible nor consistent with Rawls's defense of the difference principle and the right to abort.[29] As an alternative, Dworkin develops *ethical* arguments for liberal principles of justice that dispense with the claim that citizens' endorsement of the political principles that constrain them is required by political

---

[27] Ibid., pp. 343–5.   [28] *PL*, p. 24.   [29] Dworkin, "Rawls and the Law," pp. 251–4.

morality. While there is not space to discuss it here, it is not clear that Dworkin's critique of Rawls's "political" conception of justice is particularly convincing.[30]

There is, however, a different reply that Dworkin could offer, to wit, that it is not obvious that a thick veil of ignorance is required even if we accept Rawls's ideal of publicly acceptable justification. If Rawls is right then political philosophers and public officials must not appeal to controversial conceptions of the good in articulating or defending their favored principles of justice. But equality of resources appears to conform to that requirement, because it too secures for citizens various civil and political liberties and sets out rules for economic justice that do not rest on any controversial account of what it means to live well. Because free and equal citizens disagree about what makes one's life go well we need a metric for identifying relative advantage that does not invoke any of the controversial conceptions of living well. Dworkin's (continuous) account of equality of resources fits the bill, because the envy test operates by including everyone's distinctive ethical convictions. Its account of relative advantage makes reference to what each individual values for his own life. According to it, Quentin is not disadvantaged compared to Puja even if Puja has more income at her disposal, because he doesn't value the well-remunerated farming life that she pursues. In this way, each is entitled to resource transfers from others only if she believes herself to be worse off than them according to the ethical ideals that *she* affirms. Accordingly, Dworkin's elaboration of equal concern and respect seems to be an attractive conception of economic justice for a community that values public acceptance of the principles of justice, because it does not employ a metric to judge whether someone is worse off than another; rather, it insists that people express their claims to resources in a way that is faithful to their own ethical convictions and it responds to everyone's claim regardless of the soundness of the conception of the good that motivates it.

We might further argue on Dworkin's behalf that his conception may be superior to Rawls's metric of primary social goods for comparing people's lives for the purposes of justice. Rawls's view disregards citizens' ethical convictions and proceeds on the basis of what individuals need to develop and exercise their interests in freedom and equality and to pursue their particular conceptions of the good. But, as Dworkin suggests, such an account is not as fine-tuned as it needs to be, because people differ in the degree to

---

[30] For a critical assessment of Dworkin's objection, see the final section of Clayton, "Liberal Equality," forthcoming.

which they need or value wealth and income, say, in pursuit of their conception of the good. In our example, Quentin is not particularly bothered about income and wealth. Since that is the case, it seems odd to have a principle governing the economic system that is justified on the basis that it is in his interest to have access to more rather than less wealth and income. Couldn't Quentin object to economic arrangements that are premised on the claim that, other things equal, it is in everyone's interest to possess income and wealth? By disregarding people's ethical convictions, then, Rawls's method for comparing people's lives – primary goods – may fall foul of his own requirement that his principles be acceptable to everyone. Dworkin's account, which seeks to *accommodate* rather than disregard individuals' ambitions for their own ethical lives, might be better placed to serve as a publicly acceptable conception of economic justice.[31]

This suggestion of a broadly Rawlsian defense of equality of resources faces a rejoinder. Recall that in the hypothetical insurance market, because of the difficulty in determining the insurance decisions of particular people, Dworkin advocates a scheme for compensating individuals with disabilities that mimics what the majority of people, or the average person, would insure to provide. Surely that is an instance of one's entitlements being determined by the ambitions of others, and so it violates Rawls's requirement of public justification. For example, in a society in which the majority are content with taking health risks, imagine that a minority are, in fact, risk averse. Why is it just for an ill person's entitlement to assistance or resources to be lower than it might be because the majority do not share her aversion to risk?

In response to this kind of challenge, Dworkin invites the critic to articulate an alternative conception of justice that strikes us as more just. It is appropriate that rules for the distribution of health care, for example, should apply to everyone. Any set of principles will be controversial, imposing a health care regime on some who might have chosen differently in the hypothetical insurance scheme. Dworkin insists that, given the impossibility of knowing how any particular individual would have insured if he didn't know his particular propensity to ill health, it is "fair enough to ask him to be satisfied" with the insurance package chosen by the average person.[32] The burden is on those who support a different health care regime to explain how that alternative view is superior to the insurance model.

---

[31] I set out this argument for a political liberal defense of equality of resources at greater length in "Liberal Equality."

[32] Dworkin, *Sovereign Virtue*, p. 345.

5.8 Conclusion

As suggested above, both Rawls and Dworkin deploy hypothetical reasoning in their respective conceptions of justice, but they disagree about how to characterize the appropriate context in which political principles should be chosen. Rawls's thick veil of ignorance deprives representatives in the original position of knowledge of the general distribution of good and bad luck in society and of their clients' conception of the good. Although individuals in Dworkin's hypothetical insurance scheme are, like Rawls's parties, ignorant of whether they, in particular, are the recipients of good or bad luck, they have information about the society-wide distribution of luck and they consult their own ethical convictions when deciding whether and how much to insure themselves against being the victim of bad brute luck.

Dworkin's thinner veil of ignorance is motivated by his belief that justice should be responsive to what individuals care about; we ought to identify whether individuals are disadvantaged, and should compensate them for their disadvantages, in a way that makes reference to their own beliefs about whether they are worse off than others and their own views about the risks they want to run in their own lives.

Whereas Dworkin's thinner veil of ignorance corresponds to an ambition-sensitive approach to justice, Rawls's thick veil relies on a conception of our needs as free and equal citizens as specified by his set of primary goods. Dworkin objects that discontinuous accounts like Rawls's are counterintuitive and, furthermore, that Rawls's particular conception fails to produce sufficiently fine-grained and plausible principles of socioeconomic justice. These objections represent important challenges to the Rawlsian project in general as well as to Rawls's characterization and use of the original position.

6 Feminist receptions of the original position

Amy R. Baehr

6.1 Introduction

Does the original position accommodate feminist considered convictions? What I mean by this is: does the original position allow us to identify as unjust the arrangements that feminist considered convictions highlight? An answer to this question will be of interest to those wondering about the feminist content of Rawlsian liberalism. The question may also be understood as a step in exploring the possibility of a feminist liberalism that is contractualist.[1]

To answer this question, we need a list of feminist considered convictions, which I provide below. I show that much of what the feminist considered convictions identify as injustice is recognized as such by the original position; but much of it is not. I show also that the original position underwrites necessary effective coercive remedies for some of the injustices it recognizes, but not for all of them. So, I argue, we must say that some injustices recognized by the original position may endure in a Rawlsian well-ordered society. I then explore a feminist use of the original position associated with the work of Susan Okin that captures more of what feminists identify as injustice; but, I argue, this approach fails to fully accommodate feminist considered convictions about dependency. I ask whether an initial situation could be designed that accommodates feminist considered convictions about dependency and is also part of a liberal view.

For helpful discussion of an earlier version of this chapter, thanks are due to Ken Baynes, Asha Bhandary, David Estlund, Timothy Hinton, Cindy Stark, and Lori Watson.

[1] Martha Nussbaum's feminist liberalism is non-contractualist (Nussbaum, *Sex and Social Justice*). But much feminist liberal writing is solidly in the contractualist tradition. For just a few examples, see Alstott, *No Exit*; Baehr, "Liberal Feminism Comprehensive"; Cudd, *Analyzing Oppression*; Hampton, "Feminist Contractarianism"; Hartley and Watson, "Is Feminist?"; Lloyd, "Toward a Liberal"; Neufeld and Van Schoelandt, "Political Liberalism"; and Okin, *Justice, Gender and the Family*.

The chapter follows the process of reflective equilibrium, which Rawls tells us goes on "indefinitely"[2] (*PL*, p. 97). I begin by pointing out a discrepancy between a set of considered convictions on the one hand and Rawls's favored interpretation of the initial situation, the original position, on the other. In the face of this discrepancy one might opt to modify the feminist considered convictions; I show how the original position facilitates such modification. Alternatively, one might opt to modify the original position; I explore some modifications that feminists have suggested. If feminist liberalism is basically contractualist, the truth of the feminist considered convictions may not be assumed but must be established, perhaps through a process of reflective equilibrium. This chapter presents some first steps in that process.

6.2 Feminist considered convictions

The list of feminist considered convictions I offer here is culled from the family of social movements and doctrines that is feminism. Each conviction points not to a discrete incidence of harm or rights violation, or some other wrong, but to "social institutions, practices and norms" that work systematically and synergistically to constrain, burden, or reduce women.[3] I propose that we conceive of the arrangements to which the feminist considered convictions point as, together, constituting what I will call the "gender system."[4] I am not interested in establishing that societies like the United States are characterized by the gender system as I describe it. I leave that argumentation to others. Nor do I propose the list of feminist considered convictions as the correct account of feminism, though I hope to have captured in this list a good deal of what feminists believe is unjust:

1 It is unjust when women or girls are regularly subject to and fear violence (sexual and otherwise) at the hands of family members, intimate partners,

---

[2] Rawls explains that "justice as fairness is the hypothesis that the principles which would be chosen in the original position are identical with those that match our considered judgments... [Reflective equilibrium is reached once a person] has weighed various proposed conceptions and he has either revised his judgments to accord with one of them or held fast to his initial convictions (and the corresponding conception)" (*TJ*, p. 48).

[3] Cudd, *Analyzing Oppression*, p. 23.

[4] I take the term "gender system" from Okin, *Justice*, p. 101; see also p. 6. Rawls also uses it (*JFR*, p. 167). Our accounts of the gender system are not identical, but they are similar enough. As I understand it, the gender system works synergistically with other systems of oppression like those of class, "race," and sexuality. Trans women and girls are included when women and girls are mentioned.

acquaintances, or strangers. This includes, but is not limited to, racist and homophobic violence against women or girls, violence against gender non-conformists, disabled women or girls, and women who are sex workers.

2 It is unjust when opportunities are curtailed for women or girls because they are women or girls, are women or girls with non-conforming gender or sexual orientation, are of a particular ethnicity or "race," or are disabled. This includes, but is not limited to when opportunities are curtailed for women or girls because they have caregiving responsibilities.

3 It is unjust when women or girls carry more of the burdens and enjoy fewer of the benefits of domestic association, in particular when they shoulder more of the (unremunerated) burdens of housework and caregiving, yet enjoy fewer liberties, opportunities, or material resources, such as when they are disfavored in the distribution of educational resources.

4 It is unjust when girls are socialized to disadvantaging and subordinating social roles, for example when girls are raised to believe that their purpose is to serve others, or that it is proper to neglect their own needs and the development of their own talents.

5 It is unjust when providing the care one's dependents need is incompatible with one's economic independence, the development of one's talents, or assuming positions of cultural, economic, or political power.

6 It is unjust when women, or women of color, and their dependents are disproportionately represented among the poor.

7 It is unjust when those who require it do not receive adequate care.

8 It is unjust when social arrangements render individuals unable to provide or procure the care their dependents need.

9 It is unjust when men, or affluent white men, monopolize economic, political, and cultural power.

10 It is unjust when certain ways of being a woman or a girl are socially stigmatized, such as being a poor or single woman or a woman of color with children, being a prostitute, or having non-conforming gender or sexual identity. For example, it is unjust when laws regulating wealth transfers to single mothers express social disapprobation, when law enforcement fails to address violence against sex workers, or when families or schools denigrate the expression of non-conforming gender, sexual identity, or sexual preference.[5]

---

[5] The feminist conviction I have in mind here does not suggest that all social stigma is unjust.

6.3 A first response to fix ideas

Our question is whether the original position recognizes as unjust the arrangements these convictions highlight. Consider a first response to this question. (I don't think this response represents anyone's considered view; I offer it to fix ideas.) The original position accommodates the feminist considered convictions because it provides the guidance necessary to identify as unjust the social arrangements they highlight. The well-ordered society – whose basic structure is in full compliance with the principles of justice chosen in the original position – necessarily lacks these arrangements because they are ruled out by those principles.

One might take this to be Rawls's view. After all, Rawls tells us: "Justice as fairness ... would certainly be seriously defective should [it] lack the resources to articulate the political values essential to justify the legal and social institutions needed to secure the equality of women and minorities" (*JFR*, p. 66). In addition he says: "If we say the gender system includes whatever social arrangements adversely affect the equal basic liberties and opportunities of women, as well as of those of their children as future citizens, then surely that system is subject to critique by the principles of justice" (*JFR*, pp. 167–8). And finally Rawls says, "since wives are equally citizens with their husbands, they have all the same basic rights and liberties and fair opportunities as their husbands... together with the correct application of the other principles of justice, [this] should suffice to secure their equality and independence" (*JFR*, p. 164).

But when Rawls asks directly "whether the fulfillment of ... [the principles of justice] ... suffices to remedy the [gender] system's faults" (*JFR*, p. 168) he suggests two reasons why aspects of the gender system might endure in a well-ordered society. The first is an application of the dictum that "ought implies can." There might be certain fixed features of the social world that inevitably produce relevant aspects of the gender system. Rawls does not speculate about which aspect(s) the gender system might be unavoidable in this way. Whether any such feature exists, we are told, is an issue to be taken up by "social theory and human psychology" (*JFR*, p. 168).

We no longer think it likely that men are, say, "hard wired" for rape, or women for servility. But if human beings were hard wired in these ways, would justice for that reason not require that men refrain from rape, or not require that servile roles for women be criticized? It might be useful here to appeal to David Estlund's argument that an inability to "muster the will"[6] is

---

[6] Estlund, "Human nature," p. 208.

not the kind of fixedness that cancels an ought.[7] So the fact, should it be a fact, that folks are not able to will the conduct necessary to remedy the arrangements the feminist considered convictions highlight does not mean that justice does not call for a remedy. Note that if any aspects of the gender system are fixed, they are probably fixed only in this "can't will" kind of way. Add to this that Rawls tells us elsewhere that we are not to think of what we can will as fixed but as influenced by social arrangements (*TJ*, p. 259 and *PL*, p. 269). Nonetheless, Rawls is quite clear in *JFR* that some causes of the gender system might be ineradicable in ways that are ought canceling. I lack space to explore whether Estlund's proposal can be accepted without altering something essential in the Rawlsian view.[8]

A second reason Rawls offers for thinking that some aspects of the gender system might endure in a well-ordered society is that they might be amenable to correction only by measures ruled out by the principles of justice. Discussing an example, Rawls writes: "One cannot propose that equal division of labor in the family be simply mandated, or its absence in some way penalized at law... This is ruled out because the division of labor in question is connected with basic liberties" (*CP*, p. 600).

So on Rawls's view, even full compliance with the principles of justice might not suffice to remedy the gender system's "faults" (*JFR*, p. 168). Some of them may endure in a well-ordered society because they are unavoidable or not justly remediable. Nonetheless, Rawls expresses confidence that the principles suffice to "secure [women's] equality and independence" (*JFR*, p. 164) that is, I take it, to secure justice for women.

6.4 The original position, the well-ordered society, and coercive remedies

To better grasp Rawls's view, consider that he maintains that the principles of justice apply to the basic structure of society, understood as that complex of social arrangements whose "effects are ... profound and present from the start" (*TJ*, p. 7). G. A. Cohen argues that despite Rawls's claim that the subject of justice is the basic structure of society, justice as fairness involves application of the principles of justice to only a subset of those arrangements, namely to those that are *legally coercive*.[9] Blaine Neufeld and Chad van Schoelandt

---

[7] Ibid., p. 213.   [8] Estlund is doubtful ("Human Nature," pp. 225–7).
[9] Cohen, "Where the Action Is," p. 18. Cohen argues that there is no good reason to limit the scope of application of the principles of justice in this way (pp. 21–3).

offer clarification; they write: "rather than understand institutions as belonging entirely to, or falling entirely outside of, the basic structure ... it is more perspicuous to focus on what *aspects of institutions*, understood as components in an overall system of social cooperation, must be regulated by coercively maintained principles."[10] This clarification is intended as feminist friendly since social arrangements traditionally considered private – like families – will have "aspects" that must be coercively regulated.

In the discussion of the feminist considered convictions below, some of the presuppositions and requirements of the principles of justice will play an important role. For example, on Rawls's view, arrangements are not just if they interfere with the exercise of the first moral power,[11] and if they fail to afford individuals "a sense of their own worth" (*TJ*, p. 178). For this reason parties to the original position choose the natural "duty of mutual respect" (*TJ*, p. 337). Parties also choose the natural duty "to support and to comply with just institutions" (*TJ*, p. 115) and Rawls explains that just arrangements produce individuals with an appropriate sense of justice (*TJ*, p. 567). We should note here also that on the Rawlsian view the political liberties must have a fair value for each citizen (*JFR*, pp. 148–50). Since these factors are presupposed or required by the principles of justice, we expect the Rawlsian view to be that they may and should be coercively secured and thus that a well-ordered society will lack arrangements that systematically undermine them.[12]

It is evident now that three questions are in play. First is whether the original position allows us to identify as unjust the arrangements the feminist considered convictions highlight. Second is whether it allows or requires coercive measures if they are necessary to ensure that particular unjust arrangements don't obtain.[13] And third is whether the well-ordered society necessarily lacks these arrangements. Rawls expects answers to these questions to track one another. But the discussion of the feminist considered convictions below shows that things don't shake out that way. The original position fails to recognize as unjust some of the arrangements the feminist considered convictions highlight. From the standpoint of the original

---

[10] Neufeld and van Schoelandt, "Political Liberalism," p. 88; my emphasis.

[11] This is the "capacity to have, to revise, and rationally to pursue a conception of the good" (*JFR*, p. 19).

[12] Scheffler writes: "One of the functions of just social institutions is to shape individuals' characters in such a way as to discourage desires and motivations that are incompatible with justice" (Scheffler, "Is the Basic Structure?" p. 125).

[13] Since Rawls proposes justice as fairness as "realistically utopian" (*JFR*, p. 4) achievement of a threshold may suffice.

position, other arrangements are recognized as unjust and effective coercive measures are allowed and required. These will be lacking in a well-ordered society. But there is a third category of arrangements the original position recognizes as unjust, but for which necessary effective coercive remedies may be disallowed; these arrangements may endure in a well-ordered society.

Discussing the possibility of arrangements of this third kind, Samuel Scheffler writes: "If family law were thoroughly egalitarian, and if norms of gender equality pervaded other areas of the law that have served to enforce gender differences, it is far from obvious to me that ... egregious sexist patterns could indeed survive and flourish."[14] Elizabeth Anderson, not so sure, writes:

> The plurality of conceptions of the good that are likely to survive in a world in which the state has done all it can be reasonably and justly expected to do [that is, a well-ordered society] will include a host of unreasonable conceptions of the good, some of which may well be patriarchal. If enough people uphold such conceptions of the good, their normative expectations and norm-guided conduct, even if not mediated by state power, will unjustly constrain women.[15]

Of course, of the two, we hope Scheffler is right. But which one of them is right is an empirical question.

Since Rawls's view is that the well-orderedness of a society just is its full compliance with the principles of justice one might be surprised by my claim that arrangements recognized as unjust by the original position may endure in a well-ordered society. But the discussion of the feminist considered convictions below vindicates this way of talking. One could, though I won't here, reserve the adjective "well-ordered" for a society characterized by full compliance with the principles of justice applied to the coercive basic structure plus the good fortune that no arrangements obtain that are recognized as unjust but are not susceptible to a just coercive remedy; or perhaps plus the good fortune that all such arrangements not obtaining is caused (though not entailed) by the coercive basic structure's being in full compliance with those principles. This way of talking is also problematic. If a society's well-orderedness is in this way a matter of good fortune, a well-ordered society is a bit less "realistically practicable" than I think Rawls intends (*JFR*, p. 13).

---

[14] Scheffler, "Is the Basic Structure?" p. 126.   [15] Anderson, "Toward a Non-ideal," p. 131.

6.5 The Rawlsian response: pruning and adjusting the feminist considered convictions

Rawls explains that when a description of the initial situation fails to accommodate some considered convictions we have two choices. On the one hand "we can ... modify the account of the initial situation"; on the other, "we can revise our existing judgments ... conforming them to principle," rendering them "duly pruned and adjusted" (*TJ*, p. 20). The Rawlsian response to the question of whether the original position accommodates the feminist considered convictions is that it does so as long as those convictions are pruned and adjusted. In this section, I show how the original position facilitates such pruning and adjusting. So note in the discussion that follows when the original position identifies as unjust some arrangement the feminist considered convictions highlight and calls for an effective coercive remedy. Note also when the original position does not recognize some such arrangement as unjust and does not allow or require a coercive remedy. But further, note examples of the third category of arrangements, which the original position identifies as unjust but for which necessary effective coercive remedies may be disallowed and thus which may endure in a well-ordered society.

6.5.1 Violence

The original position accommodates the feminist considered conviction that it is unjust when women and girls are regularly subject to, and fear, violence (conviction (1)). Since systematic violence violates liberty protected by the first principle, such violence against women and girls is recognized as unjust wherever it occurs (*CP*, p. 599). "No institution or association ... can [justly] violate [women's] rights as citizens" (*CP*, p. 598, see also p. 597; and *JFR*, p. 166). "Gender distinctions limiting ... rights and liberties are excluded" (*CP*, p. 599) as are distinctions like "race," ethnicity, gender expression, disability status, or profession. Perhaps we should say then that the well-ordered society lacks systematic violence because the principles underwrite necessary effective coercive remedies. But we must be sure that the causes of such violence are not fixed – or not fixed in the relevant way – and that necessary effective coercive remedies do not violate the first principle. Surely Rawls thought that among the favorable circumstances necessary for the possibility of justice as fairness is that the causes of systematic violence are not fixed in a way that is ought canceling. And I assume that Rawls thought effective coercive remedies can satisfy the first principle; so, for example, the legal prohibition of violent pornography either does not violate it or is not necessary.[16]

6.5.2 Discrimination, female primary parenting and socialization to disadvantaging and subordinating social roles

Consider convictions (2)–(5). Rawls intends the principle of fair equality of opportunity to prohibit discrimination by the state, employers, and public accommodations against women and girls. I take this to include other bases of discrimination such as "race" or ethnicity, disability status, gender presentation, or sexuality. This underwrites something like conventional anti-discrimination law. I think the Rawlsian view must be that if the causes of sex discrimination are fixed – if men (or women) are unable to treat women as men's equals in relevant respects – then such discrimination is not unjust. Surely Rawls did not anticipate that the causes of discrimination could be unavoidable in this way. It could, of course, turn out that any of the arrangements the feminist considered convictions highlight are unavoidable, in which case they would not be recognized as unjust. With Rawls, we must assume favorable circumstances.

Rawls tells us that the principle of fair equality of opportunity is violated when women's opportunities are curtailed because of "the burden of bearing, raising, and educating children ... [falling] more heavily on women" (*JFR*, p. 11). The remedy, Rawls explains, is to either eliminate the disadvantage or compensate for it.[17] But it is not altogether clear what the Rawlsian reason is for this. To be sure, Rawls is insisting that dependency work be recognized as a form of social cooperation that entitles one to a share of benefits. This is why he endorses the basic idea behind Susan Okin's paycheck sharing proposal (*JFR*, p. 167). We must accept that women have been forced to take on the role of primary parent by an unjust lack of opportunity elsewhere, and that women have been coerced to take on this social role by law and with the law's sanction by family and community. All this counts as unjust on the Rawlsian view. And the well-ordered society lacks these features because the principles of justice underwrite necessary effective coercive remedies.

Female primary parenting may contribute to systematic under-investment in girls, or to training of girls to disadvantaging and subordinating social

---

[16] At issue here is whether violent pornography causes violence against women. For an excellent discussion, see Eaton, "A Sensible Anti-porn Feminism."

[17] Rawls calls for "special provisions ... in family law (and no doubt elsewhere)" (*JFR*, p. 11).

roles, by family and community pursuant to sexist comprehensive doctrines. Such socialization (including female primary parenting if it plays a role) is recognized as unjust if it causes girls to lack the ability to exercise the first moral power upon adulthood, or if it leaves them lacking self-respect; or if it produces individuals who lack the requisite sense of justice, fail to support just institutions, or are incapable of mutual respect; or if it undermines the fair value of the political liberties. It is not clear what kinds of socialization in fact have these consequences to the requisite degree. Many report coming to feminist consciousness through struggle in profoundly sexist communities. It is also important to note that coercive measures might turn out to be less effective than persuasive ones. But if we were able to identify relevant examples, we should expect that effective coercive remedies would be allowed and required and that a well-ordered society would necessarily lack this socialization.

There is agreement among Rawlsians that children's prospective liberty and opportunity requires schooling that promotes the development of their moral powers and the fair value of their political liberties. But what if such schooling does not effectively counteract the relevant effects of sexist socialization? Are coercive measures that aim directly at socialization in families and other associations allowed or required if they are the sole effective measures available? As we have seen, Rawls thinks coercive measures disallowing a gendered division of labor in the home violate the first principle. It is likely he would think the same about, say, parental licensing with a gender-egalitarian litmus test. Feminist Rawlsians may push at this point, stressing the importance of preserving the moral powers – especially the first, since it is presupposed by the first principle. A liberty-maximizing approach might help here. We could try to figure out whether protecting children's moral powers on the one hand or the relevant liberties of parents and other association members on the other maximizes liberty. Maybe the former does. Rawls doesn't rule out a liberty-maximizing approach in the context of partial compliance theory (*TJ*, p. 213). Or one could argue that the prerequisites of liberty take precedence over the liberties themselves, and thus that one could violate the first principle in order to secure the first moral power; it is not clear whether Rawls foresees such a move in partial compliance theory.[18] Or one could argue that coercive measures that aim directly at socialization in families and associations are justified to protect the fair value of the political liberties. Although Rawls

[18] Thanks to David Estlund for correspondence on this point.

suggests that ideal theory should help us with "the moral dilemmas that arise in partial compliance theory" (*TJ*, p. 242), it is not clear what to say at this point, given Rawls's rejection of sample remedies that aim directly at socialization in families. I will take Rawls's considered position to be embodied in what he says about coercive measures that aim directly at socialization in families and other associations, namely that they are disallowed. So sexist socialization might be an example of the third category of arrangements; that category includes arrangements that are recognized as unjust by the original position but may not be susceptible to coercive remedies and therefore may endure in a well-ordered society.

Note that we have been talking about girl-disadvantaging socialization that is moral power destroying. Disadvantage that results from socialization that is not moral power destroying is not recognized as unjust by the original position. It is among the opportunity-undermining consequences of families that justice as fairness generally permits and for which the difference principle compensates (*TJ*, p. 74). Even if a society wanted to effectively remedy this disadvantage, coercive measures may be disallowed for reasons just discussed.

What if female primary parenting disadvantages female parents but is not the result of formal or informal coercion, or unjust lack of opportunity elsewhere, and does not have moral-power and fair-value-of-the-political-liberties destroying effects? Since dependency work counts as cooperation, the difference principle applies. But there doesn't seem to be a Rawlsian reason why disadvantage resulting from primary parenting must be remedied beyond application of the difference principle. To see this, compare the way choosing to become a mother[19] reduces opportunity with the way choosing to become a monk does. The social world pits being a monk against taking up other opportunities, but this is not a violation of fair equality of opportunity. The point of Rawlsian fair equality of opportunity isn't that no one ought to be able to reduce their own opportunities by choice. If the social world pits mothering against taking up other opportunities, this is no more unjust than in the monk's case. So the resulting disadvantage is not recognized as unjust from the point of view of the original position. To be sure, a society could adopt coercive measures to remedy this disadvantage, for example restructuring the workplace or making high quality daycare accessible. Such measures are not disallowed. But it would not count as unjust if a society characterized by such disadvantage failed to adopt them.

---

[19] In the absence of coercion or unjust lack of opportunity elsewhere, and without moral-power and fair-value-of-the-political-liberties destroying effects.

6.5.3 Poverty

Conviction (6) says it is unjust when women and their dependents, or women of color and their dependents, are disproportionately represented among the poor. As we have seen, on Rawls's view, care-giving is a form of social cooperation so the difference principle applies to care-givers. The original position's parties represent those who are "normally active and fully cooperating members of society over a complete life" with "physical and psychological capacities within a certain normal range" (*CP*, p. 368). So in addition to care-givers (of any ethnicity or "race"), we count among those to whom the difference principle applies children who will become fully cooperating, the temporarily infirm who will return to being so, and the infirm elderly who once were. But note that the difference principle is compatible with care-givers and their dependents clustering at the bottom of the wealth and income distribution. Note also that the difference principle does not apply to the not fully cooperating.[20] It is reasonable to assume, as Asha Bhandary does, that this includes those who care for the not fully cooperating.[21] To be sure, a well-ordered society could adopt coercive measures to improve the economic standing of the not fully cooperating (and their care-givers); this is not disallowed. But it would not count as unjust if a society failed to do so.[22]

6.5.4 Receipt of adequate care

Conviction (7) says that it is unjust when those who require it do not receive adequate care. As feminists have emphasized, we are all, as infants and young children, utterly dependent upon the care of others for our very survival. Also, many of us will become temporarily and some of us permanently disabled; this will render us even as adults dependent on the occasional or constant ministrations of others to survive and to thrive.[23] Following Bhandary, let us understand receipt of care as among the social bases of self-respect.[24] If each individual is to enjoy the social bases of self-respect to the requisite degree,

---

[20] Stark, "How to Include," p. 134.   [21] Bhandary, "Dependency in Justice," p. 150.

[22] But see Stark, "How to Include," pp. 136–40.

[23] One aspect of the gender system is that women can be counted on to provide care to those who are dependent – even when women's doing so is to their disadvantage. When receipt of care is recognized as a matter of justice, the social arrangements themselves, through which care is provided, become a matter of justice as well.

[24] Bhandary, "Dependency," p. 149.

receipt of adequate care must be ensured. So the original position would seem to accommodate this feminist considered conviction. But, as Bhandary notes, the free choice of occupation protected by the first principle prohibits coerced provision of care,[25] so there could be a care deficit in a well-ordered society. This worry is compounded by the fact that care is sometimes adequate only if it is loving care; and while care can be obtained coercively (though it shouldn't be), loving care can't be. Also, since parties to the original position do not represent the not fully cooperating, failure on their part to receive adequate care may not count as unjust. To be sure, Rawls says: "I take it as obvious, and accepted as common sense, that we have a duty towards all human beings however severely handicapped" (*JFR*, p. 176 n. 59). But as Cynthia Stark points out, "Rawls does not tell us whether these are duties of justice."[26] It may well be that duties of justice to the not fully cooperating can be derived in some way other than through the original position;[27] but that underscores the fact that the original position is not the ground of such duties.

6.5.5 Providing care

Conviction (8) says it is an injustice to care-givers when social arrangements make them unable to provide or procure the care their dependents require.[28] This reflects the experience of women who have, by social circumstances, been rendered unable to provide care. Think of enslaved women unable to care for children sold away, or impoverished women forced by circumstances to care for others' children while their own are bereft. Receipt of care may be a social basis of self-respect, but providing or procuring care for one's dependents is simply one of the many ends had by individuals whom parties to the original position represent. Arrangements that render a care-giver unable to provide or procure adequate care may be recognized as unjust to a potential care-giver if they represent an unjust interference with her liberty or opportunity, or result from lack of income and wealth to which she is entitled. But otherwise such arrangements are a misfortune, not an injustice. Perhaps it is unlikely that care-givers will in fact be unable to provide or procure care (at least to the fully cooperating) in a well-ordered society, since the difference principle probably ensures funds sufficient to support care-giving activities.

---

[25] Bhandary, "Liberal Dependency."   [26] Stark, "How to Include," p. 130 n.10.
[27] James, "Constructing Justice," p. 312.   [28] Kittay, *Love's Labor*, p. 154; see also p. 69.

But arrangements that undermine care-givers' ability to provide or procure care are not recognized as, in themselves, unjust.

6.5.6 Monopolization of economic, political, and cultural power, and stigmatization

Finally, recall convictions (9) and (10), which concern male, or affluent white male monopolization of economic, political, and cultural power, and the stigmatization of various ways of being a woman or a girl.[29] The original position underwrites the coercive securing of property-owning democracy. This calls for capital to be widely dispersed, likely amounting to a basic income (*JFR*, p. 139). As Ingrid Robeyns suggests, while a basic income would represent an improvement over the status quo for many women and their dependents, it could reinforce women's tendency to forgo labor market participation in favor of unremunerated care-giving, entrenching attendant disadvantages. Moreover, under conditions of limited resources, the wide dispersal foreseen by property-owning democracy could compete with social investments necessary to lighten the burden of dependency work.[30]

Parties to the original position insist on the fair value of the political liberties. Rawls understands this to underwrite coercive measures to ensure wide dispersal of political influence. This means that women's marginalization, or the marginalization of poor women, or women of color, from influence over political decision-making is recognized as unjust. The causes of this exclusion are complex.[31] If it results from some of the arrangements for which the principles disallow effective remedies – such as female primary parenting and sexist socialization – then it too may endure in a well-ordered society.

Stigmatization of groups is recognized as unjust if it systematically undermines the first moral power, self-respect, or the sense of justice; if it undermines the ability to support and further just institutions, or to demonstrate respect; or if it reduces the value of women's political liberties, for example by undermining the plausibility of women's claims to social goods. Of course, it is hard to know precisely which cultural representations do this to the requisite degree; stigma can spur protest and counteract these effects. But if we were able to identify relevant examples, we might expect that the original position would underwrite necessary effective coercive remedies. The original position does indeed allow some moderately coercive measures like school

---

[29] See note 5.   [30] Robeyns, "Gender, Care," p. 173.
[31] For an overview see Baehr, "Liberal Feminism," section 1.2.2.

curricula targeting stigma, and anti-discrimination law. But if permissible measures were ineffective, more intrusive measures – like hate speech regulations or media censorship – would be disallowed because they violate the first principle. Of course a Rawlsian would hope for the good fortune that unjust stigma does not persist in a well-ordered society. But it may, since effective remedies may be disallowed.

6.5.7 Reconciliation to the gender system

I have shown that the original position fails to recognize as unjust some of the arrangements the feminist considered convictions highlight. Other arrangements are recognized as unjust, and for them effective coercive remedies are allowed and required. Still other arrangements are recognized as unjust but may endure in a well-ordered society since necessary effective coercive remedies may be disallowed.

Rawls claims that an important role of political philosophy is reconciliation. Political philosophy can "calm our frustration and rage against" our society and lead us to "accept and affirm our social world positively, not merely to be resigned to it" (*JFR*, p. 3). Rawls does not mean our being reconciled to unjust arrangements, but to those that offend us without rising to the level of injustice. Among them are, of course, arrangements the feminist considered convictions highlight but which the original position does not recognize as unjust. Does justice as fairness recommend reconciliation also in the case of those arrangements the original position recognizes as unjust but for which necessary effective coercive remedies may be disallowed, and thus which may endure in a well-ordered society? I think it does. The purpose of reconciliation is to put to rest our desire to use state power in ways justice disallows; and as we have seen, on the Rawlsian view justice may disallow effective coercive remedies for much of the injustice the feminist considered convictions highlight. We must conclude that justice as fairness would recommend reconciliation to significant aspects of the gender system.

To be sure, a Rawlsian could applaud the full demise of the gender system. But the normative ground for her applause would not be the Rawlsian original position. The original position underwrites feminist activism to harness state power to remedy some of the injustices that feminist considered convictions highlight, namely those for which the original position allows or requires an effective coercive remedy. It underwrites non-coercive activism to remedy injustice that the original position recognizes but for which coercive measures would be disallowed. One might append to justice as fairness a gender-egalitarian ethos that would recommend non-coercive feminist action to remedy the arrangements the feminist considered convictions condemn but the original position does not.[32] But the normative ground of such an ethos would not be the Rawlsian original position.

6.6 Feminist proposal 1: extending the scope of the original position

I noted above that when an interpretation of the initial situation fails to accommodate a set of considered convictions we may opt to prune and adjust them. Another option would be to modify the initial situation, in this case, the original position. One way to modify the original position to accommodate more of the feminist considered convictions would be to extend the scope of application of its principles. One proposal, associated with the work of Susan Okin, is to apply the original position's principles directly to the internal workings of the many arrangements that constitute the basic structure of society, that is, whose effects are "profound and present from the start" (*TJ*, p. 7). Applying the principle of equality of opportunity directly to the internal workings of the family would rule out disadvantaging gendered division of labor and distribution of resources. And it would rule out the socialization of girls to disadvantaging and subordinating social roles. Applying principles directly to the internal workings of families and associations makes them, in G. A. Cohen's words, "principles for individuals."[33]

Sometimes Okin's objection to the gendered division of labor in families rests on this principles for individuals view. But sometimes it rests on another view of how to extend the scope of application of the principles of justice.[34] This other view – call it "the feminist full basic structure view" – differs from Rawls's insofar as it has principles of justice apply to the complex of social arrangements whose influence is "profound and from the start" (*TJ*, p. 7), and not just to the subset of those arrangements that may be coercively maintained. Unlike the principles for individuals view, the feminist full basic structure view does not have principles apply to the internal workings of the various institutions but to the complex of arrangements that make up the basic structure. In addition, this view appreciates gender – in Okin's words

---

[32] Neufeld and van Schoelandt propose such an ethos in their defense of Rawls ("Political Liberalism").

[33] Cohen, *Rescuing Justice*, pp. 358–9.   [34] Okin, *Justice*, p. 184.

"the deeply entrenched institutionalization of sexual difference"[35] – as a particularly influential aspect of this complex of arrangements.[36]

To appreciate the difference between the principles for individuals view and the feminist full basic structure view, consider Okin's claim that justice requires housework and caregiving to be shared 50–50 in families. On the principles for individuals view, 50–50 sharing is a direct requirement of justice. It follows from the application of the principle of equality of opportunity directly to families: for women and girls to enjoy equality of opportunity within each family, housework and caregiving must be shared 50–50 by the sexes. The feminist full basic structure view notes that the gendered division of labor in the home can be an important cause of women's and girls' disadvantaged social positions, but that there are other causes as well; think for example of the gendered structure of the workplace and the meanings of femininity and masculinity in popular culture. The feminist full basic structure view would apply the principle of equality of opportunity to the complex of arrangements that make up the basic structure and call for measures to remedy the disadvantage; 50–50 sharing would be just one of a number of possible remedies.

Distinguishing the feminist full basic structure view from the principles for individuals view allows us to appreciate the objection some liberal feminists – otherwise quite sympathetic to Okin – have to her 50–50 sharing proposal. Linda Alstott, for example, writes: "The egalitarian family is, even in principle, a troubling ideal. Strictly equal sharing seems unduly constraining, not merely because families today deviate from the idea, but because free people might want to organize their lives differently."[37] As I understand this objection, it is not simply that it would be unjust for the state to enforce 50–50 sharing, since Okin agrees with this.[38] On this view, the reason to object to the distribution of domestic labor – if there is a reason – is not that families ought to be internally structured by Rawls's principles of justice; it is that such a distribution can curtail women's opportunity in society more generally.

Cohen argues that the principles for individuals view is *the form* of the feminist critique of Rawls. He writes: "in supposing that [Rawls] could include family relations, Okin shows a failure to grasp *the* form of the feminist critique of Rawls."[39] If I am right that the feminist full basic structure view is also a critical feminist use of the original position, then the principles for individuals view is not *the* form of the feminist critique of Rawls. It is not clear

---

[35] Ibid., p. 6.   [36] Ibid.   [37] Alstott, *No Exit*, p. 113.   [38] Okin, *Justice*, p. 171.
[39] Cohen, "Where the Action Is," p. 4. Italics mine.

that Okin appreciated the difference between the two views at work in her thinking about the original position. To be sure, one can help oneself to both views at once. But I do think that, held separately, they produce two distinct liberal feminisms.

It is important to note that Okin does not think coercive measures are an appropriate response to all injustice. For example, she endorses paycheck sharing as a coercive measure[40] but not 50–50 sharing of domestic work.[41] Okin does not explain why some injustices get a coercive remedy and others do not. She can't be relying on the original position's principles for the distinction, since her application of the principles to the family yields the 50–50 proposal, which she does not think ought to be coercively enforced. Indeed, in Okin's hands, the original position is no longer a guide to the distinction between permissible and impermissible coercive measures.[42]

6.7 Feminist proposal 2: situating dependency in an initial situation

The feminisms produced by extending the scope of application of the original position do not fully accommodate feminist considered convictions about dependency. Those feminisms extend the scope of application of the Rawlsian initial situation. We have seen that, among the conditions of the original position are that parties don't represent the not fully cooperating and that the interest in providing or procuring adequate care for one's dependents is merely one interest among the many that individuals might have. Thus on the Rawlsian view it is not unjust when the not fully cooperating fail to receive adequate care; nor is it (in itself) unjust when individuals are unable to provide or procure the care their dependents require. Might it be possible to design an initial situation that accommodates feminist considered convictions about dependency? Might it be possible to do this as part of an overall liberal view? The literature includes no fully worked out attempt to answer this question.[43]

If an alternative initial situation were to be worked out, it would begin with the normative conception of society implicit in the feminist considered convictions about dependency. According to such a conception, society is an intergenerational association of fully and not fully cooperating individuals

---

[40] Okin, *Justice*, pp. 180–1.   [41] Ibid., p. 171.

[42] This may be a concern to feminist liberals interested in an account of the just uses of coercive state power to feminist ends. See for example Baehr, "Liberal Feminism Comprehensive."

[43] For some suggestions see Bhandary, "Dependency"; Lloyd, "Toward a Liberal"; Thompson, "What do Women Want?"

who have an interest in exercising the two moral powers to the extent that this is possible, but also in giving and receiving adequate care. Parties representing such individuals seek social arrangements that make it possible for adequate care to be given and received, and for care-giving to be compatible with the exercise of the first moral power. Concerned to maximize the least advantageous outcome, parties would want to avoid several situations. (I don't intend this as an order of priority.) The first outcome parties would want to avoid is having the individuals they represent generally be unable to pursue their ends as a result of the burdens of care-giving. The second situation to be avoided is their being unable to provide or procure adequate care for their dependents. And third is their receiving inadequate care themselves. Shares of Rawlsian primary goods – liberties, opportunities, income and wealth, and the social bases of self-respect – are surely part of the story here. But an alternative initial situation may suggest that valid claims would need to be couched in other terms. For example, while on the Rawlsian view receipt of care may be a social basis of self-respect, on the alternative account, "the social bases of caring relations"[44] may stand alone on the list of primary goods.[45]

Cynthia Stark doubts an initial situation can accommodate both the fully cooperating and the not fully cooperating. This is because, on Stark's view, the fully cooperating's claims to shares of social goods must be tied to contributions made, whereas the not fully cooperating's claims cannot be.[46] A feminist re-design of the original position will need to grapple with the question of whether an alternative initial situation can be designed that accommodates differing kinds of claims to social goods. Also, of particular interest is whether such an initial situation can accommodate all of the feminist considered convictions, not just those concerned with dependency. And those of us interested in the possibility of a feminist liberalism will want to know whether a feminist re-design of the original position can also accommodate common liberal considered convictions, and thus be part of an overall liberal view.

6.8 Conclusion

As we have seen, much of what feminists identify as injustice is recognized by the original position as such, but much is not. And the original position

---

[44] This expression is due to Elizabeth Brake (*Minimizing Marriage*, p. 175).
[45] That the state may *support* caring relations but cannot directly distribute adequate care will be a problem for any account of distributive justice.
[46] Stark, "Contractarianism," p. 87.

underwrites necessary effective coercive remedies for some of the injustices recognized by the original position, but not for all of them. This means that some of the injustices recognized by the original position may endure in a well-ordered society. Okin's application of the principles of justice to the many arrangements that make up the basic structure – and not just those that are coercive – allows the original position to accommodate more of the feminist considered convictions, but it fails to accommodate feminist convictions about dependency. The jury is out on whether an initial situation can be designed that accommodates those convictions and is part of an overall liberal view.

Rawls tells us that, "from time to time, we must ask whether justice as fairness, or any other view, is 'ideological . . . in Marx's sense,' that is, whether it is 'a defense of an unjust and unworthy status quo'" (*JFR*, p. 4 n. 4). Should we take the fact that the original position does not fully accommodate the feminist considered convictions as indication that justice as fairness is an ideological defense in this way? There are two reasons to resist this conclusion. First, a defense is a justification, and justice as fairness doesn't directly justify the gender system. To be sure, it justifies arrangements that are compatible with much of the gender system; it recommends that we reconcile ourselves to much of it; and if the feminist considered convictions are true (or reasonable), the original position would throw us off the trail of injustice. The second reason to resist this conclusion is that we cannot assume that the feminist considered convictions are true (or reasonable); we cannot assume that they tell the truth about what is unjust. If we are contractualists, at least, we may no more assume that the feminist considered convictions are true than assume that Rawls's original position is the correct account of the initial situation. We must take up Rawls's invitation and continue the process of reflective equilibrium. This chapter has presented some first steps in that process.

7 G. A. Cohen's critique of the original position

David Estlund

7.1 Introduction

G. A. Cohen seeks to "rescue" justice from, primarily, John Rawls. His challenge to Rawlsian philosophy is widely thought to be one of the most powerful we have. Cohen's writings on this topic over many years culminate in his densely argued volume, *Rescuing Justice and Equality*.[1] While no thorough evaluation is possible here, I will tentatively defend Rawls, but with reservations.

Rawls's reliance on the original position is at the heart of Cohen's critique, with Cohen charging that this method makes the principles of justice depend on non-moral facts in ways that are fundamentally misguided. Cohen pursues both metaethical and normative prongs of this attack, and I shall be looking at both. On Cohen's view, Rawls's employment of the original position rests on the erroneous assumption that the fundamental principles of justice are fact dependent and, moreover, it leads the content of the principles chosen there to be distorted by categories of non-moral fact that themselves have nothing to do with justice. He argues that both of these shortcomings reveal that the original position method generates a conception of justice that is mistaken because it is less egalitarian than it should be. I will refer to these as the critique of "fact-dependent foundations," and the critique of "justice as regulation." I will conclude, briefly, with a discussion of a third form of sensitivity to facts suggested but not developed by Cohen, namely the role that the original position method must give to morally bad facts.

I presume no prior familiarity with Cohen's arguments, though some familiarity with Rawls is taken for granted. The stage can briefly be set with a reminder of what I will call Rawls's original position method.[2] I will

---

[1] All page and chapter references to Cohen's writing will be to this work. I am grateful to Amy Baehr, David Brink, Timothy Hinton, Tim Syme, and Paul Weithman for comments on a previous draft.

[2] There are some later developments, but the canonical presentation of the original position is in *TJ*.

sometimes follow Cohen in referring to it as Rawls's "constructivism." Rawls's seminal development of the argument from the original position stems from the following methodological proposal. Oftentimes, disagreements about what is to be done can be narrowed or settled if the answer is to be provided by a procedure whose authority is less controversial. We might not agree about which restaurant would be the best choice, and yet we might agree that this ought to be decided by voting after discussing it. We don't disagree about that procedure as intractably as we do about which choice would be correct (judged by some procedure-independent standard). Rawls proposes something similar for the case of disputes about the content of social justice: these disputes might be more tractable if we could devise a procedure (it is bound to be only hypothetical, but that would suffice) about which there is less (reasonable, at least) dispute, in the following respect: it might be seen as effectively designed so as to select principles that serve people's interests impartially, when they are conceived as morally free and equal. If such a procedure favors certain views of the content of justice over others, this ought to weigh in favor of those views as a form of evidence or support. It might give pause even to those who hold to their original views with more conviction than they can invest in the proposed procedure, perhaps leading them to appreciate the decency and seriousness with which their opponents' view can be supported. Surely, that would be something.

Famously, Rawls develops an elaborate procedure to serve this role.[3] Individuals are represented in this hypothetical original position by parties who are able to know all that science and good sense can tell us about how the competing principles would be likely to bear on certain fundamental "primary social goods." These parties will each prefer the principles that would do best for them, though they are, in their special original position office, not to concern themselves with the fate of the clients of the other choosers. However, the choosers are behind a "veil of ignorance": they are not to know which of the people in the real principle-governed society is their client. They naturally must consider the possibility that it might be anyone.

Cohen's objections to this whole approach stem from the fact that the results are partly, but crucially, driven by the non-moral facts that the parties are aware of. As I have said, Cohen mounts three lines of attack, to which I now turn.

---

[3] For a thorough introduction to the original position in Rawls see Freeman, "The Original Position," *Stanford Encyclopedia of Philosophy*.

7.2 Fact-free foundations

Cohen mounts a general and abstract argument about the nature of moral principles that begins from the claim that facts have whatever moral significance they have in virtue of principles. Thus, fact-independent principles are morally more basic than, because they explain, fact-dependent ones. Certainly, some moral principles depend on non-moral facts.[4] For example,

Principle 1: It is wrong, except in special conditions, to physically *strike* another person,

and this is partly because of certain facts. That is,

Fact basis 1: Principle 1 is true partly because striking people tends to hurt or injure them.

The fact that hitting will tend to have this effect is not a moral truth, but a non-moral fact derivable (if necessary) from physics, physiology, and psychology. The moral wrongness rests on this non-moral fact in the following respect: hitting people would be less wrong, or perhaps even permissible if, and then because, it did not hurt people. Cohen accepts this, of course. But he argues that all such fact-dependent moral principles rest, in their turn, on principles that are independent of the non-moral facts in question. In the case of the wrongness of hitting, the following principle seems to be implicated, and yet it is not dependent on non-moral facts about how hitting affects people:

Principle 2: It is wrong, except in special conditions, to *hurt* people.

This is a deeper principle than (1) in the following sense: (2) grounds (1), and not vice versa. We will not try to say exactly what this grounding relation is, but we can note a few features of it that indicate the sense in which (2) grounds, or underlies (1). Notice that (1)'s truth depends on (2)'s truth. If this were denied, it would be inexplicable why the fact that hitting hurts is stated as a fact upon which (1) depends. How could this fact support (1) unless it was normally wrong to hurt people, which is principle (2)? Citing the fact that hitting hurts as a basis for the wrongness of hitting evidently presupposes, as an explanation, the wrongness of hurting. So (1) must be granted to rest on (2).

---

[4] The arguments I attribute to Cohen in this section appear in his own words in Chapter 6, section 5.

But (2) does not similarly rest on (1), of course. The wrongness of hurting does not rest or depend on any facts about whether hitting happens to hurt people. If hitting did not hurt people, then we would have less interest in the morality of hitting, but we are not now asking what moral principles are of interest given the facts as they are. We are asking what things are right and wrong. So there is this asymmetrical relation of depth. We will mark these ostensibly deeper principles with higher numbers, as measures of increasing depth. So (2) indicates more depth relative to (1).

So, the wrongness of hitting rests on the wrongness of hurting, but the wrongness of hurting does not rest on the wrongness of hitting. Principle (2), the principle about the wrongness of hurting, obtains independently of the facts that ground (1). But (2) might be thought in turn to rest on some other non-moral facts. In that case we would not yet have to accept that there are any fact-independent moral principles. Cohen's argument, however, contains two importantly different claims, one of which we have just seen an argument for:

> *Relative claim* (of fact-independence): For any principle that does depend on certain facts, there is a deeper grounding principle that does not depend on *those* facts.

This leaves open the possibility of an infinite stack of deeper principles, each of which depends on some facts, albeit owing to a deeper principle yet. But Cohen denies that this is so in his second claim, which is the

> *Ultimate claim* (of fact-independence): Every principle that depends on facts is grounded, directly or indirectly, in a principle that depends on no facts at all.[5]

Unless the ultimate claim is true, principle (2), which grounds the wrongness of hitting in the wrongness of hurting, might itself depend on some non-moral fact. It is not, as we saw, grounded in the fact that hitting hurts, so it would have to be some other fact. What might it be? There might be something deeper to say *morally* about what is wrong with hurting people, but we are asking whether it is wrong to hurt people owing to some *non-moral* facts. I cannot think of any plausible candidates, but even if there were such grounding facts, Cohen challenges us to recapitulate these questions at the next deeper level and to see if we can find grounding facts yet again. Cohen

---

[5] I paraphrase what Cohen says at p. 232 and elsewhere.

argues, from such examples, that this procedure will always eventually (and usually quite quickly, he thinks) terminate in a principle that does not rest on any non-moral facts at all.

Since it will figure importantly below, we want a handy name for Cohen's movement (in the manner of the "relative claim") from any fact-dependent principle to a deeper, relatively fact-independent principle that explains the moral relevance of those facts. I will call this "unearthing" the deeper principle.[6] In asking what grounds the fact that hitting is wrong in virtue of hurting, we can unearth the deeper principle that hurting is wrong. Cohen hopes to use this strategy against the original position method.

7.3 A formal objection: Cohen's unearthing strategy

As we have seen, Rawls argues that principles of social justice are "constructed"[7] partly through engagement with non-moral facts. The question that guides the Rawlsian approach is how things would work out in practice, in certain ways, if the basic social structure met certain principles rather than others. "In practice" is not meant to tie the principles to all the expected contingencies of our world going forward. It idealizes in particular ways. For example, parties to the original position are to choose principles of justice on the assumption, clearly contrary to fact, that there would be, among other "favorable conditions," publicly recognized full compliance with the rules and norms of the basic structure. Still, the parties who are selecting the principles in the hypothesized choice situation will bring to bear their general knowledge of such non-moral facts as characteristic human motives and concerns, cognitive abilities, characteristic patterns of moral development, predictable strains in keeping certain commitments, not to mention the whole universe of facts about how nature itself operates.[8]

The derivation of the fundamental principles of social justice in the original position renders those principles dependent on, and explained partly by, the non-moral facts about people and nature that lead the parties to select them. Rawls is explicit about this. He writes, "There is no necessity

---

[6] The pun is intended, though no part of my present point. Cohen agrees with Plato that, "justice transcends the facts of the world . . . [and] that justice is the self-same thing across, and independently of, history. But that extreme anti-relativism is no part of the doctrine here defended that justice is, ultimately, facts-free" (pp. 291–2).

[7] *PL*, p. 103.

[8] Freeman pulls together the main textual sources for roughly this list in "The Original Position."

to invoke theological or metaphysical doctrines to support [these] principles ... Conceptions of justice must be justified by the conditions of our life as we know it or not at all."[9]

At this point, of course, we should bring to bear Cohen's strategy of unearthing the fact-independent principles that are alleged to ground any fact-dependent ones. If Rawls is right that the two principles of justice as fairness are grounded wholly or partly in the non-moral facts about the "conditions of our life as we know it," there must be, Cohen argues, a deeper principle that explains the particular moral relevance of those facts. This would suffice to show, Cohen thinks, that the principles generated by the original position cannot be the fundamental principles of social justice. The normative force of Rawls's two principles would be explained by some more fundamental principle, one that does not depend on those facts. To get to the fundamental principle or principles, we must unearth them by scraping away the facts whose relevance is grounded by something deeper.

Suppose Cohen's argument were conceded up to this point. It might seem to undermine the original position as an appropriate way to generate or arrive at the content of principles of social justice. And suppose a Rawlsian were to acquiesce in the demand for further unearthing. She then reports on her findings:

> **The unearthed Rawlsian principle:** The fundamental principle is this – institutions ought to meet principles, whatever they are, that would be chosen in the original position, with its sensitivity to the facts whatever they might be.

This principle is now independent of any of the facts that the original position brings to bear, just as the wrongness of hurting is independent of the fact that hitting hurts. It is the kind of grounding principle, possibly independent of any facts at all, that Cohen has urged us to seek.

Obviously, a key question is whether or not the unearthed Rawlsian principle would necessitate any revision of the content of Rawls's two principles of justice. On the face of it, it seems that their content would remain exactly the same. And indeed, Cohen acknowledges this.[10]

Moreover, the unearthed principle also grounds the content of justice by grounding the exact same moral relevance of the facts of our life that Rawls had

[9] *TJR*, p. 398.

[10] Pp. 262–3. My point here can allow that there would be even deeper principles required to "justify the use of the original position machine" underlying even the unearthed Rawlsian principle.

originally maintained. It grounds the whole original position methodology unchanged. It merely adds that in a certain sense, the famous two principles, which depend on facts, are not fundamental because they are explained by a deeper principle – the unearthed Rawlsian principle – which does not depend on the facts. But this is uninformative normatively, and it leaves in place the grounding relation between the facts and the principles Rawls had alleged.

Cohen still has a complaint here. Let's call it a *formal complaint,* because it is a complaint about how Rawls formulates the theory, not about its normative substance. (In that sense, we could also call it "metaethical.") Let's look more closely at the formal complaint before turning to a *substantive complaint* as well, but one quite independent of the unearthing strategy.

The unearthing move to the fact-independent principle is so simple that it does not appear to make any substantial difference in Rawls's theory at all.[11] But there is, first of all, an important metaethical lesson here, and Cohen is right to think it is philosophically significant. It is structurally similar to the point (as I see it) of the famous Euthyphro problem:[12] If "[i]t is wrong to murder" depends on the fact that God forbids murder, there is a deeper principle that does not depend on that fact about God, namely: "[i]t is wrong to disobey God's will, whatever it might require." On the divine command view this principle is more fundamental than "it is wrong to murder," because it morally explains the force of that prohibition. Similar points can be made for any view according to which moral principles stem from the outcome of a certain specified agency or procedure of any kind. Such views ascribe a certain moral authority to the agency or procedure. It looks to be a deeper (maybe fundamental, maybe not) normative truth that they have that authority to begin with. And that deeper normative force or authority does not stem from or depend on what those agencies or procedures do or say at all.[13] The structure of Cohen's point, then, has an ancient resonance in a broadly Platonic cast of thought.[14]

---

[11] Several authors have explored the simplicity or triviality of the ungrounding move, for example Pogge, "Cohen to the Rescue."

[12] Plato's *Euthyphro.*

[13] This is related to Valentini and Ronzoni's argument in "On the Meta-ethical Status," p. 403. They argue that the unearthed Rawlsian principle might be grounded in a fact, but a methodological one about how to construct justifications. Cohen would surely ask what it is that accounts for the particular moral significance of that method of construction, if not a deeper principle?

[14] Cohen aligns himself with Plato in certain respects at p. 291. For Cohen's views about Plato's views more generally, including his "reactionary" political position relative to the sophists, see his *Lectures*, Chapter 1.

Cohen believes that, in this way, he has identified a deep metaethical disagreement between himself and Rawls.[15] He believes that his own view, in which the unearthed principle is the fundamental one, is in conflict with Rawls's view in which the original position-generated principles are the fundamental principles of justice. I take Cohen to be arguing that Rawls is committed to denying that moral principles are ultimately grounded in fundamental fact-independent principles. This appears to be a metaethical disagreement in the sense that it is independent of disputes about what the content of moral requirements might be. So Cohen takes Rawls to be committed to a faulty (because fact-bound) metaethics.

There is a way of interpreting Rawls that would avoid any metaethical tussle with Cohen, one hinted at in the quotation just above, in which Rawls says, "There is no necessity to invoke theological or metaphysical doctrines to support [these] principles." This is importantly not the same as asserting the metaphysical view that *there is no deeper grounding principle* for the relevance ascribed to the facts in the original position method. Rawls says, instead, more modestly, that the metaphysics (and here, metaethics) is beside the point if we are interested in the content and justification of the principles of social justice. Whether because God says so, or because there is a quasi-Platonic fact-free principle to this effect, Rawls may still assert that the principles of justice are justified by their appeal to the parties in the original position in light of the facts of human life. Nothing *about what would be just* is added by pointing to the unearthed fact-independent principle (whether God-given, Platonic, or otherwise) that says, simply: "Those are the principles of justice, justified by the original position argument which appeals to those very facts." The quoted passage from Rawls, "Conceptions of justice must be justified by the conditions of our life as we know it or not at all," is no support for Cohen's evident suggestion that Rawls is metaethically committed against this kind of "rational intuitionism." Indeed, that very quotation could be read as an endorsement by Rawls of a fact-independent principle, one that can be unearthed, in Cohen's own fashion, in looking for further grounding for the method of the original position. That is, to say that principles of justice are to be justified by the facts of human life or not at all, is not to deny that there may be some deeper philosophical support for this very view.[16] Contrary to

---

[15] Chapter 6, especially section 18.

[16] As Cohen points out, Rawls "disparages" rational intuitionism (p. 258), but my suggestion is that his target is only rational intuitionism about the content of justice. "[O]nly the substantive principles specifying content of political right and justice are constructed. The procedure

what Cohen argues, the original position method, in which principles are justified by facts, is not committed to denying that there is some fact-free basis for any such moral relevance of the facts in a deeper normative principle.

7.4 A substantive objection: regulation and non-justice values

Cohen denies that the facts of human life rightfully play any role in determining the content of justice, and we will consider his arguments shortly, but this is neither implied by, nor does it imply, the unearthing point about fact-free fundamental principles. We should have names for two separate issues about the relation of facts to principles. Cohen's unearthing strategy uncovers principles that do not *rest on facts*. This leaves entirely open whether those principles *operate on facts*. To say that principles operate on facts is to say that their normative implications vary in accordance with relevant variations in the facts. Consider, again, the unearthed Rawlsian principle. It says that the content of justice is given by principles chosen in the original position in light of the non-moral facts of human life and nature, whatever they might be. As we have seen, this principle does not rest on any facts, such as those of human nature. Rather, the principle grounds the moral significance of those facts. But this shows that the principle operates on certain non-moral facts. It gives them a certain moral significance. The principle's normative implications vary depending on facts about "the conditions of our life."

Every normative principle operates on facts, by saying which facts have what kind of moral significance. If this is right, then the way to understand Cohen's substantive complaint about the original position method, as represented by the unearthed Rawlsian principle, must be that it operates on the wrong facts and/or that it operates on facts in the wrong way. Cohen's substantive objection is that the original position method can be shown to mix questions of justice with other considerations, as if one were choosing rules of social regulation rather than (the real project at hand) trying to ascertain the true or genuine principles of justice. We might keep the issue clearer if we distinguish the formal *objection from facts*, which we discussed in the previous section, from this substantive *objection from regulation*. In a way, it is a coincidence that this second issue also happens to be about facts

itself is simply laid out" (*PL*, p. 104). On the question of whether there is a deeper principle that explains how facts have the moral importance they are given in the original position method, I believe Rawls can and does stay neutral in affirming a "constructivist conception" that is "political and not metaphysical" (*PL*, p. 97).

allegedly playing too great a role. I believe we get a clearer view of Cohen's substantive worry if we refrain from continually casting it, as Cohen tends to do, as (to put it roughly) anti-fact. The crux of this point is that the original position method wrongly assimilates principles of justice to rules of social regulation.

The explicit distinction between rules of social regulation and principles of social justice is, as far as I know, original to Cohen and it is powerful. A precise account of rules of regulation is not needed in order to see the distinction Cohen is after.[17] It rests on the powerful observation that when we make choices, there are often reasons in place that count for or against certain alternatives. Rules of social regulation are things we choose or adopt, and we do so for certain reasons. Among the reasons to consider are reasons of justice. Once adopted, rules of regulation bear on how certain things are to be done, sometimes in the form of laws, sometimes in less formal norms. Being normative in that way, they are easily confused with principles of justice. But we do not choose principles of justice. Rather, they are among the considerations we consult in our choice of rules of regulation.

This important distinction allows that our convictions about social justice might include principles that we do not, on balance, have reason to adopt as rules of social regulation under the conditions we happen to face. Such regulatory reasoning might recommend adopting (in practice) rules with a different content from the principles of justice we have compelling reason to accept as a matter of conviction, and we will consider examples in the next section. Cohen argues that this dissonance can arise because among the great variety of considerations that will bear on the question of which rules to adopt, it will be relevant how one set of rules of regulation would work out in various respects – engaging values other than justice, such as efficiency or stability – as compared to an alternative set of rules.

Here is one interpretation of Cohen's line of thought:

1 The original position, with its regulatory reasoning, requires that the choice, by the parties, of principles be made in light of whatever might affect people's interests – effects stemming from the adoption of one or another set of rules.
2 Not just anything about how adopting certain rules affects individual interests is a consideration of justice.

---

[17] For more on the distinction in Cohen, see pp. 276–7.

3 Therefore, the original position's regulatory approach lets the choice of principles be determined by non-justice considerations, and so does not reliably identify justice.

(To be clear, (3) does not say that the original position approach *guarantees* that the choice of principles will actually turn on non-justice considerations; it says that such considerations are included among the ones that will, taken together, determine the choice.) On one meaning of "a consideration of justice" (in premise (2)) this would be a puzzling complaint. In the original position method it would be fatally circular to have the choosers bring ideas of justice to their deliberations. The aim of the original position method is to understand justice in terms of other ideas. A less puzzling interpretation of the complaint, and the one I believe Cohen intends, does not suggest that the parties should employ the idea of justice. Rather, the objection is that some of the considerations relevant to the parties' regulatory reasoning arise from values that are (so we philosophers determine) no part of justice.

Of course, the Rawlsian should flatly deny this. So we want to know what argument Cohen gives in support of this charge, and what can be said against it. We know that Cohen endorses an interpretation of distributive equality that differs from and conflicts with Rawls's with respect to a number of values and considerations that might move the parties, but that is beside the point Cohen is focusing on. He denies that the stylized regulatory reasoning is suited to track or constitute justice in any case, whether or not it happened to select principles he (Cohen) endorses.

The polemical situation is similar to the one raised by Nozick in his early charge that the original position method is designed from the beginning in a way that is blind to the possibility that justice is simply whatever would result from free market exchanges under protection of a minimal state. As Cohen writes, "the original position also excludes a concern for how much one person gets compared with somebody else: what I get by comparison with others finds no representation within that position, and believers in the claim to justice of relational equality should therefore be as wary of the original position, as a criterion of justice, as Nozick is."[18]

There are two subtly different lines of objection to consider here. One is that the original position argument is, roughly, question begging by, in effect, premising its argument, whose conclusion rules out Nozickean entitlement theory and Cohen-style egalitarianism, on the assumption that they are false.

---

[18] Pp. 159–60.

It is not clear, though, which side (putting Nozick and Cohen on one side, with Rawls on the other) is best seen as begging the question. All sides are supposing for the sake of the present argument that Rawlsian premises do indeed entail the Rawlsian conclusion, thus ruling out the others. And, as Nozick notices,[19] any good deductive argument will be logically valid, in which case no one who rejects the conclusion can consistently accept the premises. To show that the argument is question begging, then, must take more than showing that the premises logically entail the conclusions, but neither Nozick nor Cohen rises to this challenge. And, in fact, they both suggest that their doubt about the premises is based on and justified by their own theories of justice. It is patently question begging, as an argument against the Rawlsian original position premises, to object on the grounds that those premises do not entail Cohen's or Nozick's preferred principles of justice. What is needed by these critics is an argument against the original position which does not presume the truth of any particular account of justice.

A second line of objection by Cohen can be seen as taking this more promising form, arguing that the original position involves the parties in (hypothetically situated) regulatory reasoning, and that such reasoning is bound to introduce considerations that have nothing to do with justice as intuitively understood (and not assumed to be Cohen's egalitarianism or anything like it). So the question becomes this: which of the considerations that must influence the parties to an original position can be persuasively shown by Cohen to be considerations that do not, intuitively, bear on social justice?

After all, here is the Rawlsian position, put into Cohen's terms, which he must argue against: principles of justice are properly identified with possible rules of social regulation that parties to an original position would choose behind a veil of ignorance and under certain idealizing assumptions such as full compliance.

Notice that even what Cohen casts as regulatory reasoning is itself a morally defined enterprise. The question of what rules of regulation we should have in our society is, surely, a moral question. For example, in answering this regulatory question presumably no one's interests should count more heavily than anyone else's, and this is for moral reasons. And, arguably, the sum of interest-satisfaction is not a morally significant quantity, since it does not represent the good of any agent at all, again a moral point. So

---

[19] *ASU*, p. 203.

the original position might seem to emerge as a good method for answering this moral question: which rules of regulation should we have for our society? Indeed, Cohen writes,

> The present charge is not a criticism of the particular device, that is, the original position, that Rawls employs to *answer* the question, namely, what rules should we choose, that the denizens of the original position answer … Instead, I protest against the identification of the answer to *that* question with the answer to the question "What is justice?"[20]

But, importantly, Rawls is not proposing the original position or the two principles as answers to the latter question, for (at least) the reason that the parties are choosing under the false assumption of full compliance. Cohen tends to exaggerate the regulatory character of the original position method in this way, and it is a distraction from his main point. For example, he often writes of "identifying justice with optimal rules of regulation."[21] Rawls is certainly not asking what rules of regulation we should have in the real world. He is enquiring into what justice would be for this world. The parties, while they are sometimes said to know all "general" facts – those that would not allow any of them to know which individual they will be – are actually fed at least one important factual falsehood, namely that there will be full compliance with the chosen principles. For that reason, the resulting principles, if translated into social rules, would not be sure to serve their intended purpose in a world in which compliance was only partial. Thus the original position is neither intended nor suited to selecting good principles of regulation for any plausible society. It is not perspicuous to say, then, that the account identifies optimal rules of regulation for a society with the principles of justice for that society. The original position identifies justice with appropriate rules for a certain hypothetical scenario. Indeed, Rawls could perfectly well agree with Cohen that principles of justice are not the sort of things we get to choose.

Cohen's central point is not damaged by this clarification, however. Even with the idealization about full compliance, the parties are engaged in what we might call "regulatory reasoning," and this is where the issue lies. The hypothetical society they seek to regulate is an unrealistically compliant one, but nevertheless, by selecting principles for that society on the basis of what would best promote their interests the parties are (so Cohen argues) necessarily concerning themselves not only with considerations of justice, but

---

[20] Pp. 277–8.   [21] P. 277.

also with non-justice considerations such as efficiency and stability. That is the more important charge, rather than the charge that Rawls thinks that principles of justice are subject to real social choices, or that the choosers in the original position are selecting appropriate rules of regulation for real societies.

We should accept Cohen's argument here up to a point. It is hard to deny that such values as efficiency and stability will influence the parties' choices. What remains disputable, then, is whether Cohen has strong arguments showing that these values are not considerations that bear on justice. Cohen appears to believe that it is simply obvious. He writes, "I have... asked you to agree ... with the ... overwhelmingly intuitive claim, that the sorts of facts about practicality and feasibility that control the content of sound rules of regulation do not affect the content of justice itself."[22] He argues that, "Constructivism about justice lacks the conceptual resources to describe justifiable trade-offs between justice and other desiderata, because those desiderata (improperly) constrain what constructivism deems to be just,"[23] but what we are looking for is an argument that justice is the sort of thing that should be balanced against practicality and efficiency rather than *being the appropriate way of balancing them*, as constructivism, with its regulatory reasoning, would hold. Cohen's argument for this lies mainly in his discussion of a number of problems of social policy or regulation, including the structure of tax rate schedules, the problem of differential care (roughly, moral hazard), and issues around publicity and stability.[24] For reasons of space, I consider only the first two here, arguing that they do not succeed.

7.5 Tax brackets and exactness

Cohen argues that step-wise tax brackets are bound to be less than perfectly just, and yet they must be irresistible to a constructivist theory of justice for reasons of administrability. This puts daylight between the original position method and considerations of justice. How could the person whose property or income is greater than another person's by the single dollar that kicks him into the higher tax (or rate) owe, *as a matter of justice*, much more tax – not just a little more – than that other person, and yet owe exactly the same as

---

[22] Pp. 278–9.   [23] P. 312.

[24] Richard Arneson, by contrast to my reading, finds Cohen's "terminological" choice here to be undefended. See "Justice Is Not Equality."

significantly richer rate-mates? Of course, it might be impractical to spend vast sums of public money to implement a highly refined tax schedule, and in that case it ought not to be done. That does not, however, make the step-wise tax rates as just as the more refined ones would be.

Cohen argues that the parties to the original position would not insist on an extremely fine-grained tax schedule if it would be vastly more expensive than a moderately fine-grained schedule. This is because they will be sensitive to how those extra resources might be used to benefit them in other ways. He takes this to show that a constructivist method must be prepared to trade greater justice off against gains with respect to other values such as efficiency.

Does this objection really show that Rawls's original position method forces the parties to engage in regulatory reasoning? It is fair to ask to what extent the original position addresses such things as tax rates at all. The answer is that it mostly leaves tax rules aside as a subsidiary question about how the basic social structure could be brought to meet the difference principle (subject to the other Rawlsian principles). So Rawls's view seems to be that tax rates are not directly matters upon which justice takes a position. A given tax rate is just in the purely procedural sense if it is the product of a just basic structure where legislators duly aim to maintain the structure's justice by conforming it to the basic principles.

Cohen might reply that Rawls's original position argument forces him to deny that there is anything unjust about, say, taxing the poor at a higher rate than the rich, if that should turn out to be the most sensible policy all things considered. But, of course, it doesn't quite say that. It says that there would be nothing unjust about doing that *so long as* that scheme is part of a basic social structure that meets the difference principle and the other principles. Rawls could argue that no such tax system is remotely likely to meet that proviso, thus explaining the absurdity in the suggestion that it might be just. But some will agree with Cohen that this does not accommodate the deep intuition that some tax rates are unfair, even if there are other good reasons for adopting them, irrespective of their downstream effects on distribution.

7.6 Differential care

The case of what Cohen calls "differential care," similar to what is often called "moral hazard," is a second example he uses to support his view that Rawls's constructivist method in the original position incorporates values that have nothing to do with justice. He sketches an example, which I slightly simplify here. Suppose that there are two possible schemes S1 and S2 for publicly compensating homeowners should storms damage their property. Under S1 everyone gets fully compensated for any damage. However, some people might rely on this program and reduce the amount of care they take to prevent storm damage. When compensation is provided, this would seem to be unfair to homeowners who had, at their own expense, taken greater care and minimized their property damage. To reduce that kind of unfairness, we might prefer scheme S2, which requires anyone who claims benefits to bear the first $200 of repairs themselves. This provides people with an incentive not to skimp in their preparations in the hopes of being bailed out later, thus reducing the unfairness produced by compensation under S1. Of course, the "deductible" in S2 is crude in that it is not scaled to each homeowner's incentive. Therefore, there might remain homeowners who will still do little or nothing even though the first $200 will be their own responsibility, calculating that their preventive costs would be considerably more than their expected compensation (the amount in excess of $200 multiplied by the probability of its occurring, say). Finally, suppose that while we could, at great expense, determine just how conscientiously each homeowner prepared her house for storms, and thereby tailor compensation so as to avoid such free riding,[25] this scheme, S3, would be very expensive. To recap: S1 compensates for damages with no deductible, S2 compensates but with a $200 deductible to discourage skimping, and S3 expensively compensates each, partly according to how thoroughly she prepared. Cohen argues that, (a) if there are free riders, S3 would be the most just, but (b) the original position approach to justice, with its reliance on regulatory reasoning, would, if S3 is expensive enough, select S2. The Rawlsian method, then, trades off justice against non-justice values such as efficiency.

S3's allegedly greater justice seems to presuppose that unequal outcomes are only just if they reflect factors for which individuals are responsible.[26] It might look as though Cohen's argument here assumes that "luck egalitarian" standard of justice, indicting the original position method on the grounds that it doesn't select that principle. That would be question begging in a dispute about whether justice truly has that content. But there is another way of reading Cohen's complaint against constructivism, namely as asserting only that to count against a policy the fact that it would be very expensive is to give weight to a consideration – total expense – that is not an ingredient of justice at all, but a different value altogether. The original position method's reliance

---

[25] See Cohen's more elaborate example at pp. 308ff.   [26] P. 313.

on regulatory reasoning evidently selects for less expensive options other things equal, and it thereby disqualifies itself as a reliable method for determining the content of justice. To avoid the question-begging form of argument, we must be willing to grant – whether or not we accept luck egalitarianism – that the overall expense of an arrangement does not count against its justice.

It might be asked how we supposedly know that a scheme's overall expense is not any part of its justice? Grant that parties to the original position would, other things equal, disprefer an arrangement that is more expensive. Can we infer that the original position set-up forces Rawls to be indifferent to comparative benefits? Supposing that we were to grant to Cohen that social justice, whatever more precisely it is, cannot be completely indifferent to comparative benefits, that would be damning. Surely we cannot infer it, though, since the parties in the original position might give some weight to inequality and also some weight to aggregate benefit – overall cost. Cohen tells us that he rejects the view, "that distributive justice doesn't have a compara- tive aspect at all. And as long as it (at least also) does so, then [constructi- vism's sensitivity to the non-comparative issue of efficiency] will be (at least) in one way a deviation from justice."[27] That is a dubious argument, which resembles the following fallacious reasoning: a crust is an aspect of what it is to be a pie. So pumpkin pie, by including pumpkin, which contains no crust, deviates from pie-ness "(at least) in one way." The fact that a certain consider- ation (such as Pareto efficiency or overall cost) is not a comparative consider- ation does not establish that an account in which it is one consideration among others is not comparative.

It is worth noting that Cohen eschews, without explanation, the name "moral hazard," for the issue he calls "differential care," even though in earlier drafts of the book he did use the more familiar name.[28] One possible explan- ation leads us into an important issue. The term "moral hazard" suggests that when certain protective policies induce reduced care or increased risk-taking this operates by way of some moral deficiency on the part of those who reduce their care or take greater risks. Cohen points out, however, that while some reduced care might be intended to exploit the care of others, this needn't be the case. Some people might reduce their care in response to the protective policy without any intention of exploiting others, and so there needn't be any element of moral defect, but simply a an economic calculation. An alternative

---

[27] P. 323.   [28] See September 2003 and September 2006 drafts, on file with the author.

explanation is that strictly speaking, the familiar problem of moral hazard is not about "differential care" – some exercising less care than others – at all, but about some or all (maybe even equally) reducing their care in response to the policy, still with the clear implication that their doing so is a "moral" wrong. In any case, we can see that Cohen wishes to focus on the case of differentially reduced care, and without the assumption that it is morally wrong. His point, as we have seen, is that even if no one is morally misbehaving, a policy that leads to such differentially reduced care will be unfair to those who reduce their care less or not at all, even though it might be the appropriate policy in light of the costs of fairer policies.

Summarizing, the differential care example of Cohen's might show that Rawlsian constructivism will tend to trade off equality of a luck egalitarian kind for the sake of efficiency (less overall cost). But that doesn't show that this deviates from justice unless it is question-beggingly assumed that justice is luck egalitarian in content. The simpler point that the original position method will be sensitive to overall expense, or to Pareto efficiency (which is not a comparative consideration), shows neither that justice is essentially comparative in nature, nor that, even if it is, constructivism is indifferent to (other) comparative considerations.[29]

7.7 Bad facts

We have seen two ways in which Cohen criticizes the original position method for bowing to facts. The first was his formal objection that Rawls fails to recognize that facts are only morally relevant owing to principles that determine their relevance. Call this his objection to Rawls's reliance, in a certain way, on *facts as such*. The second and independent complaint was that the original position bends its results to facts that have nothing to do with social justice, facts concerning such things as efficiency or stability. Call this his complaint about constructivism's reliance on *facts irrelevant to justice*.

In his treatment of the case of differential care, we glimpse a third kind of complaint about reliance on facts, but one that Cohen does not clearly demarcate as different from the other two. Repeatedly, as I will illustrate, Cohen rhetorically leverages the moral deficiency represented by some of the

---

[29] Space prevents consideration of Cohen's treatment of stability and publicity. His argument that the original position method deviates from justice succeeds overall if it succeeds in any of these cases.

facts to which constructivism bends its results. Call this a complaint about constructivism's reliance on *bad facts.*[30]

In discussing the differential care case discussed above, he observes that

> The root cause. . . that induces a compromise with justice in the "exploiter" variant of the differential care phenomenon is a certain human moral infirmity: Constructivists are, therefore, in the questionable position that they must defer to facts of human moral infirmity in the determination of what fundamental (nonrectificatory) justice is.[31]

Cohen acknowledges that under full justice-compliance, which Rawls assumes to be in place, there might not be any exploitation, but only innocent differential care. Even if there is no exploitation, there might be reasonable fear of exploitation, which he says is enough for his purposes. And yet he continues to suppose that "moral infirmity" might well be part of the differential care profile: "It would be transparently wrong to say that the facts about moral weaknesses and so on make S2 just (without qualification), as opposed to more worthy of selection."[32]

It might have seemed from the very beginning that Cohen objected to the original position's sensitivity to, in particular, bad facts. He complained that if talented citizens decide to withhold socially productive labor unless they are paid more than others, the original position will lead to the conclusion that justice requires paying them more even though such a demand seems to put them outside the publicly shared sense of justice. To that extent, they look bad. But Cohen never quite embraced this route. Even in the earliest setting, he did not complain that justice is being bent to accommodate bad behavior, but complained, more obliquely, only that in that case the talented would not count as in "justificatory community" with the other citizens – quite a different point.[33] And true to form, in the much later treatment of differential care in *Rescuing*, he refers only glancingly to the inadequacy of "moral weaknesses *and so on*" (emphasis added) to qualify the original position's results as just. He does not make clear whether the original position is disqualified partly by the fact that its results are bent to make the best out

---

[30] I briefly discuss a part of this question in "Human Nature," pp. 225ff.   [31] P. 309.

[32] P. 311.

[33] "Incentives, Inequality, and Community," pp. 263–329. There, he says that the original position "generates an argument for inequality that requires a model of society in breach of an elementary condition of community" (p. 268).

of *morally* bad situations – adjusting not only to facts as such, or to justice-irrelevant facts, but to bad facts.[34]

Even if Cohen never offered that line of criticism in full voice, it poses an important challenge to the original position method. If a certain predictable moral deficiency in some or all people – maybe indefensible selfishness or partiality, or maybe a certain ineluctable level of bigotry – leads the original position to reject certain arrangements as infeasible or unreasonably expensive, it may strain credulity to accept that justice is being reliably tracked. That is, suppose one disagreed with Cohen's view that feasibility or expense are values foreign to justice, holding that they are among the values that ought properly to be balanced in the constitution of justice, as the original position method holds. Nevertheless, when an arrangement is rejected because it would be too expensive, but where the expense stems from moral deficiencies people would have under the hypothesized conditions, there is, arguably, an untoward capitulation to vice that seems foreign to the idea of full social justice. (Cohen seems to me unclearly to be running both objections at once in the passages I have quoted above concerning differential care.) That would be a third of three lines of objection to letting justice be sensitive to facts: to facts as such, to justice-irrelevant facts, and to morally bad facts.

One possible reply is to say that even if the original position procedure is, in principle, sensitive to such bad facts, as it happens, it turns out they make no difference to the choice of principles of social justice. It seems likely that Cohen would reject this as a defense, being essentially the kind of defense of utilitarianism that he explicitly rejects.[35] Whether a reply along those lines is successful is a further question. A second possible reply would be to say that an account of justice would not be tainted by its sensitivity to justice-*irrelevant* bad facts, and that justice-*relevant* bad facts are put aside by the Rawlsian assumption of full justice-compliance. Why think that moral defects that are not themselves any violation of the principles of justice are justice tainting in the way the bad facts objection alleges? There is more worth thinking about in this third, barely broached, line of objection to the original position method's sensitivity to facts, but I must leave the matter here.

---

[34] At pp. 178–80, Cohen trenchantly scrutinizes several short texts from across Rawls's career on this question, but still does not suggest that his (Cohen's) critique of Rawls's argument relies on the badness of the facts in question.

[35] Pp. 263–7.

8 Liberals, radicals, and the original position

8.1 The role of the original position in the dispute between liberals and radicals

Although political philosophy has been dominated by liberalism ever since the publication of *TJ*, this hegemony has not gone unchallenged by radicals. For the most part, the disputes between liberals and radicals have focused on matters of principle, including deep disagreements over how best to understand the central values of liberty and equality. As significant as these substantive disagreements are, there are equally important methodological differences between liberals and radicals that have not been the focus of as much philosophical attention.

In this chapter, I want to show how Rawls's political philosophy, in particular, is animated by certain key assumptions about history and social theory that radicals can and should contest. Because these deeper assumptions shape our understanding of questions of principle, I shall treat them in tandem with a substantive dispute between liberals and radicals over the content of constitutional liberties. My aim is to use the lens of the original position as a way to scrutinize these assumptions in order to bring out their connection with principles of justice. My thesis is that our commitments in social theory profoundly shape our principles.

I begin by examining Rawls's original position argument for a set of distinctively liberal freedoms. I will then interrogate some of the key background stipulations that work to support Rawls's case for those freedoms. I will then indicate how radicals can reasonably contest those stipulations, proceeding to show how that contestation would play out in an original position framework more congenial to radicals.[1]

For comments on an earlier version, I would like to thank David Brink, David Estlund, Michael Pendlebury, and Paul Weithman.

[1] I have learned a great deal from three early radical responses to Rawls's original position argument: Fisk, "History and Reason" and Miller "Rawls and Marxism," both in Daniels (ed.), *Reading Rawls* and Wolff, *Understanding Rawls*.

8.2 The primacy of the liberal freedoms

I begin with Rawls's defense of the primacy in justice of the liberal freedoms. We should bear in mind that Rawls never wavered in his belief that whether or not people can correctly be said to be free is "*determined by* the rights and duties established by the major institutions of [their] society" (*TJ*, p. 63, my emphasis). I take this to show that the dominant conception of liberty in Rawls's work is form of liberal legalism.[2] According to liberal legalism, taken here to be a distinctive view of liberty, there is no such thing as liberty *per se*, there are only basic *liberties*, understood as fundamental legal rights to be free from certain specified restrictions. So, in the course of emphasizing his rejection of liberty *per se*, in the Tanner Lectures, Rawls reformulated his first principle of justice to say: "Each person has an equal right to a fully adequate scheme of equal basic liberties which is compatible with a similar scheme of liberties for all" (*PL*, p. 291).

But, and this point is utterly crucial for what is to come, Rawls simply offers a stipulative definition of the content of this principle in terms of a distinctive array of constitutional liberties. The list making up the specified content is as follows:

> freedom of thought and liberty of conscience; the political liberties and freedom of association, as well as freedoms specified by the liberty and integrity of the person; and finally, the rights and liberties covered by the rule of law. (*PL*, p. 291)

We can take Rawls to be maintaining that, in a just society, all and only these freedoms have priority over all other potentially competing values.[3] In particular, as he puts it, they have "an absolute weight" in comparison with any reasons for restricting them that could be derived from considerations of mere utility or from perfectionist values.

In his writings, Rawls developed one central argument from the original position for the priority of the liberal freedoms. He presented it in two slightly different versions, first in *TJ*, and then in the Tanner Lecture subsequently included in *PL*.[4] Since the latter is the version favored by Rawls himself, it is, for the most part, the one on which I shall be focusing.

---

[2] I have discussed the connections between liberal legalism and the radical critique of liberalism in "Liberalism."

[3] In *TJ*, the priority of the basic liberties forms part of the priority rules comprising Rawls's special conception of justice. See *TJ*, p. 250.

[4] See *PL*, pp. 294–324 and *TJ*, §§ 32–9, and 82.

The basic idea is to characterize the original position in such a way that the parties in it, presented with a choice between Rawls's first principle, on the one hand, and either utilitarianism, or perfectionism, on the other, would have compelling reasons to favor the former. And Rawls's fundamental point here is surely very plausible. If utilitarian principles were to be given primacy in a society, that would make it permissible for the government to limit legal rights whenever doing so would make people, on the whole, better off. Likewise, if perfectionist principles were given first ranking, then legal rights could be restricted whenever doing so would give people a better chance of living in whatever exalted way was deemed by the government to be most worthwhile. Either way, the core liberal freedoms would be jeopardized.

Rawls grounds his argument on an appeal to the moral importance of two powers possessed by human beings. The first of these, the capacity for a sense of justice, involves being able to understand, apply, and to be motivated to act from the basic principles of justice. The other basic moral power is the capacity to form, revise, and rationally pursue a conception of the good, that is,

> a conception of what we regard for us as a worthwhile human life. A conception of the good normally consists of a determinate scheme of final ends and aims, and of desires that certain persons and associations, as objects of attachments and loyalties, should flourish. Also included in such a conception is a view of our relation to the world – religious, philosophical, or moral – by reference to which these ends and attachments are understood. (*PL*, p. 302)

The parties in the original position are conceived of as representatives charged with acting in the best interests of certain unspecified individuals on whose behalf they are selecting the basic principles of justice. In their deliberations, the parties are trying to choose those principles that will turn out to be maximally advantageous to the people they represent. But since they are choosing behind the veil of ignorance, their reasons for deciding on principles are restricted in various ways. Crucially, they do not know which particular conception of the good is actually affirmed by the person they represent. And, as a result, they must rely on considerations of a general kind to make their choice, that is, the considerations must apply to and be in the service of any number of such conceptions.

Rawls must now show why, in the light of a concern to promote the basic interests of the people they represent, the parties in the original position would have decisive reason to reject utilitarian and perfectionist principles in favor of his first principle of justice. In making his case, Rawls focuses on the example of liberty of conscience in particular. The argument has two main parts: the first speaks to the moral power connected with a conception of the good, and the second to the moral power connected with a sense of justice. Given my purposes, I shall present a stripped down version of Rawls's argument, beginning with the idea of a determinate conception of the good.

Thanks to the veil of ignorance, the parties are forced to acknowledge that those they represent may have deep commitments of a broadly ethical or spiritual kind, and that these commitments will turn out to be fundamental to their sense of what it would take for their lives to go well. In virtue of the significance of these values and convictions, anyone possessing them would have strong reason not to jeopardize them – indeed to protect and promote them – unless they had no other alternative.

Consequently, the only rationally defensible choice for the parties in the original position is to select a principle guaranteeing equal liberty of conscience for all. Choosing either the principle of utility or any version of perfectionism might make it permissible for proponents of a society's dominant religious or ethical view to suppress or persecute anyone who dissented from it. But since the parties do not know *which* particular religious or ethical doctrine is held by those they represent, they cannot rule out the possibility that those people will end up as dissenters. To choose any principle that might restrict the freedom of conscience of dissenters would be tantamount to gambling on the likelihood that those they represent belong to the majority religion. And taking such a risk involves a grievous misunderstanding of the role that such values and convictions play in human life. As Rawls expresses it, the parties are forced to think of people's conceptions of the good as "non-negotiable" (*PL*, p. 311).

Turning now to Rawls's reasoning based on the moral power of developing and acting from a sense of justice, for my purposes, only his argument from self-respect is significant. Rawls thinks of self-respect as having two elements. It involves, for one thing, being securely confident that our own conception of the good is worth carrying out and, in addition, it means having a strong sense of our own value, where this is taken to be rooted in our belief that we will be able to live our lives in accordance with our view of what ultimately matters. If the liberal freedoms are guaranteed, Rawls says, then people are much more likely to feel that their view of a worthwhile life is indeed worth carrying out. This is because such a guarantee makes it possible for both their capacity for a conception of the good and their sense of justice to be fully exercised. And because the guarantee of those freedoms would be part of the political culture in a liberal democracy, there is a public affirmation of worth of each citizen (*PL*, pp. 318–19).

8.3 The relevance of history and social theory

So much, then, for Rawls's central original position argument for the primacy in justice of the liberal freedoms. I want now to examine some of its deeper assumptions.

To demonstrate that the original position is an excellent way to shed light on the methodological differences between radicals and liberals, I want to focus on what Theodore Adorno called "socially produced evil," an expression I take to refer to all evils arising in the course of human history as a result of human attitudes, actions, and institutions.[5] Judging by the importance it has for Rawls's arguments for his first principle of justice, it seems that he took the most pressing of socially produced evils to be religious intolerance: the sectarian attempt by some to impose their religious views on others. And it is precisely this focus that sets Rawls apart from radicals, or at any rate from those radicals for whom the most urgent socially produced evils are economic exploitation, and social and political domination based on such features of human beings as their race and gender.

I believe that this difference reveals something of great importance, namely that Rawls's set-up of the original position is deeply shaped by a prior, and largely unargued for, conception of socially produced evil.

Let me press this point a little further by distinguishing between two sharply different ways of factoring history into one's thinking about justice. The first of these is what I'll call an ideal-historical approach because it employs a conception of close-to-perfect history, in which there are no major historical injustices, because there is, for the most part, strict compliance on the part of historical agents with the demands of justice. A good example would be the use Nozick makes of history in *ASU*. Although he proudly describes his own theory of justice as "historical," Nozick simply stipulates that in the social world he has in mind, "people generally satisfy moral constraints and generally act as they should." He means of course that people generally act in accordance with the requirements of Lockean justice as Nozick interprets them.[6]

The other way of figuring history into one's views about justice makes explicit use of real history. Here an attempt is made to offer an account of the

---

[5] Adorno uses this expression in *Metaphysics*, p. 105.

[6] *ASU*, p. 5. It is noteworthy that, elsewhere in the book, Nozick admits that, given the effects of profound historical injustices on actual societies, his arguments for libertarianism cannot be used without further careful historical analysis to condemn any particular system of taxation (p. 231).

actual course of historical development, focusing on the ways in which history has been marked by profound injustices between people.

It is perhaps worth pointing out that my distinction between ideal and real-historical approaches is not quite the same as Rawls's distinction between ideal and non-ideal theories of justice. This is because Rawls's distinction focuses on the kinds of societies to which the basic principles of justice ought, in the first instance, to apply. In employing an ideal theory of justice, we are supposed to apply its principles to societies in which we stipulate that there is strict compliance with those principles on the part of the citizenry. When we make use of a non-ideal theory of justice, we are concerned, instead, with principles of justice that apply in the absence of strict compliance. So Rawls's distinction is meant to serve a methodological insistence that we start from general compliance, and then, once we have in hand the principles we think would regulate people's interactions in that ideal case, we can work backwards to identify principles for dealing with historical injustice. My distinction, on the other hand, bears on the question of how, if at all, knowledge of the actual course of human history ought to enter into our deliberations about the demands of justice.

There is a further distinction I want to draw, which involves differentiating between thick and thin social theories. A thin social theory, I shall say, is one that can only be formulated by using thin or formal concepts like those of rational choice or utility. Good examples of such theories would include Arrow's impossibility theorem and the theoretical foundations of microeconomics. A thick social theory, by contrast, is one that makes free use of thick normative or evaluative language in its attempt to explain people's behavior. Examples might include Marx's account of capitalist exploitation in *Capital* I, and Weber's explanation of the origins of capitalism in *The Protestant Ethic and the Spirit of Capitalism*.

This pair of distinctions enables us to enquire with greater precision as to exactly where the parties in the Rawlsian original position stand when it comes to their knowledge of history and social theory. Since Rawls says nothing about this in the Tanner Lectures, I shall work with the account presented in *TJ*. In that text, Rawls stipulates that the parties know "the first principles of social theory," together with the consequences that follow from them (*TJ*, p. 200). Elsewhere in *TJ*, he says

> they know the general facts about human society. They understand political affairs and the principles of economic theory; they know the basis of social organization and the laws of human psychology. (*TJ*, p. 137)

The parties also make knowledgable inferences from the fact that their society is in the circumstances of justice. This means that they know that in their society, there are personal and material circumstances that make it both possible and necessary for human beings to cooperate with each other. But, because they are behind the veil of ignorance, Rawls insists that "the course of history is closed to them" (*TJ*, p. 200).

It is not unfair to conclude that the parties in Rawls's original position are, in an important sense, officially meant to be historically blind. Relatedly, Rawls clearly envisages them as adopting an ideal-historical approach to understanding human history, and as working with a thin social theory. It is precisely on these two points that Rawls's use of his theoretical construction is open to profound challenge by radicals.

But before I say any more about that challenge, I need to draw attention to what Rawls says about cases in which the original position generates principles which turn out to be discordant with the rest of our beliefs. In such circumstances, he says

> we have a choice. We can either modify the account of the initial situation or we can revise our existing judgments ... By going back and forth, sometimes altering the conditions of the contractual circumstances, at others withdrawing our judgments and conforming them to principle, I assume that eventually we shall find a description of the initial situation that both expresses reasonable conditions and yields principles which match our considered judgments duly pruned and adjusted. (*TJ*, p. 20)

An obvious question that arises here concerns the reference of the "we" in this passage. I'm going to assume that if Rawls means "we liberals," then his argument for the first principle succeeds: he has shown that a commitment to his list of basic liberties can be derived from the original position. But if Rawls means anything more catholic than that, then he is almost certainly wrong. For instance, radicals would insist against many liberals that restrictions on racist hate speech do not violate anyone's basic liberties. In that case, the Rawlsian set-up of the original position has produced a basic principle that radicals have reason to reject.[7] But as this passage shows, Rawls is open to the rational revisability of the original position itself: its stipulations can be

---

[7] I am assuming here that Rawlsian liberals take the view that racist hate speech counts as a permissible exercise of freedom of thought. To be sure, Rawls himself was silent about whether this was the case, and there is clearly room for a Rawlsian to agree with radicals that such speech may be subject to legal regulation.

changed when and because it fails to deliver principles that have the right kind of fit with our own beliefs about justice.

8.4 Racial capitalism and the historically sensitive original position

Accordingly, I shall treat Rawls's willingness to countenance rational revisions to the original position as an invitation to imagine a rather different set-up for it, one in which the parties hold a distinctive thick social theory, deeply informed by a real-historical narrative. I have in mind an abstract critical theory that I call the theory of racial capitalism.[8] For present purposes, the theory has two main components, one of which is factual, and the other explanatory.

The factual part is simply the claim that the development of capitalism in the modern world went hand in hand with the emergence of white domination and of various forms of resistance to that domination on the part of people of color. White domination is here to be understood as a complex ensemble of social relations that emerged during the early capitalist period and persisted for most of the twentieth century. The ensemble consisted of relations of domination and subordination, as well as of a series of closely linked socioeconomic inequalities. As a result of the workings of white domination, white people systematically exercised authority – both formal and informal – over black people, and white people systematically had access to more wealth and better opportunities than black people.

The explanatory part of the theory of racial capitalism can be encapsulated in the claim that the best way to account for the existence of white domination is that one group of human beings had the power and the resources to put in place a broad array of conventions – both formal and informal – whose basic terms involved a more or less explicit categorization of human beings into two basic groups: whites and blacks. Fundamental to this process was the fact that the members of these respective groups were deemed to have

---

[8] Two exiled South African scholars, Harold Wolpe and Martin Legassick, developed the theory of racial capitalism in the 1970s to explain the main features of South Africa's economy: that it was both capitalist and marked by systematic racial domination by whites. See for instance Wolpe's classic article "Capitalism and Cheap Labour-power," Wolpe's *Race, Class, and the Apartheid State*, and Lichtenstern, "An interview with Martin Legassick." I have obviously generalized their view and made it much more abstract than they might be willing to accept. In doing so, I have drawn heavily on Charles Mills's *The Racial Contract* (hereafter *RC*). For Mills's own attitude towards Rawls's treatment of race, see his "Rawls on Race."

radically unequal moral, social, and political status. Consequently, by virtue of these conventions, those human beings designated by various criteria to be *white* were, in effect, deemed to command the status of being fully human, while those designated by the same sorts of criteria to be *black* were, in effect, deemed to be morally and politically less than human, that is to say, beings possessing an inferior moral, social, and political status that legitimated all manner of their ill treatment by whites.[9]

Some striking evidence for this explanatory claim is adduced by Charles Mills, who documents the emergence of what he calls a racial polity, which typically took one of two main historical forms. One of these was the *white settler states* in which pre-existing non-white populations were deliberately killed off in order to make room for the whites who came to exercise political sovereignty there. The other Mills calls *white sojourner colonies.* These involved a substantial white presence whose main function was to exercise colonial domination over existing non-white societies. In white settler states, non-whites were typically held to be (or were treated as being) in a permanently pre-political or non-political state, and hence seen as "savages" belonging in a permanent state of nature marked by wildness and lawlessness (*RC*, p. 13). In sojourner colonies, by contrast, the existence of non-white societies alongside the society of "civilized" whites was acknowledged, but these societies were held to be fundamentally deficient, marked by social decadence or stagnation. In these cases, non-white natives were considered to be more like barbaric children incapable of self-rule, so that whites could and would rule for them.

Either way, non-white people were deemed to be by nature both "*unfree* and *un*equal" (*RC*, p. 16). At the core of these racial polities was a profoundly hierarchical social ontology that is, a social world containing what were called "subject races" who were dominated politically, economically, culturally, and psychologically by white people (see *RC*, pp.16–17). I take it to be a crucial part of this theory that the hierarchical social ontology in question is primarily a lived or practical ontology. We are not talking here about an idle theoretical picture of the universe, but a vast and ramified pattern of ways of treating people. For instance in a racial polity, the state would assign people to particular races, by virtue of whichever criteria were taken to be operative

---

[9] The theory advances a second key explanatory claim, which I mention only to set aside as irrelevant to my concerns in this chapter. This is that white domination came into existence because it best served the interests of capitalist expansion in early modernity and it remained in existence because of that effect.

at the time. This official racial identity would then have profound consequences for the life of the individuals in question. Political and legal rights were often unequally distributed, with black people typically being excluded from the full exercise of political power and from full rights of due process. A person's official racial identity would also be of fundamental economic significance, determining such things as the kinds of occupations she could take up or her right to take part in collective bargaining. No less importantly, the practical ontology of racial categorization was deeply woven into the fabric of ordinary face-to-face encounters. Hierarchical social expectations differentially shaped how people of different races were expected to behave in each other's presence, what kinds of gaze, or bodily posture, or form of words could be used by whom and when. And this practical ontology of race was always firmly undergirded by mechanisms of extreme violence deployed both by representatives of the state and by ordinary whites aiming to keep black people in their socially assigned place.

This explains why one of the central concepts in the theory of racial capitalism is that of racial oppression, which picks out social relations between people in which, as it were, at least some of the more important prison bars are internal to the human subject. Instead of unfreedom being merely a matter of external restrictions on what people may do, unfreedom is conceptualized to consist in part, in the internalization of a deeply distorted conception of one's own humanity. Inhabiting such a distorted self-understanding makes it immeasurably harder for anyone to be free to be themselves. So it is not just that oppressed human beings face a restricted array of options (which, of course, they do), but that their very subjectivity is lacking in freedom. But, importantly for theorists of racial capitalism, the oppression must be seen as taking a specifically racialized form. Some human beings are oppressed just by virtue of their membership in a wider group of people whose race they are taken to share. Racial oppression, then, is more than skin deep: it deeply affects how people see themselves and their place in the social world which they inhabit.

The searing after-effects of this practical ontology remain with us today. This is because people's lives have been so deeply shaped by it that it forms part of the background understanding of modern societies. But, more importantly, aspects of it still form part of the self-understanding of most people in these societies. As we noted, in consequence of the system of racial conventions, human beings became racialized subjects, with white people seeing themselves as essentially white, and as possessing a status that is morally and political superior to that of black people. Black people, similarly, came to see themselves as essentially black, permanently occupying the status of inferiors.

I want now to place these historical and theoretical considerations in a broader original position framework. I shall say that contracting parties are in a historically sensitive original position when all of the following conditions are satisfied. First, they accept the theory of racial capitalism I have just rehearsed. Second, they know that the society for which they are choosing principles of justice could have been profoundly shaped by white domination. And third, they are ignorant about the race of the people they represent.[10]

In keeping with the general structure of original position arguments, what is needed is a pairwise comparison in which the parties are called upon to make a choice. I propose we imagine the parties as having to choose between two quite different versions of the abstract principle to which Rawls assigns primacy in justice, the one that said "Each person has an equal right to a fully adequate scheme of equal basic liberties which is compatible with a similar scheme of liberties for all" (*PL*, p. 291).

In order to explain the difference between the two versions of this principle that I have in mind, I need to dig a little deeper into the place of considerations of liberty in the original position. At one point in *TJ*, Rawls remarks:

> under favorable circumstances, the fundamental interest in determining our plan of life eventually assumes a prior place... Thus the desire for liberty is the chief regulative interest that the parties must suppose they all will have in common. (*TJ*, p. 543)

In speaking here of the parties' "desire for liberty," I take Rawls to be arguing as follows: provided that you took your society to be in reasonably favorable material conditions, behind the veil of ignorance you would place a premium on the protection of what I'll call *telic autonomy*. Taking the *telos* in question here to refer to what Rawls describes as one's system of final ends, telic autonomy refers to the freedom to form, revise, and live out one's conception of the good based on that system of ends. Now, there can be no doubt of the importance of telic autonomy both from the perspective of the parties in the original position and, more importantly, for modern human beings. It is a form of freedom that we rightly cherish, and indeed, I would think, cherish for many of the reasons Rawls supplies in his argument for the priority the liberal freedoms.

---

[10] Compare with Rawls's stipulation in *JFR*, that "a person's race and ethnic group" are hidden behind the veil of ignorance (p. 15).

But I want to picture a version of the original position in which the parties are obliged to weigh up telic autonomy against the importance of a different kind of freedom, which I call individual sovereignty. Fundamentally, individual sovereignty is a matter of enjoying rightful authority over yourself in society, something that can only be done when other people recognize and fully affirm your status as a self-determining individual. Understood in this way, the sovereignty of human beings is relevantly diminished or undermined whenever they stand in relations of deference or domination. To dominate another is to treat her as your inferior, not merely as a means to your ends, but as someone who owes you homage and deferential service. In other words, sovereignty is a relation of normative authority: to enjoy it is to be authorized to make decisions about what becomes of you without having to consult anyone else or to defer to their wishes. What is required for universal telic autonomy is that everyone be free to choose their final ends; what is necessary for universal sovereignty, on the other hand, is living in a society utterly without social hierarchies in which some dominate others.

To bring out the contrast more clearly, we might picture someone held in slavery in the ancient world. Imagine his master to be kind and benevolent, someone who decides to provide his slave with the best education possible. After a thoroughgoing philosophical formation that enables him to reflect carefully on various conceptions of the good, the slave determines that he will henceforth live his life as a Stoic. His master is happy to allow him to do so. Furthermore, being a man of good will, he always consults the slave before making any decisions that will affect the latter's happiness. The slave dies having lived a life shaped by his chosen conception of the good. It seems perfectly clear that this man, while he has obviously enjoyed telic autonomy, has been deprived of sovereignty over himself.[11]

I return now to my argument. In order to give it a properly Rawlsian form, I propose that we imagine that the parties placed in my historically sensitive original position have a choice between two different specifications of Rawls's equal basic liberties principle. The first is Rawls's preferred interpretation (whose wording I have drawn from *JFR*), and which I'll call

> *The liberal-democratic specification*: the basic liberties are: "freedom of thought and liberty of conscience; political liberties (for example, the

---

[11] My account of individual sovereignty shares much with Philip Pettit's conception of liberty as non-domination. For a brief discussion of some of the differences see my "Equality."

right to vote and to participate in politics) and freedom of association, as well as the rights and liberties specified by the liberty and integrity (physical and psychological) of the person; and finally, the rights and liberties covered by the rule of law."[12]

The second interpretation is

The radical-democratic specification: the basic liberties are: a right to equality that forbids both the state and private citizens from discriminating against anyone on grounds of race, ethnicity, gender, sexual orientation, disability, religion, or marital status; a right to have one's dignity respected and protected; a right to freedom and security of the person; a right not to be subjected to slavery, servitude, or forced labor; a right to freedom of conscience, religion, thought, belief and opinion; a right to freedom of expression that does not extend to advocacy of hatred based on race, ethnicity, gender, sexual orientation, disability, religion, or marital status; a right to peaceful unarmed assembly and demonstration; a right to freedom of association; rights of political participation; rights of due process under law.[13]

The core of my argument is that, confronted with this pair of options, the parties in a historically sensitive original position would have overwhelming reasons to favor the radical-democratic specification over its liberal-democratic rival. This is because, in the light of their acceptance of the theory of racial capitalism, they will consider freedom from racial domination to be more important than the freedom to choose one's system of final ends, and they will reason that the radical-democratic specification provides much more robust protection for the former than its liberal-democratic competitor. In the light of their social theoretical commitments, they will strongly prefer a

---

[12] *JFR*, p. 44.

[13] I have taken the wording of this specification directly from the South African Constitution of 1996. Of course, one could read the liberal-democratic specification as being co-extensive with the radical-democratic one, and it is certainly possible that that is the reading Rawls himself would have embraced. But, one could equally well read the former in a much less radical way, as, for instance, simply committing one to a kind of color-blind liberalism, according to which any mention of race in a statute or court ruling is subject to special scrutiny. This could then be used to justify eradicating programs of affirmative action, say, on grounds of their use of the concept of race. Such a position, I take it, depends on the claim that equality between black people and white people has already been achieved. The radical-democratic specification implicitly denies that claim, and is intended to eliminate all vestiges of white domination from society.

specification of the basic liberties that explicitly rules out systematic racial oppression, not one that could (in principle and charitably) be read as doing so.

My first argument for this claim appeals to Rawls's remark that "the parties in the original position would wish to avoid *at almost any cost* conditions that undermine self-respect" (*TJ*, p. 440, my emphasis). There can be little doubt that a system of racial domination profoundly undermines the self-respect of the people who are dominated by it. To live under such domination is to be treated as someone who is morally and socially inferior: it is to live with an ongoing sense of being the bearer of a defective humanity. As we have seen, in a society characterized by white domination, the color of one's skin becomes the main social marker of that inferiority. This affects the self-respect of black people in two relevant ways. The first is that members of the dominant race – whites – treat members of the subordinate race – blacks – as their inferiors, that is to say, as people who lack full standing. Black people are expected to show public deference to whites, their opinions are not taken seriously and, in the worst cases, those who display any behavior regarded by whites as improper are liable to heavy penalties. This means that the public standing of black people is radically different from that of whites. But in addition, this sense of inferiority is either internalized or else has to be constantly fought against by its victims. This imposes an immense psychological burden on people of color. The provisions of the radical-democratic specification – especially the prohibitions against racial discrimination and advocacy of race hatred – constitute a much more effective way of guaranteeing what Rawls calls "the social bases of self-respect" than those embodied in the liberal-democratic specification.

My second argument is that without freedom from racial domination, it becomes exceedingly difficult, if not impossible, for everyone in a society to develop telic autonomy. I suggested earlier that racial oppression is more than skin deep because it prevents black people from exercising sovereign agency: they must always take into account what whites will be able to do to them as a result of what they do and say. But this clearly makes it much harder for its victims to set about forming their own systems of ends. Indeed, as the testimony of countless black writers who have struggled with being victims of racism shows, before you can think yourself into your own final ends, you have to think yourself out of the shackles of oppression. Rawls's original position argument elegantly shows that everyone's telic autonomy matters. But in order for everyone's telic autonomy to matter it must be impossible for some to use their freedom in the service of promoting or maintaining a hierarchical social order in which black people are regarded as inferior. While both specifications of Rawls's first principle honor people's freedom of conscience, only the radical-democratic one does so in a manner that properly befits the equal dignity of black people. Knowing this, the parties would have compelling reason to favor it.[14]

Let me briefly retrace my steps. I began by announcing my intention to employ the original position in clarifying the deeper disagreements between radicals and liberals. I have maintained that Rawls's argument for the primacy of the liberal freedoms rests on an eminently contestable view of the place of history and social theory in our thinking about justice. I then showed that, if the veil of ignorance is lifted slightly to allow the parties knowledge of precisely those matters, they would choose a conception of the basic liberties that is much more congenial to radicals than Rawls's. In this way, I have shown that one's social theoretical commitments profoundly shape the principles of justice to which one is committed.

8.5 The second principle

Before considering some objections that might be entered against my argument, I feel I should say something about its bearing on Rawls's conception of distributive justice.

In the course of deriving his second principle of justice in the original position, the first pairwise comparison that Rawls sets before the parties involves a choice between his own two principles and that of average utility. Since controversial claims about history and social theory are not at issue in the dispute between Rawls and the utilitarians, questions of history and social theory appear to play no role at all in this part of the argument.

But this appearance is misleading. For a central plank of the original position argument is the parties' reliance on the primary goods as the appropriate metric of advantage by reference to which they are to assess their options.[15] Rawls's official justification for the use of the primary goods in the

---

[14] To be sure, Rawls could insist that his commitment to the fair value of citizens' political liberties and to fair equality of opportunity sets limits on permissible social inequalities. But his commitment to measuring inequalities in terms of rights, opportunities, and income and wealth makes it harder for his theory to track (and correct for) unjust social hierarchies.

[15] By "the primary goods" Rawls means the resources needed by people in order to realize their two moral powers (their capacity for a conception of the good and their capacity to act on the principles of justice). But those goods also function as "all-purpose means" that enable people to live well, whatever their conception of living well turns out to be. The list of primary goods

original position appeals to his conception of the person, with its two attendant moral powers. But a careful reading of *TJ* reveals that his reliance on the
primary goods is derived, in equal measure, from the thin ideal-historical
social theory that underpins his account of democratic equality in §§12–13 of
that text. There, Rawls pictures the economic part of the basic structure as
issuing in a series of self-replicating economic cycles, at the beginning of each
of which there is a particular allocation of goods, while at the end of which
there is a determinate economic outcome. The latter, in turn, becomes the
initial allocation of goods at the outset of a subsequent cycle, and so on. Rawls
suggests that two main features explain the overall distributive effects of the
economy theorized in this way. The first is "the initial distribution of income
and wealth" (that is to say: who owns what to begin with), while the second is
"the cumulative effect of prior distributions of natural assets" (that is to say:
the overall array of talents that people are born with) insofar as these are
shaped by social relations and historical accidents (*TJ*, p. 72).

In the course of diagnosing the ills of the systems of natural liberty –
unfettered capitalism – and liberal equality – capitalism constrained by measures intended to guarantee everyone a fair chance of success – the only socially
produced economic evils that Rawls recognizes are inequalities in people's
shares of opportunities, income, and wealth. And it is these that Rawls's second
principle is meant to regulate directly. The problem that taxes him is an
arbitrarily unequal division of goods, and his solution is to maximize the shares
enjoyed by the least advantaged. When refracted through the lens of the
original position, the claim becomes: the major social ills which the parties
have reason to avoid are inequalities in opportunities, income, and wealth.

Here again radicals might well object that Rawls's reliance on such a thin
ideal-historical social theory has led him astray. This time, it results in a
fundamental misdiagnosis of the problems of capitalism. For radicals, the
most significant evils of capitalism are not primarily the inequalities it
generates in people's shares of income and wealth, vile and vast though they
have turned out to be. These are merely symptoms of the real problem,
namely that capitalists are in a position to take systematic advantage of the
fundamental vulnerability of working people. This vulnerability was made
possible by the forcible expropriation of the agricultural populace from the
land in Europe, and by the brutal varieties of colonial depredation that

---

includes: the basic liberties, freedom of movement and of occupation, the powers attending
occupancy of offices and positions of responsibility, income and wealth, and the social bases
of self-respect.

decisively shaped the history of the rest of the world. The structure of actually existing capitalist societies is such that workers can only survive by laboring on means of production that are owned by capitalists. Within the capitalist labor process itself, these workers produce valuable products, and capitalists – thanks to their structural position – appropriate a large proportion of the value of these products. As a result, workers receive less value than the value of the products they create, and in this way, they are exploited by capitalists.[16]

It seems plausible that parties in a historically sensitive original position who accepted this account of the evils of capitalism – rather than Rawls's – would be unlikely to embrace the second principle if there was some alternative principle on hand which offered a better prospect of more directly addressing those evils. This because the kind of social hierarchy that marks the capitalist labor process is inconsistent with the individual sovereignty of working people. Whether there is any such alternative principle is not a question I shall take up here.[17] What is clear is that Rawls's own conception of the original position seems artificially to foreclose discussion on this crucially important topic.[18]

I turn now to some objections to my argument.

8.6 Three objections

The first essentially works by invoking Ockham's razor, on the basis of which someone might say: "Rawls quite rightly wants to set up the original position using the weakest premises possible. Your historically sensitive version of his argument is too prolix to pass muster, since it turns on the acceptance of something highly contentious, namely the theory of racial capitalism."

---

[16] I am drawing here on Allen Wood's account of exploitation as laid out in his *Karl Marx*, second edition, and G. A. Cohen's work on the kind of unfreedom characteristic of working people in capitalist societies, especially "The Structure of Proletarian."

[17] One candidate would be what I have elsewhere called the *common ownership formula*: each citizen of a democratic society, as a co-owner of its resources, may use those resources provided that the terms of their use are in conformity with principles that no democratic co-owner could reasonably reject as the basis of an informed, unforced general agreement between all democratic co-owners who sought to find equitable principles for dividing the resources of their society (see my "Equality").

[18] It is clearly possible that Rawls could address some, perhaps most, of these concerns by insisting – as he does in *JFR* – that justice as fairness would best be realized in a property-owning democracy. For recent work on this topic, see O'Neill and Williamson, *Property-Owning Democracy*.

My initial move would be to question what sometimes amounts to an excessively uncritical use of the ideal of theoretical simplicity in analytical philosophy. In the present context, Ockham's razor should be understood to say not "use the simplest and least controversial premises you can" but "use the simplest and least controversial premises you need to get things right." And so, I say: you need the theory of racial capitalism to get the right principles of justice. I simply find it incredible that anyone could figure out what justice requires without knowing about the actual deep direction of human history and without some kind of explanation of its overall dynamics.

My other reply is to acknowledge that my set-up for the original position is undeniably more controversial than Rawls's. But then I would point out that Rawls himself cannot so easily dismiss all of the claims of the theory of racial capitalism. Recall that one of the fixed points from which Rawls himself begins is the belief that racial discrimination is unjust (see *TJ*, p. 19). There seem to be two ways of accounting for what that belief comes to.

The first we might call racism as unfair discrimination. Discrimination, in this context, would be counted as unfair just in case it was a matter of explicitly drawing invidious distinctions between people on the basis of the color of their skin – say, by screening out all applicants for a job because they were black. The second account sees racism as unfair discrimination in that way, but adds that the invidious distinctions are being made against a background of structural inequalities between people of different races. That Rawls himself quite clearly subscribes to this second view, is shown by his statement that "racial ... discrimination presupposes that some hold a favorable place in the social system which they are willing to exploit to their advantage" (*TJ*, p. 149). So I take his position to entail that overtly racist actions are mere symptoms of a deeper and much more systematic array of social, legal, and economic practices which work to the ongoing disadvantage of black people because they are black.

But if you accept this second account of racism, then you can't so readily ignore the theory of racial capitalism in thinking about historical injustice precisely because it purports to offer a deeper explanation both of what racist structures are and of how they came into being.

Next, I take up an objection that appeals to the fact that Rawls envisaged a four-stage sequence for connecting principles of justice with determinate laws.[19] The original position marks the first stage because, in it, the most

---

[19] See *TJ*, pp. 195–201.

fundamental principles of justice are chosen. Then comes the constitutional stage in which a group of delegates, employing the two principles of justice, fashion a constitution to shape their society. This is followed by a legislative stage in which laws are enacted in accordance with the constitution and a judicial stage in which the laws are subject to legal interpretation and review.

It might be said that my argument is vitiated because I am applying reasoning which is only appropriate to the constitutional stage in the original position. In doing so, I am conflating stages. For this reason, someone might reject my comparison between the liberal-democratic specification and the radical-democratic specification of Rawls's first principle as simply irrelevant from the standpoint of the original position.

My response to this worry is that Rawls's own approach invites the employment of constitutional language in the original position. Recall his stipulation that "the equal basic liberties in the first principle of justice are specified by a list," which list includes such items as freedom of thought and liberty of conscience; the political liberties and so on (*PL*, p. 291). One might have thought (and the early Rawls clearly did think) that when it comes to matters of first principle, one needs to stick with a general or abstract formula, such as one that said "each person ... has an equal right to the most extensive liberty compatible with a like liberty for all" (*CP*, p. 48). For good reason, Rawls felt compelled to abandon this conception of a first principle, opting instead for one that manifestly employs constitutional language. If Rawls himself saw fit to do so in the original position, I see nothing objectionable in my own practice.

Finally, I consider an objection that will no doubt have already occurred to you. I call it *the ideal theory objection*. According to this, Rawls's entire project involves a search for principles meant to govern the ideal case, a society in which most citizens comply with the principles of justice and whose most important institutions conform and are publicly acknowledged to conform to those very principles. In arguing for the radical-democratic specification of the first principle, I have focused on the non-ideal, and indeed that focus has proved central to making my case. But in doing so, someone might say, I am simply talking past Rawls.

My first reply to this objection is that Rawls himself prioritizes ideal theory only in order to get guidance for real-world non-ideal cases, since those are, morally speaking, by his own admission, where the real action lies.[20] In other

---

[20] As Rawls says in *TJ*, "The reason for beginning with ideal theory is that it provides, I believe, the only basis for the systematic grasp of these more pressing problems [such as civil disobedience and questions of compensatory justice]" (*TJ*, p. 9).

words, as we might put it, even on Rawls's own view, the non-ideal has moral – although manifestly not methodological – priority over the ideal. But the problem with embracing Rawls's commitment to the liberal freedoms is that they offer very little illumination when it comes to combating the injustices left in the wake of the system of racial domination that marked the emergence of capitalist modernity.

My second response probes the role that history actually plays in Rawls's argument for the liberal freedoms. I have so far simply granted for the sake of argument that the parties in Rawls's original position are entirely lacking in historical knowledge and that they know only the thinnest of social theories. But it's well worth asking whether anyone could knowledgably infer from those exiguous premises alone that religious persecution is such a clear and terrifying historical danger. What I mean is that surely only someone familiar with the actual historical record of an expansionist religion like Christianity would know that adherents of such religions cannot be trusted to respect people's rights to freedom of conscience in the absence of robust constitutional protections. I suspect that, like most of us, the parties in the original position believe in freedom of conscience because they know how likely religious persecution would be without it. But that is a piece of knowledge that cannot be inferred by someone who is historically blind.

But having said that much, let me end by simply conceding the point: let's make the disagreement straightforwardly about non-ideal theory. In that case we would be using the original position to shed light on actual historical injustices. But then the result, I suggest, would be to make it even more obvious that the radical-democratic specification of the first principle illuminates social reality much better than Rawls's own specification.

9 The original position and Scanlon's contractualism

Joshua Cohen

In "Contractualism and Utilitarianism," Scanlon first presents his contractualist theory of moral rightness.[1] According to that theory, elaborated in his subsequent work, conduct is morally wrong just in case it conflicts with "any set of principles for the general regulation of behavior that no one could reasonably reject as a basis for informed, unforced general agreement."[2] Lying and stealing, for example, are wrong because principles that permit lying or stealing can reasonably be rejected as a basis for such agreement. Intuitively, when you lie or steal, you act in ways that you cannot justify to others.

Scanlon's contractualism shares with other contract theories the concern about justifiability to others. A distinctive feature of Scanlon's view is that, in conducting such mutual justification, the contracting parties themselves use a normative notion of reasonableness. When we reason about right and wrong, we ask ourselves whether a proposed principle is reasonable for others to accept or reject. The notion of reasonableness is distinct from and irreducible to rationality. When I assess a proposed principle for the general regulation of behavior, I do not ask whether compliance with the principle is rationally advantageous – an effective means for achieving my aims. Instead, I ask whether the principle is reasonable to accept or reject.

As Scanlon emphasizes in "Contractualism," moral contractualism contrasts on this point with Rawls's social-contract theory of justice. In *TJ*, Rawls observes that different contract theories – those developed by Hobbes, Locke, Rousseau, and Kant, for example – all employ an idea of justification via

I wrote the first draft of this paper for an October 2008 workshop at Princeton University on T. M. Scanlon's moral and political philosophy. I am grateful to the participants, and especially to Samuel Freeman and Seana Shiffrin, for comments. I presented the ideas in political philosophy seminars at Stanford University in spring 2008 and spring 2014 and received many helpful suggestions. I wish to thank Tim Hinton for his excellent editorial advice on the final drafts.
[1] In Sen and Williams (eds.), *Utilitarianism and Beyond*.
[2] Scanlon, *What We Owe*, p. 153 (references will appear parenthetically in the text as *WWO*).

universal agreement in an "initial situation."[3] They differ in how they interpret that initial situation. In Rawls's preferred interpretation of the initial situation – the original position – the parties, reasoning under informational constraints, make a rational choice of principles. Each person asks what the most effective way is of advancing his or her good. Parties in the Rawlsian initial choice situation thus make no use of the notion of reasonableness. The original position relies instead on what I will be calling the *Rational Advantage Model*.

To be clear, Rawls does not suppose that people in a just society (or any society) act solely on the basis of judgments of rational advantage. In a just society, people act in part on the basis of their sense of justice, as specified by a set of principles of justice. The original position, with its Rational Advantage Model, is not a description of motivation; it is a "device of representation."[4] It is developed for the purpose of explaining and justifying principles of justice. The device is designed to model fair conditions of agreement and acceptable restrictions on reasons for defending principles of justice.

In this chapter I will explore the idea that the original position is a device of representation. I have two main aims. After explaining how the original position is meant to serve as a device of representation (sections 9.1–9.2), I will raise some doubts (section 9.3) about the Rational Advantage Model as a device of representation. Focusing on the issue of self-respect, I will show how the form of representation – modeling arguments about justice as arguments about our rational advantage – forces on us substantive claims that arguably weaken the normative arguments it aims to model. My concern is that the form of representation distorts what it is meant to represent.

Second, I will distinguish two kinds of individualism that we find in contractualist views: *judgmental* and *substantive* individualism. Rawls's Rational Advantage Model embraces judgmental individualism as well as a particular form of substantive individualism. In *TJR*, Rawls *also* suggests a form of ethical contractualism that is judgmentally individualistic, but not committed to substantive individualism (*TJR*, p. 512). This ethical contractualism, mentioned only briefly, is continuous with the notion of public reason in Rawls's political liberalism (*PL*, Lecture VI). In section 9.4, I discuss Scanlon's moral contractualism in light of the judgmental/substantive distinction. While Scanlon rejects the Rational Advantage Model, his notion of reasonable rejection preserves a form of substantive individualism.

---

[3] *TJR*, pp. 10–15, 102–5, 511–12.   [4] *PL*, p. 24.

I conclude with some reflections on why this endorsement of substantive individualism may not be an advantage of Scanlon's contractualism.

9.1 Basic question

Rawls's theory of justice is organized around the idea of a fair system of social cooperation. The cooperators in such a system are understood as free and equal persons. Their cooperation proceeds by reference to a public conception of justice, as public as it would be if it were the object of an agreement.[5] Rawls asks: what principles of justice are best suited to providing public standards of fair cooperation among persons thus understood (*JFR*, pp. 14–15)? He answers by asking what principles would be agreed to by people who will use the principles to regulate their own cooperation. In choosing principles, the parties reason as if they did not know their social class position, natural talents, sex, race, or ethnicity, conception of the good, religious convictions, or anything else that distinguishes among them, understood as free and equal moral persons. Reasoning under this *veil of ignorance*, they refrain from offering any arguments they are drawn to only in virtue of their knowledge of these "contingencies."

Some considerations fall behind a *thinner* veil, some behind a *thicker* one (*PL*, pp. 24, 273). The thinner veil keeps us from knowing our social position or natural talents; the thicker veil keeps us from knowing our conception of the good, or the religious and philosophical doctrines that support our conception. I will return later to the rationale for the veil(s) of ignorance. Generally speaking, the animating idea is that certain considerations are irrelevant to the problem of working out principles of fair cooperation among free and equal moral persons. The veil of ignorance is used to model our convictions about the (ir)relevance of certain considerations in deciding what justice requires in the relations among free and equal persons (*PL*, p. 24).

For example, if social class is judged irrelevant, then assume we do not know it; if our final ends are judged irrelevant, then assume we do not know them. The veil prevents us from arguing for principles of justice by reference to the considerations antecedently judged irrelevant in specifying fair terms of cooperation among free and equal persons. The veil of ignorance, in short, models irrelevance through ignorance.

Under ignorance, then, we make a *rational* choice, which means that we choose the most effective means to promote our own good (or the good of the

---

[5] John Rawls, *JFR*, p. 5.

persons we represent). Because we reason under the veil, the only information we have about the good of those we represent is that they need social primary goods. Taking the most effective means to advancing their ends implies, then, evaluating principles in terms of an expected level of primary goods and picking the principles that give the highest expectation.

Moreover, the choice is "mutually disinterested": each party is concerned solely with advancing the ends of those he or she represents, and not with the level of primary goods of others, and is thus unconcerned with relative positions.

The essential point is that reasoning in the original position is reasoning about what best promotes one's advantage. Within the original position, we never ask what is reasonable, or how best to fulfill our responsibilities to ourselves or others, or what is fair. That we are reasoning about justice is not relevant to how we reason, just as considerations about truth are not in view when we prove theorems within some formal system – though we know from the semantics and soundness proof that the reasoning will lead us to truths, and that that is the point of the exercise.

Reasoning within the original position is, then, different from reasoning about how to set up the original position; different from reflecting on the relevant/irrelevant distinction or thinking about how to express or model that distinction. Moreover, it is different from what we do in a just society, when we use moral-political ideas in individual reflection and public reasoning. Still, it is intended as a way to answer the fundamental question: what conception of justice provides "the most appropriate moral basis for a democratic society" (*TJR*, p. xviii), understood as a fair system of cooperation among free and equal moral persons?

The proposal, then, is that a conception of justice is explained and justified by a rational choice of principles of justice subject to informational constraints. The constraints model our ideas about relevance/irrelevance to justice. The parties making the choice aim to get the highest expected level of primary goods. And the interest in primary goods is stipulated for the parties in the original position, and explained by reference to a conception of persons as free and equal (*PL*, pp. 187–90).

In the original position, then, parties make a constrained rational choice. They aim to advance the good of the individuals whose interests they represent. Their choices are based on judgments of rational advantage, under the veil of ignorance. That is not true about actual people, certainly not in a well-ordered society, whose members are assumed to have and to be motivated by a sense of justice. Nor is it true about *us* when we think about what the right standards of justice are. We might be concerned, for example, that some arrangements give insufficient importance to the value of choice, or permit extreme burdens to fall on some solely because of a large sum of small benefits for others, or subject some to contempt, disdain, or humiliation. We are assumed to have a sense of the distinction between considerations that are relevant and considerations that are irrelevant to justice. That sense is modeled by the original position, not deployed within it.

All of which prompts the question: why present the case for principles of justice in terms of judgments of rational advantage made under the veil of ignorance? Why have a strategy of argument for explaining and justifying principles that is so different from how moral-political argument actually proceeds? According to the Rational Advantage Model, principles of justice are explained and justified by reference to judgments by individuals of what principles would be rationally advantageous under conditions of ignorance, judgments that are very different from the claims about what is right, fair, and reasonable that are made by members of a well-ordered society to one another. Why the Rational Advantage Model?

9.2 Why the veil of ignorance?

To focus the issue, let's back up and ask: why impose the constraints of the veil of ignorance? Sometimes Rawls defends these constraints by arguing that they keep people from pressing their own advantage in ways that are inappropriate when basic issues of justice are at stake: "we must nullify the effects of specific contingencies which put men at odds and tempt them to exploit social and natural circumstances to their own advantage. Now in order to do this I assume that parties are situated behind a veil of ignorance" (*TJR*, p. 118).

Such concerns about nullifying self-interest or other forms of partiality – essentially about ensuring fair conditions for pursuing individual and group interests – will not suffice as a rationale for the thick veil, but at most for the thin. It is not a good reason in favor of some principles that those principles would benefit the rich, or would be especially good for men. The fact that the principle would benefit men is not a reason that counts in support of it: the fact that it benefits women or the poor is only derivatively a reason, not because it is women or the poor, but because of assumptions about how those categories may be proxies for unjust disadvantages. We model the irrelevance of this consideration in the idea that people are to reason under the assumption that they do not know whether they are men or women. In general, we can make sense of the thin veil as an effort to capture the idea that the choice of principles should not be affected by biases and threats, which introduce plainly irrelevant considerations into our assessment of principles.

But suppose I endorse a relatively weak principle of liberty that permits the enforcement of morality: say, I hold to a natural-law moral theory, according to which certain conduct is naturally wrong because it violates natural standards of rectitude; that lives are made worse by engaging in such violations; and that political communities are made unacceptably worse by permitting members to lead such bad lives. In this case, I am not trying to win advantage for myself or my group, nor obviously yielding to a bias.

Still, we may think that considerations that come from a much-disputed religious or moral or ethical outlook are not suitable reasons in support of a conception of justice, given the role of the conception in shaping the basic institutions under which we all will live, as free and equal persons. Such considerations are matters on which free and equal persons reasonably disagree. Because we are looking for principles suited to fair cooperation among free and equal persons, we may judge these considerations to be irrelevant, thus appropriately placed behind the thicker veil, though not because they represent forms of self- or group-interest. I am not here arguing that those considerations *are* irrelevant, but simply underscoring that the veil of ignorance expresses antecedent convictions about the relevance of different considerations in establishing the correctness of principles of justice. And some considerations may be thought irrelevant even if we think they are not matters of self-interest or partiality.

We begin, then, from the idea that certain kinds of considerations are not relevant to settling on public standards of fair cooperation among free and equal persons. We get to the thick veil by considering exclusively the features of persons thus conceived. We model the irrelevance of other features by putting knowledge of them behind the veil of ignorance. In general, the slogan is: *model moral irrelevance through ignorance.*

The fundamental idea is that while some considerations provide reasons relevant to fixing public standards of fair cooperation among free and equal persons, other considerations are irrelevant. We are looking for a way to permit only the relevant considerations to play a role. Instead of, say, using a referee – a kind of Walrasian auctioneer who announces which arguments are acceptable – we make an assumption of ignorance. Rawls expresses the essential point this way:

> The idea here is simply to make vivid to ourselves the restrictions that it seems reasonable to *impose on arguments for principles of justice*, and

therefore on these principles themselves. Thus it seems reasonable and generally acceptable that no one should be advantaged or disadvantaged by natural fortune or social circumstances in the choice of principles ... The aim is to rule out those principles that it would be rational to propose for acceptance, however little the chance of success, only if one knew certain things that are *irrelevant from the standpoint of justice*. For example, if a man knew that he was wealthy, he might find it rational to advance the principle that various taxes for welfare measures be counted unjust; if he knew that he was poor, he would most likely propose the contrary principle. *To represent the desired restrictions one imagines a situation in which everyone is deprived of this sort of information.* One excludes the knowledge of those contingencies which sets men at odds and allows them to be guided by their prejudices. In this manner the veil of ignorance is arrived at in a natural way. This concept should cause no difficulty *if we keep in mind the constraints on arguments* that it is meant to express. At any time we can enter the original position, so to speak, simply by following a certain procedure, namely, by arguing for principles of justice in accordance with these restrictions. (*TJR*, pp. 16–17, emphases added)

The central idea is about acceptable arguments. The point is to represent constraints on arguments (reasons). We are assumed to have a grasp already of the relevant constraints, understand their rationale, and be drawn to use them in our informal arguments about justice. For example,

if we are reasonable, it is one of our considered convictions that the fact that we occupy a particular social position, say, is not a good reason for us to accept, or to expect others to accept, a conception of justice that favors those in that position. If we are wealthy, or poor, we do not expect anyone else to accept a basic structure favoring the wealthy, or the poor, simply for that reason. To model this and similar convictions, we do not let the parties know the social position of the persons they represent. (*JFR*, p. 18)

But now we face a puzzle. How do we get from the idea that the original position reflects a judgment about suitable restrictions on reasons *to the idea of rational choice under conditions of ignorance*? How, that is, do we get to the idea that we are to choose principles by asking, subject to the constraints of the veil of ignorance, about what is rationally advantageous?

Suppose I say, on behalf of a principle, that if it were followed, it would advance the good of all citizens, the general welfare, or would encourage great trust and civility in the conduct of our political relations. Or suppose I say that it would foster fair cooperation by mitigating the impact on the lives of free and equal persons of the morally adventitious distribution of natural and social fortune. These considerations seem plainly relevant in deciding what justice requires. But these relevant considerations end up behind the veil of ignorance. They cannot themselves figure in original position reasoning, because they do not point directly to a benefit that flows to individuals. On the Rational Advantage Model only considerations about what works to the benefit of individuals, what is good for them, figure in the reasoning.

To be sure, these other relevant considerations – like a concern to advance the common good – figure in a different way, and it is essential to understanding the original position as a model to see how. Consider the relevant claim that a principle would advance the good of each person. Arguably, we get the effect of this consideration through the joint work of a rational choice of means by individual parties and the veil of ignorance. In choosing principles I try to promote the fundamental interests of the person I represent. Unable to specify who that person is, I must arguably choose principles that advance the basic interests of each person.

So the fact that some institutions and laws would advance the basic interests of each person is relevant; the theoretical issue is how to model the relevant consideration. The original position models this consideration without using it. The fact that some principles would promote the basic interests of each person is not a reason *within the original position* in support of principles. Instead, the original position models the relevant consideration through the combined efforts of the veil of ignorance, primary goods, and the assumption of mutually disinterested rationality. Indeed, if the original position did not give us standards of the common advantage, then we would have to change the design. The design would need to be changed because that consideration is relevant, and needs to be captured somehow.

Rawls thinks this line of reasoning supports the following "conjecture":

> that the principles of justice the parties would agree to ... would specify *the terms of cooperation that we regard – here and now – as fair and supported by the best reasons.* This is because, in that case, the original position would have succeeded in modeling in a suitable manner what we think on due reflection are the reasonable considerations to ground the principles of a political conception of justice. (*JFR*, p. 17; *PL*, p. 26, emphasis added)

This claim is a conjecture because we are not to suppose that justice consists in being the object of a rational choice under conditions of ignorance – or that the latter is an analysis of the former. The idea instead is that we will be able to see in the end how the Rational Advantage Model gives us the principles that the relevant considerations taken together would lead us to. Only then has the original position "succeeded in modeling ... the reasonable considerations."

This sketch provides an answer to the concern about how we could use the Rational Advantage Model to specify principles of justice. The parties in the original position do not use normative considerations (other than rationality) in their reflections. But the original position models other normative considerations through the combined work of the veil of ignorance, the assumption of mutually disinterested rationality, and the account of primary goods. At no point is the construction driven by some pretended aspiration to moral neutrality, much less by an exclusive concern with rational advantage, though a narrow focus on how reasoning proceeds within the original position might suggest that.

Still, the italicized phrase "the terms of cooperation that we regard – here and now – as fair and supported by the best reasons" suggests that we ought to be able to arrive at the principles of justice without going through the original position at all. We could instead consider, more directly, which principles are supported by the balance of reasons: by having considerations about what is reasonable in relations among free and equal citizens appear directly in our argument about what justice requires.

Rawls makes precisely this point in a passage near the end of *TJ*. Addressing the rationale for the Rational Advantage Model, he says:

> If justice as fairness is more convincing than the older presentations of the contract doctrine, I believe that it is because the original position, as indicated above, unites in one conception a reasonably clear problem of choice with conditions that are widely recognized as fitting to impose on the adoption of moral principles. This initial situation combines the requisite clarity with the relevant ethical constraints. It is partly to preserve this clarity that I have avoided attributing to the parties any ethical motivation. They decide solely on the basis of what seems best calculated to further their interests so far as they can ascertain them. In this way we can exploit the intuitive idea of rational prudential choice. We can, however, define ethical variations of the initial situation by supposing the parties to be influenced by moral considerations ... I have simply divided up the description of the original position so that these elements do not occur in the characterization of the parties, although even here there might be a question as to what counts as a moral element and what does not. There is no need to settle this problem. What is important is that the

various features of the original position should be expressed in the simplest and most compelling way.

Occasionally I have touched upon some possible ethical variations of the initial situation (§17). For example, one might assume that the parties hold the principle that no one should be advantaged by unmerited assets and contingencies, and therefore they choose a conception of justice that mitigates the effects of natural accident and social fortune. Or else they may be said to accept a principle of reciprocity requiring that distributive arrangements always lie on the upward sloping portion of the contribution curve ... There is no a priori reason for thinking that these variations must be less convincing, or the moral constraints they express less widely shared. Moreover, we have seen that the possibilities just mentioned appear to confirm the difference principle, lending further support to it. Although I have not proposed a view of this kind, they certainly deserve further examination. The crucial thing is not to use principles that are contested. (*TJR*, pp. 511–12)

Here Rawls imagines a contract argument in which the parties use the relevant normative considerations – say, those Rawls mentions in the second paragraph above – to arrive at an account of fair terms for free and equal persons. He suggests no case for the Rational Advantage Model beyond the analytical clarity that it might arguably bring and the conjecture that things will work out plausibly if we use it.

An ethical variation of the initial situation of choice may seem puzzling: how is the reasoning we use when we adopt an ethical variant, in which parties are directly "influenced by moral considerations" (*TJR*, p. 512), a kind of contract theory? The ethical variant seems to lack a feature essential to the contract idea, whether understood as a form of political justification, as in the social contract tradition, or as a more general moral theory about what we owe to each other, as in Scanlon's view. In particular, the ethical interpretation may appear to move away from what Scanlon has called the "individualistic basis of contractualism" (*WWO*, p. 234).

To understand how it appears to move away from the individualistic basis, consider a line of argument that Rawls offers for his principles of justice in his *JFR*. The argument in question is assumed to be used in the original position, but it does not "*focus on the individual good of citizens.*" Instead, it

focuses on the nature of the public political culture realized by the two principles of justice and the desirable effects of that culture on the moral quality of public life and on citizens' political character. The parties try in effect to fashion a certain kind of social world ... They view the best agreement as one that guarantees background justice for all, *encourages the spirit of cooperation between citizens on a footing of mutual respect*, and allows within itself sufficient social space for (permissible) ways of life fully worthy of citizens' allegiance. (*JFR*, p. 118, emphases added)

Here we have an argument that is supposed to support an initial agreement on the two principles of justice. But the reason does not focus on the good of individual citizens, or make any explicit reference to their good; instead, it is about achieving the important social value of cooperation on a basis of mutual respect. It illustrates the kind of argument that works in an ethical interpretation of the initial situation.

To understand why the ethical interpretation is nevertheless a kind of contract view, we need to distinguish two interpretations of what Scanlon calls the "individualistic basis of contractualism": *judgmental individualism* and *substantive individualism*. Judgmental individualism says that justification of principles of cooperation requires making a case to the considered judgment of each person who will be expected to regulate his/her conduct by reference to the proposed standards. Justification is addressed to individuals. This condition, taken by itself, does not restrict the content of the reasons that do the justifying to considerations about how the person him/herself is treated. Judgmental individualism is preserved by Rawls's ethical interpretation. That, I assume, is why he thinks of the ethical interpretation of the initial situation as a kind of contract view.

Substantive individualism in contrast does restrict the content of the reasons that have a role in justification. It has at least two variants. One version of substantive individualism – suggested by the Rational Advantage Model – confines the considerations that play a role in the case for principles of right conduct to considerations about what is *good for* the persons who will be using the principles. Another version – call it the Reasonable Objection view, expressed in Scanlon's moral contractualism – confines the considerations to (roughly) concerns by an individual about how he or she is treated, and the kind of treatment that he or she can reasonably object to. The consideration that Rawls mentions in the argument in *JFR* – about the "nature of the public political culture realized by the two principles of justice and the desirable effects of that culture on the moral quality of public life and on citizens' political character" – is not individualistic in either of these ways. I will return to these variants in section 9.4.

Why, then, take the route through the original position: an interpretation of the initial situation that uses the Rational Advantage Model? Rawls says that this is a way to model the relevant/irrelevant distinction, and that it has the virtue of analytical tractability. But I want now to suggest some costs to the choice of model: the form of representation, I will argue, has contentious implications.

9.3 Respect and rational advantage

To make the case, I will sketch one of the central arguments for the difference principle. Call it *the argument from self-respect*.[6] I will sketch the original position argument from self-respect, and then see how it could have been presented more directly, by using the relevant reasons themselves, rather than by modeling them with the Rational Advantage Model. I am not concerned to defend the argument, but only to use it as illustration of the issue I am raising about the costs of using the Rational Advantage Model as a device of representation.

The basic elements of self-respect (following Rawls) are: (i) a person affirms some aims, and is more or less confident that he/she can achieve them; (ii) the person believes that his/her aims are worth achieving (*TJR*, p. 386). Self-respect, thus understood, is relevant to the choice of principles of justice for three reasons.

First, self-respect is a fundamental good whose presence is almost certainly required if our conditions are to be acceptable:

> When we feel that our plans are of little value, we cannot pursue them with pleasure or take delight in their execution. Nor plagued by failure and self-doubt can we continue in our endeavors. It is clear then why self-respect is a primary good. Without it nothing may seem worth doing, or if some things have value for us, we lack the will to strive for them. All desire and activity becomes empty and vain, and we sink into apathy and cynicism. Therefore the parties in the original position would wish to avoid at almost any cost the social conditions that undermine self-respect. (*TJR*, p. 386)

So we have:

> Further Fact One: Self-respect is a fundamental good for the person who has it, in part because having self-respect is needed to pursue aims that the person values pursuing.

Further Fact One asserts the instrumental importance of self-respect: having self-respect is an important means in that it enables us to pursue what matters to us. (On the reason for the term "further fact," see section 9.4 below.)

---

[6] The sketch of the argument from self-respect draws on Cohen, "Democratic Equality."

Second, while self-respect itself is not socially distributed, certain social conditions that support self-respect are: the social bases of self-respect. Two such social bases, corresponding to the two aspects of self-respect, are: first, that our circumstances enable us to develop aspirations and to pursue them with confidence in our success. Call this the "objective side" of self-respect. Second, that we associate with others in such a way that we experience their respect for us; without such experience, our sense of our own worth and that our aspirations are worth pursuing may be hard to sustain. "Our self-respect normally depends on the respect of others. Unless we feel that our endeavors are respected by them, it is difficult if not impossible for us to maintain the conviction that our ends are worth advancing" (*TJR*, pp. 155–6). Call this the "recognitional side" of self-respect. Here, then, we have:

> Further Fact Two: Self-respect is hard to sustain without respect from others.

The two further facts together imply that respect from others has great instrumental importance (not that it is solely of instrumentally importance). Respect from others is important for self-respect; and self-respect is important to the successful pursuit of the ends that matter to us.

Third, social primary goods other than social bases of self-respect – including basic liberties and income – provide the two types of social bases of self-respect (objective and recognitional).

Taking these three points together, the parties in the original position need to ensure that social conditions will support their self-respect. And that means that they need to ensure that, whatever position they may land in, they have the resources that enable them to form and to pursue aspirations with confidence; and that they will be in a position to experience the respect of others.

To illustrate how this works, consider how the difference principle supports self-respect at the least advantaged position.

The difference principle only permits inequalities that contribute to lifetime expectations at the least well-off position. Smaller inequalities would reduce expectations, as would greater inequalities. Assume now that the value of liberties to a person depends (assuming a fair value of political liberty as background) on the level of resources available to that person. So the minimum value of the liberties with the difference principle is greater than the minimum value under the alternatives. Indeed, if the value of the liberties is, as proposed, a monotone-increasing function of (absolute, not relative) income and wealth, then the value of the liberties achieves its maximin when the difference principle is satisfied. But self-respect depends on the value of the liberties. For self-respect requires confidence in one's ability to successfully pursue one's aims. But that confidence is increased as resources increase. In short, then, the great value of self-respect encourages the choice of principles that maximize the minimum worth of liberty. If the two principles together achieve maximin worth of liberty, then there is a strong case for choosing them to ensure the bases of self-respect.

Furthermore, under the difference principle occupants of the least well-off position are not only guaranteed the material basis for the worth of the liberties; this guarantee is part of a public understanding about the limits of legitimate inequalities. With an acceptable minimum defined as a maximized minimum, the society agrees to ensure advantages regardless of the particulars of social position, natural endowment, and good fortune that distinguish the free and equal members of a well-ordered society. To forgo possible advantages because accepting them would keep the expectations at the minimum, and the worth of liberties at the minimum, less than they might be, expresses respect for those at the minimum position and affirms their worth. Because self-respect is so important, it is rational to want public institutions to show such respect.

So the choice of the difference principle strengthens the foundations of self-respect both by ensuring the resources required for the self-confident pursuit of aims and by contributing to the experience of respect. It builds mutual respect for one another, as free and equal, into the basic structure of the society:

> Thus a desirable feature of a conception of justice is that it should publicly express men's respect for one another. *In this way they insure a sense of their own value.* Now the two principles achieve this end. For when society follows these principles, everyone's good is included in a scheme of mutual benefit and this public affirmation in institutions of each man's endeavors supports men's self-esteem. The establishment of equal liberty and the operation of the difference principle are bound to have this effect. The two principles are equivalent, as I have remarked, to an undertaking to regard the distribution of natural abilities in some respects as a collective asset so that the more fortunate are to benefit only in ways that help those who have lost out (§17). I do not say that the parties are moved by the ethical propriety of this idea. But there are reasons for them to accept this principle. For by arranging inequalities for reciprocal advantage and by abstaining from the exploitation of the contingencies of nature and social circumstance within a

framework of equal liberties, persons express their respect for one another in the very constitution of their society. *In this way they insure their self-respect as it is rational for them to do.* (*TJR*, p. 156, emphases added)

The essential point is that the *reason* for choosing the difference principle in the original position *is not* that it builds respect for each person into the basic structure of society. That cannot be the reason because that is not a matter of rational advantage for the individual parties (unless we are able to show that it is rationally advantageous to all to be in a society that shows respect for each). Still, the claim that it builds in respect for one another as equals is a *step* in the original position argument ("For by arranging inequalities for reciprocal advantage and by abstaining from the exploitation of the contingencies of nature and social circumstance within a framework of equal liberties, persons express their respect for one another in the very constitution of their society."). But the fact that persons thus express their respect for one another (assuming it is a fact) is not itself an original position-reason for choosing a principle. Instead, in order to connect that fact to an original position-reason, we need – as the two italicized sentences in the passage just quoted indicate – to connect it to the *good of individuals*. We need to connect the asserted fact – that a society that meets the two principles of justice would treat everyone with respect – to a judgment about what works to the rational advantage of those who are so treated – to a judgment about what is good for individuals. And that is precisely the role of Further Facts One and Two. Putting these two claims together, we can conclude that lack of respect from others is *bad for me*. It is not only a form of treatment that I have strong grounds for objecting to; it is not simply that I can reasonably object to treatment that reveals a lack of respect. To make the lack of respect from others relevant in the original position, we need to add that the lack of respect from others makes my life go less well: in particular, that it disables me in forming and pursuing my aims. Put otherwise, we have a relevant normative consideration: that cooperation in accordance with the two principles puts cooperation on a footing of mutual respect among equals. That relevant consideration cannot be used as a reason by parties in the original position. To represent it in the original position, with its Rational Advantage Model, the Further Facts are essential.

I am not arguing here that the Further Facts are wrong, though their plausibility is an arguable matter. My point is that Rawls uses a device of representation that *demands* the Further Facts. Consider what happens in their absence. The apparently relevant fact – relevant to determining what justice requires – that a society that uses certain principles would show respect for each person as a free and equal member, that it would "encourage the spirit of cooperation between citizens on a footing of mutual respect" (*JFR*, p. 118), cannot itself serve as a reason for parties in the original position. A person's claim that he or she is entitled to be treated with respect cannot play a role. The apparently relevant claim that treating others with respect is fitting or appropriate cannot play a role. Considerations such as these can only be made live as original position reasons via the Further Facts. The original position models these relevant considerations by drawing a connection between being treated with respect and the rational advantage of the person who is thus treated.

We have, then, a consideration, antecedently assumed to be relevant to assessing principles of cooperation among equals: namely, that cooperation regulated by certain principles provides a more compelling expression of mutual respect among equal persons. Indeed, in the brief sketch I presented above, that very consideration is a step in the argument. But the Rational Advantage Model cannot permit this relevant consideration to stand on its own. It can only play a role when we add that treating a person as it is appropriate to treat him/her is good for that person. The form of representation itself (the Rational Advantage Model) forces such Further Facts on us, in this way: only when we add them in can we make a consideration that we antecedently judge to be relevant into a consideration that can play a role in the original position.

To be sure, the claims asserted by the Further Facts may be true. And if they are, all to the good: that would help to show that a society in which people are committed to principles that express mutual respect for one another as equals is good for the members of the society. That would make such a society more attractive, perhaps more stable, and stable, moreover, for good reasons. But the relevance of concerns about cooperation on a footing of mutual respect to an account of the correct principles of fair cooperation among equals does not seem to depend on the Further Facts.

9.4 Two other models

With the self-respect argument as illustration, I want now briefly to distinguish the Rational Advantage Model from two other contractualist conceptions. Neither makes use of the model of rational choice under ignorance. They do not build reasonableness into the background of the evaluation of principles, but appeal directly to it. The first alternative, the Reasonable

Complaint Conception, is a rendering of Scanlon's contractualism (*WWO*, p. 229); the second, the Public Reason Version, interprets what Rawls describes as an ethical interpretation of the initial situation. Drawing on the distinction I introduced earlier: the Reasonable Complaint Version is both judgmentally and substantively individualistic, whereas the Public Reason Version is committed only to judgmental individualism, not substantive individualism.

For the sake of discussion, I will assume a key element in the argument from self-respect is correct. In particular, I will assume – just for concreteness – that accepting the two principles as public standards of justice and treating others in accordance with those principles, is a way to express respect for others as free and equal persons. Focus on this claim itself: that affirming the two principles of justice is a strong expression of respect for others as free and equal. Put aside the claim that being shown respect by others in these ways is good for the person who is shown respect because it bolsters self-respect, or that if we lack self-respect we will be "plagued by failure and self-doubt" and so be unable to "continue in our endeavors" (*TJR*, p. 386).

Consider Jones, who is less well off than he or she would be under the difference principle. Let's say that Jones is less well off than anyone needs to be, in that there is a scheme of laws and policies that would make Jones better off without making anyone worse off than Jones now is (I am simplifying by focusing on a person, not a social position: nothing changes with the complexity added). The Reasonable Complaint Model says that Jones has a forceful objection against the actual distribution. The distribution is objectionable because Jones is not being shown proper respect as an equal. *Jones has a complaint about how she is treated: the treatment is inappropriate, objectionably insulting, disrespectful.* To have a complaint, Jones need not say that by being treated this way, her life is made worse, or that the treatment is bad for her. In addition, Jones can complain about being treated unfairly (*WWO*, pp. 229, 231), or in some other way not being taken properly into account. Jones need not say that this lack of sufficient respect deprives her of self-respect – Jones's self-respect may remain fully intact (anyway, as intact as it was, or would otherwise be). Or if it does challenge her self-respect, she need not say that this limits her will to persist, or inhibits attentive action, or that her life is made worse in some other way by the failure to treat her with respect. Jones need not say that the failure to treat her with respect is not in her interests, that it is bad for her and undermines her well-being. Instead, all that Jones needs to say is that as an equal person – as someone who the same standing as others – she has a reasonable objection to the existing arrangements because they do not fully show her respect. The lack of respect (or diminished respect) is either unfair to her, or fails to treat her in a way that she is entitled to be treated. And unless there is some compelling reason that counts on the other side, this objection suffices to condemn the system of principles. So the complaint is like the complaint I would have against being deprived of a right that I will not use: I think the deprivation is unfair, disrespectful, perhaps insulting, even if no benefit redounds to me from having the right.

The proponent of the Reasonable Complaint Model is not introducing anything that the original position self-respect argument is not already committed to: that is why the Further Facts are called "further." In particular, the original position argument is founded on the idea that free and equal persons can reasonably demand to be treated with respect as equals, and it requires – as in the self-respect argument – making the additional case that upholding the two principles of justice is a way to show respect. The Reasonable Complaint Model agrees. But it says these things directly, so to speak: it offers as a consideration in support of the principles that we can reasonably complain against arrangements that do not treat us with respect as equals. It does not offer this consideration as a reason for setting up a choice situation focused on judgments of rational advantage in a particular way. It thus does not depend for its force on linking the complaint against being treated with disrespect to an argument about what is rationally disadvantageous. It thus gives no hostage to further-factual fortune, nor does it turn objections into complaints about debilitating wounds.

The Reasonable Complaint Model then has the advantage of not taking on the further burdens that come with trying to turn the reasonable complaint about being treated with disrespect into a case about what is rational to agree to as a way to advance our good under conditions of ignorance. Again, it does not need to say what must be said on the original position self-respect argument: that the failure to be treated with respect undermines self-respect and thereby kills the will to strive for goals. It captures the idea that being treated with respect is something you can reasonably demand of others, quite apart from any setback to your interests that might issue from the failure of others to respect that demand.

Now let me end with a brief discussion of the Public Reason Model. The Reasonable Complaint Model rejects Rational Advantage, because it turns all arguments about the kinds of treatment individuals have good reason to complain about into arguments about what works to the rational advantage of the complainant. The Public Reason Model agrees, but adds that there is no reason to insist on presenting our reflections about the appropriate public standards of fair cooperation among equals in the form of complaints by individuals about how they are themselves treated. If we are aiming to model reasons for criticizing principles – in general, to model restrictions on reasons for defending and rejecting principles – we need not assume this substantively individualistic constraint. Suppose I have a good reason to reject a principle because it imposes a severe burden on me: then others have reason to reject it because it imposes an unacceptably severe burden on someone. If I have a good reason to reject a principle because it shows contempt for me, then others have reason to reject it because it shows contempt for someone: public standards of cooperation among equals cannot allow some cooperators to be the targets of contempt.

To be sure, it helps in understanding the nature of a burden imposed on someone – or in appreciating the contempt or disrespect that is shown by, for example, permitting some to be much less well off than anyone needs to be, or requiring some people to buy their rights – to locate myself imaginatively in the shoes of the person who is burdened or treated with contempt. It will help to picture myself walking in his or her shoes. It may be impossible to properly appreciate the burden or the contempt without that imaginative act. But the importance of such imaginative grasp in appreciating the magnitude of the burden or in understanding the contempt or the disrespect does not compel us to endorse the substantively individualist thought that objections to principles are to be understood, in the first instance, as complaints by those who are subject to the objectionable treatment.

Recall the distinction between judgmental and substantive individualism. In his discussion of contractualism and aggregation, Scanlon commends contractualism for its individualism: "a contractualist theory, in which all objections to a principle must be raised by individuals," blocks aggregative justifications in which a sum of individual benefits, no matter how small those benefits are for the individuals who get them, outweighs a severe burden concentrated on a single person. And he says as well that the Complaint Model (which is narrower than what I have been calling the Reasonable Complaint Model, in that it makes complaints depend on effects on the complainants well-being) "calls attention to a central feature of contractualism that I would not want to give up: its insistence that the justifiability of a moral principle depends only on various *individuals'* reasons for objecting to that principle and alternatives to it" (*WWO*, p. 229). Or again, he insists that contractualism "confines itself to reasons for rejection arising from individual standpoints" (*WWO*, p. 230).

These references to the role of individuals' reasons – including their reasonable objections – do not distinguish the Public Reason Model from the Reasonable Complaint Model. The former preserves judgmental individualism – the importance of justifying to individuals – but does not endorse substantive individualism. The Public Reason Model accepts that objections must be raised by individuals and justifications offered to them. But it does not give any special privilege to complaints by a person about how *she herself* is treated.

Take the following consideration: that in a society of a certain kind (with excessive inequalities of rights or resources, say) the members fail to treat each other with respect as equals. This consideration does not figure as such in the original position, and also does not figure as such in the Reasonable Complaint Model, because the consideration is not expressed in the form of a complaint by any individual that he or she is not being treated with respect. But why isn't this a reasonable objection, just on its own? Anyone can object that some people are not being treated with respect as equals. In particular, the Public Reason Model can simply adopt that argument without reformulating it in terms of a concern about the good of individuals or in terms of their reasonable complaints about how they are treated. The central problem with terms of cooperation that fail to treat people with respect as equals is not that we cannot justify those terms to the very individuals who are treated with disrespect; it is that we cannot justify those terms to anyone who understands the importance of people cooperating on terms of mutual respect. The problem is not that the justification can be given to some individuals but not others (not to those who are burdened): anyone could object and everyone should.

It might be argued that the substantive individualist constraint on reasons is needed to block unacceptable aggregation:

> A contractualist theory, in which all objections to a principle must be raised by individuals, blocks such [aggregative] justifications in an intuitively appealing way. It allows the *intuitively compelling complaints of those who are severely burdened to be heard* [emphasis added], while, on the other side, the sum of the smaller benefits to others has no justificatory weight, since there is no individual who enjoys these benefits and would have to forgo them if the policy were to be allowed. (*WWO*, p. 230)

Suffice it to say that substantive individualism strikes me as an entirely unnecessary price to pay for blocking unacceptable aggregation: a price, because it requires us to present objections to severe burdens as if those

objections were available only by allowing "the intuitively compelling complaints of those who are severely burdened to be heard," and not objections
that each of us can raise in our own voice. An unnecessary price, because the
severity of the burden on some, and the minimal character of the benefit for
each of the others, suffices just by itself to give force to the objection.

9.5 Conclusion

Some social contract theories – those advanced by Thomas Hobbes and David
Gauthier, for example – use the Rational Advantage Model because they are
committed to the view that individuals, when they act for reasons, take
effective means to the pursuit of their interests. According to these theories,
then, individuals have reasons to act justly if and only if such action effectively
advances their ends (or is at least believed to advance those ends).

Rawls rejects this view of human agency. Human beings, Rawls thinks, have
a moral nature. We are moral persons, endowed with a sense of justice: a
capacity to understand and act on reasons of justice, which express an idea of
fair terms of cooperation among free and equal persons (*TJR*, pp. 440–9).
Despite this rejection, Rawls's uses the Rational Advantage Model to specify
fair terms of cooperation. He defends that model as a device of representation.
I think it was a mistake to use the Rational Advantage Model as a device of
representation. This form of representation has large substantive implications.
I focused in section 9.3 on one such implication: the need to recast arguments
about the implications of treating others with respect as arguments about the
instrumental benefits of respect from others and self-respect. The supplemen-
tary assumptions (further facts) needed for that recasting weaken the case for
his conception of justice.

Rawls also suggests an alternative to the Rational Advantage Model of
mutual justification. *TJ* describes the alternative as an ethical interpretation
of the initial situation of choice in which we assess principles of justice.
According to the ethical interpretation, we in effect justify terms of cooperation using reasons that others, understood as free and equal persons, have
reason to accept. The reasons are not limited to (though they may include)
considerations about what is in a person's rational advantage. Nor are they
restricted – as in the Reasonable Complaint Model – to considerations about
the kinds of treatment of persons that those persons have reason to object to.
Parties might, for example, directly appeal to the relevant idea that "no one
should be advantaged by unmerited assets and contingencies," and that idea
might lead them to "choose a conception of justice that mitigates the effects of

natural accident and social fortune" (*TJR*, p. 512). The ethical interpretation thus anticipates the idea of public reason in Rawls's political liberalism, which also imposes no such restrictions. To be sure, justification on grounds of public reason lacks the clarity and analytical tractability that are sometimes associated with the Rational Advantage Model and alleged to be its special advantages. Those advantages are, however, illusory. Normative political argument is what it is and cannot be represented by some other thing.

10 The "Kantian roots" of the original position

Andrews Reath

10.1 Introduction

In §40 of *TJ*, Rawls tells us that "there is a Kantian interpretation" of justice as fairness "based upon Kant's notion of autonomy" (*TJR*, p. 221), and goes on to say:

> The original position may be viewed, then, as a procedural interpretation of Kant's conception of autonomy and the categorical imperative within the framework of an empirical theory. (*TJR*, p. 226)

Likewise one of Rawls's aims in "Kantian Constructivism in Moral Theory" is "to set out the Kantian roots" of justice as fairness by showing how it incorporates "the distinctive features of Kantian constructivism" (*CP*, p. 303). Those features he summarizes as follows:

> What distinguishes the Kantian form of constructivism is essentially this: it specifies a particular conception of the person as an element in a reasonable procedure of construction, the outcome of which determines the content of the first principles of justice. Expressed another way: this kind of view sets up a certain procedure of construction which answers to certain reasonable requirements, and within this procedure persons characterized as rational agents of construction specify, through their agreements, the first principles of justice. The leading idea is to establish a suitable connection between a particular conception of the person and first principles of justice, by means of a procedure of construction. (*CP*, p. 304)

This is to say that Kantian constructivism deploys a Kantian conception of the person as free and equal agents with different rational and moral capacities, and that this conception of the person is the basis of a deliberative procedure incorporating different requirements of practical reason that is used to justify a set of normative principles. In justice as fairness, of course, the deliberative procedure is the rational choice in the original position. Furthermore, within a constructivist theory the standard of correctness for a set of normative principles is that they result from the employment of this procedure. In *PL*, where Rawls sees the need to develop justice as fairness as a political conception of justice, he pulls back from its Kantian lineage to present it as a free-standing political view that does not presuppose any comprehensive moral doctrine. Here he stresses the contrasts between political constructivism and both Kant's moral constructivism and intuitionist moral realism. Still, the structural parallels between justice as fairness as a form of political constructivism and Kant's moral constructivism remain.

By Kant's "notion of autonomy," Rawls means Kant's thesis that morality is based in the autonomy of the will – that is, that moral principles in some sense originate in the rational willing of the agents subject to them and are thus principles that moral agents (in some sense) choose or legislate for themselves through reason, independently of contingent and desire-based interests.[1] In this chapter, I'll use "Kant's notion of autonomy" to refer to this idea. A constructivist normative theory aims to make good on this notion by specifying a "procedure of construction" that represents the idealized process of reasoning that leads to the content of the moral conception.[2] The qualification "in some sense" is needed since the form of rational willing that Kant puts at the basis of morality needs to be unpacked with some care. It is "pure willing," or volition directed by "pure practical reason" independently of desire-based interests. Among other things, an account of how morality is based in the rational willing of moral agents must preserve the necessity and universality of moral requirement, avoiding the idea that either the content or the authority of

---

[1] References to Kant are to the volume and paging of the Berlin Academy edition and will be given in the text using the abbreviations listed in the bibliography.

[2] Sharon Street has argued that discussions of constructivism have overemphasized the idea of a hypothetical procedure that generates correct moral claims, and argues that the fundamental idea instead is that "the truth of a normative claim consists in its being entailed from within the practical point of view" ("What is Constructivism?" p. 367). I think that she is right that the procedure of construction is a heuristic device and that a defense of constructivism as a metaethical view should adopt her "practical standpoint characterization of constructivism," but I set this issue aside in this paper. In "Kantian Constructivism" and *PL*, Rawls does not treat constructivism as a metaethical theory. It is a moral (or political) conception in competition with conceptions such as utilitarianism, perfectionism, and intuitionism, though its account of objectivity does have metaethical implications (*PL*, p. 303). It is also worth noting that representing Kant's conception of moral reasoning as the "CI (categorical imperative)-procedure" is and is recognized by Rawls to be a great simplification. The original position is a well-defined deliberative procedure, but the "CI-procedure" is at best an approximation. Rawls develops his "schematic" account of the latter mainly to elucidate the distinguishing features and structure of Kant's moral conception. See *LHMP*, pp. 162–4.

morality are based on a discretionary choice made by individuals. Kant's thesis that moral principles are based on the purely rational willing of moral subjects is the obvious inspiration for the device of the original position, and is Rawls's model in introducing the Kantian form of constructivism.

In this chapter, I explore the "Kantian roots" of justice as fairness, both Rawls's historical debt to Kant and the structural parallels between Kant's moral conception and Rawls's conception of justice. "Justice as fairness" refers both to Rawls's two principles and to his distinctive methodology that regards the principles as the object of a fair agreement between free and equal persons (*TJR*, pp. 10–14). I will use the phrase in the second sense to refer to the set-up and use of the original position as a device for producing agreement on principles of justice for the basic structure of society. As Rawls first makes clear in "Kantian Constructivism," he bases the original position on a conception of persons as free and equal agents who are both rational and reasonable. He understands Kant's moral conception to have the same structure and suggests (correctly in my view) that the categorical imperative is likewise based on a conception of persons as free rational agents with the capacities of both pure and empirical practical reason. My overall focus will be on the ways in which each conception is driven by this conception of the person.[3] Section 10.2 gives an overview of the relevant features of Kant's moral conception, with a focus on his "notion of autonomy" (the thesis that moral principles originate in the purely rational willing of free agents). I'll aim to provide enough (but not more than is needed) to explore the Kantian roots of the original position. In some respects, the conception sketched there is a Rawlsian Kant. But Rawls was an acute reader of Kant, and his interpretation has shaped contemporary understanding of Kant's moral conception (at least in some quarters). Furthermore, since Rawls's understanding of the structure of justice as fairness offers interesting inroads into the distinctive structure of Kant's moral conception, it is appropriate to draw on his reading of Kant in an exploration of the Kantian roots of his own political conception. Section 10.3 provides an overview of the original position that will bring out the close parallels between Kant's categorical imperative (understood as a "procedure" for generating substantive moral principles) and the original position as a procedure for constructing principles of social justice. Section 10.4 briefly

---

[3] For the most part I will focus on commonalities. Rawls notes obvious differences between his conception and Kant's at *TJR*, pp. 226–7, *CP*, p. 304, pp. 339–40 and elsewhere. And I won't discuss the changes required in Rawls's conception by the move to a "political conception" of justice in *PL*.

discusses *TJ*, §40, where Rawls first takes up the Kantian basis of justice as fairness. Section 10.5 explores further parallels between Rawls and Kant, as well as one possible difference in the bases of their conception of the person.

10.2 Kant's morality of autonomy: an overview

The idea of autonomy appears mid-way through the argument of *Groundwork* II, though it is implicit in the Universal Law formulation of the categorical imperative that one is to act only on maxims that one can at the same time will as universal law. The Formula of Universal Law (FUL) is the fundamental demand of morality – to act only from maxims that can at the same time be willed as universal law – and is presented as the basic principle that determines our duties and permissions. The Formula of Humanity (FH) introduces "a matter" or "an end" for morality, i.e. the substantive value that underwrites moral thought – as we might say, that conformity to universal law or moral requirement is about respecting humanity as an end in itself. The idea of autonomy then appears in a new formulation of the categorical imperative, initially stated simply as "the idea *of the will of every rational being as a will giving universal law*" (*G* 4: 431); call this the Formula of Autonomy. Kant tells us that "the will" (or moral agent) is subject to moral principle "in such a way that it must be viewed as also giving the law to itself," that the moral agent "is subject *only to laws given by himself but still universal* and that he is bound only to act in conformity with his own will," and that a moral principle applies unconditionally only if it "arise[s] from *his* will" (*G* 4: 431, 432, 433). For these reasons Kant calls the basic principle of morality "the principle of the **autonomy** of the will" and says that it "is the sole principle of morals...[that] commands neither more nor less than just this autonomy" (*G* 4: 433, 440).

The autonomy of the will is the formative idea that shapes many components and distinctive features of Kant's moral conception. In the *Groundwork*, Kant has the twofold aim of "the seeking out and establishment of *the supreme principle of morality*" – that is, both of determining the content of the basic moral principle and establishing its rational authority. The thesis of autonomy plays a role in each task, as well as having implications for the moral standing of individual agents. Regarding the content of morality, FUL states the condition of universal validity that Kant thinks comes directly from the idea of pure practical reason, where a universally valid principle is one that all rational agents can agree is to apply to all and that accordingly is the basis of genuinely shared normative judgments about action. He derives FUL from the idea of a practical law that is built into the idea of the complete determination of action by practical reason. In this respect, FUL is the principle that pure practical reason gives to itself and it expresses practical and normative commitments that we have simply as agents with pure wills, which turns out to mean the commitments that we have simply as free rational agents. Further, the condition of universal validity is generally thought to lead to a deliberative procedure that, applied to an agent's subjective maxims of action at some level of generality, generates substantive moral principles and conclusions about duty. Kant's preferred method of deliberation is given by the Law of Nature formulation of the categorical imperative – that "one is to act as if the maxim of your action were to become by your will a universal law of nature" (*G* 4: 421). Rawls terms this method of deliberation the "categorical imperative procedure" or "CI-procedure" (*LHMP*, pp. 162–76). As most commentators understand Kant's theory, what can rationally be willed as universal law (or as a universal law of nature) is the standard of right action. That is, what makes a claim about basic moral principles correct, true, or reasonably accepted is that it follows from the correct employment of this form of reasoning.[4] Of course, there is controversy as to whether FUL or the Formula of the Law of Nature (FLN) is adequate to the task of generating a plausible moral conception, or whether it must be supplemented (for example, by reading into FUL ideas that are only made explicit in the other formulations of the categorical imperative). But assuming that such problems can be addressed, as many sympathetic commentators believe, the content of Kant's moral conception is determined or constituted by what agents will under the direction of pure practical reason – that is, through a deliberative procedure based in pure practical reason that expresses practical and normative commitments that we have simply as free rational agents.[5]

Kant himself did not think that there was much doubt about the content of ordinary moral principles, and his foundational works are more concerned to

---

[4] This point is a central feature of constructivism that Rawls calls "constitutive autonomy" – that "the so-called independent order of values does not constitute itself but is constituted by the activity, actual or ideal, of practical (human) reason itself" (*PL*, p. 99).

[5] Commentators who have argued that FUL can generate a plausible moral conception include O'Neill, *Constructions* (esp. Chapter 5), Herman, *The Practice* (esp. Chapters 3, 6, 7, 10), and Korsgaard, *Creating* (esp. Chapter 3). For an alternative approach that stresses Kant's idea of the realm of ends and that draws on the argument from the original position, see Hill, *Dignity* (Chapter 11) and *Respect* (Chapter 2). Interestingly, Rawls himself did not "believe that the CI-procedure is adequate for this purpose" (of generating the content of a reasonable moral doctrine), though "it is surely highly instructive as one of the more, if not most, illuminating formulations of the requirement to express our reasons universally when assuming a moral point of view" (*LHMP*, p. 163).

establish the authority of morality and show that the deliberative priority that commonsense morality claims for itself is genuine. Autonomy of the will is a key element of this part of Kant's moral conception. Indeed, he is led to his thesis about autonomy of the will by the need to ground the unconditional authority of moral principle: moral principles are unconditionally necessary only if based in autonomy, that is, if they originate in the rational will. Kant's central thesis here is that "[a]utonomy is the property of the will by which it is a law to itself (independently of the property of any objects of volition)" (*G* 4: 440). Very simply, I take Kant to be claiming here that the nature of rational volition by itself is the source of its basic normative principle (that principle being the categorical imperative), without the need to appeal to any object or interests given to the will from the outside. This thesis is supported by Kant's derivation of FUL from the nature of pure practical reason earlier in *Groundwork* II. The authority of the categorical imperative thus comes from the fact that it is the internal principle of the pure will, or the law that the will or practical reason is to itself.[6] Now in fact, Kant's account of the authority of morality is more complicated. The derivation of FUL shows that it is the principle of the pure will or pure practical reason, to which we are committed insofar as we are in the business of complete conformity to practical reason. But as sensibly affected beings we can still coherently ask why we should give priority to the requirements of pure practical reason when they conflict with our interest in happiness, and this question is not closed off until *Groundwork* III. The reformulation of FUL as the Formula of Autonomy sets up an argument at the beginning of *Groundwork* III to the effect that FUL – the basic principle of moral requirement – is equally the basic principle of free agency, the principle by which one exercises the capacity for free agency. Further arguments show that we human beings have this capacity, and moreover that we "necessarily act under the idea of freedom" and identify with our free agency as our proper self (*G* 4: 448, 457–8, 461). Thus ultimately the *Groundwork* aims to establish the authority of morality by showing that the categorical imperative is the principle internal to our self-conception as free agents, where that is a necessary feature of the practical standpoint.[7]

---

[6] Obviously there is a lot to say about this point. I try to say some of it in Reath, "Kant's Conception." For more on the reading of Kant sketched in this section see Reath, *Agency*, Chapters 4–5, 7.

[7] The *Critique of Practical Reason* takes a different approach to the authority of morality, arguing that the categorical imperative is given as a "fact of reason," but (though I can't elaborate here) the claim that the categorical imperative is the basic principle of free agency remains central to the argument.

Note here that we find two levels of moral principle in Kant – the categorical imperative and the particular categorical imperatives that result from its application – and they are based in autonomy in different senses. The categorical imperative is the principle that the will or practical reason gives to itself, or as we have just seen, the internal principle of free agency, and that is the basis of its authority. Particular categorical imperatives are substantive moral principles that result from the deliberative procedure associated with the categorical imperative. They are more specific principles that rational agents will through pure practical reason (content), and their normative force comes from the fact that they are in this way generated through a form of reasoning to which we are committed by our self-conception as free agents (authority).

These claims to the effect that morality is based in autonomy have implications for the moral standing of rational agents and what they are owed. If moral principle originates in the will of moral agents and does indeed have deliberative priority over other sources of reasons, then the agents subject to moral requirement are not bound by any norms given externally to their own reason. Moreover, their rational capacities give them, as Kant says, "a share... *in the giving of universal laws*" (*G* 4: 435). Moral subjects are a kind of autonomous or sovereign moral legislator, bound only to their own rational will, which itself is a legislative capacity. The autonomy of the individual, so understood, is the basis of the dignity or moral standing of persons (*G* 4: 440), and it leads to a requirement of justification that feeds into and reshapes our understanding of what persons are owed. In the appearance of FH found in the second *Critique*, Kant writes:

> Just because of this [the autonomy of his freedom] every will... is restricted to the condition of agreement with the autonomy of the rational being, that is to say, such a being is not to be subjected to any purpose that is not possible in accordance with a law that could arise from the will of the affected subject himself; hence this subject is to be used never merely as a means but as at the same time an end. (*KpV* 5: 87)

It will be useful to summarize Rawls's own understanding of "the CI-procedure" since it is the analogue in Kant's moral conception of Rawls's original position (the procedure of construction). Rawls says of the CI-procedure that "it specifies the content of the moral law as it applies to us as reasonable and rational persons in the natural world, endowed with conscience and moral sensibility, and affected by, but not determined by our natural desires and inclinations" and that it represents "in procedural form all the requirements of practical reason (both pure and empirical) as those requirements apply to our maxims" (*LHMP*, pp. 164, 165). That the requirements of practical reason admit of a "procedural representation" is important for Kant's constructivism. Rawls writes:

> An essential feature of Kant's moral constructivism is that the particular categorical imperatives that give the content of the duties of justice and virtue are viewed as specified by a procedure of construction (the CI-procedure), the form and structure of which mirror both of our two powers of practical reason as well as our status as free and equal moral persons. As we shall see, this conception of the person as both reasonable and rational, and as free and equal, Kant regards as implicit in our everyday moral consciousness, the fact of reason. (*LHMP*, p. 237)

How does the CI-procedure "represent in procedural form all the requirements of practical reason" and how does its "form and structure mirror" our powers of practical reason and our status as free and equal persons? Rawls takes Kantian maxims to represent agents' desire-based practical reasoning, and he assumes that they are instrumentally and prudentially rational. (Maxims that are not do not even get to the stage of moral assessment.) The CI-procedure applies the condition of universal validity given by pure practical reason to an agent's rationally formed maxims. It is to be used by agents with "a certain moral sensibility and a capacity for moral judgment" (*LHMP*, p. 165) who have a sincere interest in determining the permissibility of a maxim and the scope of their moral requirements – where that interest is a recognizably moral interest. So the procedure incorporates the requirements both of empirical and pure practical reason, the rational and the reasonable, and in a way that makes plain the order of priority between them. As Rawls likes to say, the "reasonable frames the rational": the condition of universal validity frames the choice of maxims and sets authoritative limits on the permissible pursuit of desirable ends. This formal feature of practical reasoning is the priority of right (cf. *CP*, p. 319). However, the requirements of practical reason incorporated into the procedure are not simply abstract principles. They are principles that we recognize and employ in everyday contexts, and thus represent the rational capacities characteristic of persons (to develop and pursue a conception of happiness, to take an interest in the justifiability of our conduct to others and in genuinely shared practical reasoning, etc.).[8] In this respect, the moral principles that make up the

---

[8] Here cf. *PL*, p. 107 (on political constructivism): "the principles of practical reason are expressed in the thought and judgment of reasonable and rational persons and applied by

content of Kant's moral conception are the product of the idealized reasoning of persons with specific rational and moral capacities.

A feature of Kant's moral constructivism that Rawls stresses that distinguishes it from other conceptions (e.g. intuitionism and utilitarianism), and which also holds for his own political constructivism, is that "a relatively complex conception of the person plays a central role in specifying the content of his moral view" (*LHMP*, p. 237). According to Rawls's understanding of both Kant's constructivism and his own political constructivism, the "procedure of construction" serves as a bridge or connecting device between the conception of the person and the content of the moral conception. Since Kant's conception of the person is indeed relatively complex, I can't give a full account here. But the obvious features are that persons have both empirical practical reason (including an interest in happiness and the capacity to set ends for oneself) and pure practical reason (including "personality" and the capacity to be moved by respect for morality),[9] they represent their rational nature as an end in itself and thus value the ability to exercise their rational capacities, they understand themselves to have autonomy and to act under the idea of freedom, they understand themselves to have equal dignity as ends in themselves, and so on. Again, for Kant these are necessary features of the practical standpoint, or of practical self-consciousness.[10]

From "Kantian Constructivism" on, Rawls presents justice as fairness as founded on and unfolding three closely linked "fundamental ideas," or "model conceptions" (as he puts it in "Kantian Constructivism") – (i) the ideal of a well-ordered society, or more generally an ideal of social cooperation (as involving fair terms of cooperation and an ideal of reciprocity that are fully realized in a well-ordered society), (ii) an idea of the person (as a free and equal moral person), and (iii) the idea of the original position (as a device for specifying the fair terms of cooperation between free and equal persons in a well-ordered society) (see *CP*, p. 308: the original position establishes "the connection between the model-conception of a moral person and the

---

them in their social and political practice. Those principles do not apply themselves, but are used by us in forming our intentions and actions, and plans and decisions, in our relations with other persons"; and *LHMP*, p. 241: "unless this conception and the powers of moral personality it includes – our humanity – are animated as it were, in human beings, the moral law would have no basis in the world."

[9] See *Religion* 6: 27–8.

[10] Regarding the interest in happiness, Kant thinks that it is a priori that human beings have this end. This end "can be presupposed surely, and a priori in the case of every human being, because it belongs to his essence" (*G* 4: 415–16).

principles of justice that characterize the relation of citizens in the model conception of a well-ordered society"). The original position is the procedure used to "construct" the content of the conception of justice, and in *PL* Rawls makes it clear that the "basis" of the procedure includes the idea of social cooperation and the ideal of a well-ordered society as well as the (political) conception of the person. Roughly, the content of the conception of justice is determined by asking what principles are rationally chosen by free and equal moral persons under fair conditions to serve as a public conception of justice that sets out the fair terms of social cooperation in a well-ordered society (where each element of the preceding phrase plays some role in determining the content of the principles). In this way "the political conception of citizens as cooperating in a well-ordered society shapes the content of political right and justice" (*PL*, p. 103). Rawls finds the same structural features in Kant's moral conception. He takes the "basis" of the CI-procedure to be Kant's conception of the person and the related ideal of moral community – "the conception of free and equal persons as reasonable and rational. . . along with the conception of a society of such persons, each of whom can be a legislative member of a realm of ends" (*LHMP*, p. 240). Again roughly, the idea is that the content of Kant's moral conception is to be derived by determining what principles reasonable and rational moral persons can will as universal law for a realm of ends, viz. that place interaction between persons on a footing of mutual respect and play the social role of enabling individuals to justify their conduct to each other.

That the conception of the person, and the associated ideals of moral community and of the social role of moral principles, are used to specify the content of Kant's moral conception (through the procedure of construction) means several things. First, since the "procedure of construction" incorporates a conception of the person and all the relevant requirements of practical reason, it models what persons who conceive of themselves as free and equal persons with certain rational and moral powers would will in conformity with these practical requirements. The normative authority of the resulting principles is based on the fact that this self-conception is a necessary feature of the practical standpoint. In this respect, the deliberative procedure is a way to specify the substantive normative commitments that are built into or follow from this self-conception. Second, I take it that Rawls thinks that unless a rich conception of the person (and the associated ideal of moral community) is incorporated into or modeled in the deliberative procedure, it could not generate a substantive moral conception. In this respect, much of the content of the moral conception is due to this complex conception of the person. For example, a procedure that applies the bare idea of universalizability to maxims would not generate interesting moral content. (Perhaps deceptive promising but not much else would be ruled out.) So one might argue that in order to address the "content problem" (*LHMP*, p. 163), FUL must be understood either to implicitly contain, or to be applied in conjunction with, ideas expressed by the other formulas of the categorical imperative, such as that of persons as agents with autonomy who are ends in themselves, the ideal of moral community expressed by the realm of ends, etc. In asking whether a maxim is rationally willed as universal law, we ask whether a principle could serve as universal law for agents with autonomy to serve the role of justification within a community of ends.[11]

The general point here is that Kant's "notion of autonomy" puts the conception of the person center stage, since it understands moral principles as resulting from an idealized process of practical reasoning to which we are committed by our (necessary) self-conception as free rational agents. The normative force of the principles that are the product of this form of reasoning is thus rooted in this self-conception.

10.3 The Kantian roots of the original position: an overview

Justice as fairness takes its inspiration from "Kant's notion of autonomy" in that it uses the idea of a fair and rational agreement between free and equal moral persons in the original position to derive principles of justice for the basic structure of society. Somewhat more specifically, justice as fairness tries to achieve consensus about the most reasonable conception of justice for a modern democratic society by determining what principles for specifying fair terms of social cooperation are reasonably chosen by free and equal moral persons simply as such persons – that is by setting out and carrying through a reasonable procedure of deliberation that models the freedom and equality of reasonable and rational moral persons and showing that this procedure leads to the two principles.

We have seen that the categorical imperative is a principle that states the fundamental requirement of morality and that (as understood by Rawls) can

---

[11] Barbara Herman develops such an approach in *The Practice*, especially Chapters 6, 7, and 10, and I pursue this line in *Agency*, Chapter 7. Note also that in Christine Korsgaard's reading of Kant (or Kantian theory) in *The Sources*, universal law by itself does not get us all the way to morality. Agents must think of themselves as citizens in a realm of ends (which is our necessary moral identity), so that the laws that they give to themselves range over all rational beings. See Korsgaard, *The Sources*, pp. 98–100.

be unpacked as a procedure that incorporates a conception of the person and represents "all the requirements of practical reason both pure and empirical" (with pure practical reason "framing" empirical practical reasoning). Working through the CI-procedure determines what more specific principles free rational agents will for themselves under the direction of practical reason (content), and moreover what principles we are committed to by our self-conception as such agents (authority). Rawls's original position is not itself a moral or political principle, but it is a procedure for "constructing" principles of social justice that "embodies all the relevant requirements of practical reason and shows how the principles of justice follow from the principles of practical reason in union with conceptions of society and person, themselves ideas of practical reason" (*PL*, p. 90). How so?

The idea, of course, is that the original position brings together an ideal of social cooperation and a conception of persons as citizens with different requirements of practical reason (of both the reasonable and the rational), including several intuitively acceptable restrictions on arguments for a conception of justice (*TJR*, pp. 15–19; *PL*, pp. 22–8). The relevant requirements of practical reason and "restrictions on reasons" (e.g. that principles of justice are to be applied in the circumstances of justice, that arbitrary inequalities in life prospects created by the basic structure are unfair) are normative ideas that individually are insufficient to ground determinate principles, but collected together in the original position do support a specific conception of justice. The original position thus shows what principles of justice for the basic structure are supported by deliberation that satisfies all the relevant requirements of practical reason among persons so conceived. It is a device for justifying and forging consensus on specific principles of justice over others by showing that they can be "unfolded out of" a complex ideal of society as a fair system of cooperation among free and equal moral persons (*PL*, pp. 27, 93) who are to establish the terms of their social cooperation themselves (*PL*, pp. 22–3). Moreover, the normative force of the principles is based in these ideas of the person and society. In effect, the principles represent normative commitments that follow from our (political) self-conception as free and equal moral persons engaged in social cooperation.

To elaborate, democratic citizens understand themselves to be free and equal moral persons. They have the two moral powers (a capacity for a sense of justice and a capacity to develop and pursue a conception of the good), a determinate conception of the good, and higher order interests in exercising their moral powers and advancing their "determinate but unknown final ends" (*CP*, p. 315). They conceive of themselves as free in various respects (as free to revise their conception of the good, as "self-originating sources of valid claims" on their institutions, and as responsible for their ends) and as having equal moral standing in virtue of possessing the moral powers to the degree needed to participate in social cooperation (*CP*, pp. 312–15, 330–3; *PL*, pp. 29–35). The original position is set up and the parties described in such a way that the parties "model" citizens as free and equal moral persons. The parties have the same moral powers and higher order interests as the citizens they represent (*CP*, pp. 312, 333–4; *PL*, pp. 73–7). Their good in abstract form is the exercise of these higher order interests. Their rationality is represented by their stipulated interest in primary social goods (as social conditions needed to act on their higher order interests), mutual disinterest among the parties (they are each concerned to advance their own higher order interests), and the assumption that the parties can enter into advantageous agreements and will not make agreements that they cannot keep (*TJR*, pp. 125–6). Note here that the rationality and mutual disinterest of the parties incorporate into the original position a number of intuitively acceptable conditions (of the rational) to impose on conceptions of justice, e.g. that the principles are to apply under the "circumstances of justice" (*TJR*, pp. 109–12), including the "fact of reasonable pluralism" that is a permanent feature of modern democratic social life (*PL*, p. 36), that a conception of social justice should protect individuals' essential interests, and that it should be stable (under the conditions of reasonable pluralism). The freedom, or "rational autonomy," of the parties (which models the freedom of citizens) has both a negative and a positive dimension that parallel Kant's conception of free agency.[12] The negative aspect, what we might call the "normative independence" of the parties, is that they are not bound by any prior principles of right but are free to make agreements in light of their own good; their independence is represented by the use of pure procedural justice in the original position (that whatever conception of justice the parties agree on is just). The positive dimension of their freedom is that they are moved by their higher order interests in exercising their moral powers and advancing their conception of

---

[12] For Kant the negative aspect of free agency is that the operation of the will "can be efficient independently of alien causes determining it" (*G* 4: 446). Kant means at least that the will operates independently of determination by natural causality – as normatively governed, it is governed other than by natural causality. Most commentators think that the negative aspect of free agency must also include a capacity for non-desire based motivation. (For a good discussion see Hill, "Kant's Argument," in *Dignity*.) The "positive concept" of freedom is the principle that positively guides the exercise of free agency – the principle that the will is to itself – that Kant identifies as the categorical imperative.

the good, again as represented by the interest in primary goods. (In Kantian terms, the interest in primary goods so understood provides the positive conception of the freedom or rational autonomy of the parties, the principle that guides their choice of principles of justice.)[13] Finally the moral equality of citizens is seen in the fact that all citizens are represented in the original position (in virtue of possessing the two moral powers "to the requisite minimum degree" (*PL*, p. 79)) and that under the veil of ignorance the choice situation is fair to all. More generally the veil of ignorance introduces a set of reasonable conditions that a conception of justice should satisfy – for example, that principles of justice should set out fair terms of cooperation that recognize citizens as moral equals, that "no one is to be advantaged or disadvantaged by natural contingencies or social chance in the adoption of principles" (*CP*, p. 310), and that arguments for a conception of justice should not be influenced by one's social position or natural endowments, that a conception of justice should be acceptable to citizens with conflicting conceptions of value, etc. Other features of the original position introduce further reasonable conditions, for example, that the basic structure of society is the first subject of justice or that principles of justice should satisfy various publicity conditions (as a way of expressing citizens' mutual respect (*TJR*, p. 156), as a condition of human freedom (*PL*, p. 68), etc.).[14] The structural features of the original position and the constraints imposed on the parties represent the "full autonomy" of citizens – roughly their capacity to affirm and to act from principles of justice that they give to themselves simply as free and equal moral persons. Once all this machinery is in place (and there is indeed a lot of machinery), Rawls can show that justice as fairness is the individually rational choice for the parties under these fair conditions, using both the maximin principle (*TJR*, §26) and the arguments from stability and self-respect (*TJR*, §29).

---

[13] Rawls points to another aspect of a version of Kantian negative freedom in his discussion of freedom as citizens' independence from their conception of the good. Citizens have the capacity to critically assess their final ends and revise them if they see reason to, for either reasons of justice or of rationality. (They also have the ability to adjust their ends to their fair share of social resources.) As Rawls says, "in this sense, they are independent from and moved by considerations other than those given by their conception of the good." The parties in the original position "do something analogous, but on a more abstract level" (*CP*, p. 335). Though the veil of ignorance deprives them of information about their final ends, they can still deliberate about and assess conceptions of justice because of their higher order interests in exercising their moral powers and pursuing their (indeterminate) conception of the good. That the parties can deliberate about conceptions of justice independently of the particulars of their actual final ends is another aspect of their "negative freedom."

[14] This list of "reasonable conditions" is not intended to be complete.

My point in going through this very familiar territory is to highlight the close structural parallels between Rawls's original position as a procedure of construction and Kant's CI-procedure (at least as Rawls understands it). By thinking through all the different features of the original position and the description of the parties, we can see how the choice in the original position models deliberation of free and equal moral persons that satisfies all the requirements of practical reason relevant to agreement on principles of social justice, both those based in individual rationality and those based in the reasonable. The "reasonable frames the rational" in the sense that the parties choose rationally based on their desire to maximize their individual share of primary goods, under the reasonable limiting conditions that are part of the structure of the original position, including the veil of ignorance. Furthermore, just as the categorical imperative determines what we will simply as free rational agents, the choice in the original position represents what principles of social justice free and equal moral persons would choose *simply as such persons*. Indeed, it is easier to give sense to this idea in Rawls's theory than in Kant's: the description of the parties as "artificial agents of construction" models the freedom, equality, and moral personality of the citizens whom they represent, and nothing more (*CP*, pp. 315–16, 321; *PL*, pp. 28, 72). Because the "thick veil of ignorance" (*CP*, pp. 335–6; *PL*, pp. 24ff.) deprives the parties of information about their circumstances and final ends, they are moved simply by the higher order interests that define their moral personality (*CP*, p. 336). What results from the original position are thus principles that free and equal moral persons have reason to choose simply as such persons.

Let me close this section by pointing to different forms of Kantian autonomy seen in justice as fairness. For Kant, autonomy of the will in the first instance is that the will gives itself its own fundamental principle, the categorical imperative: "autonomy is the property of the will by which it is a law to itself (independently of the property of any objects of volition)" (*G* 4: 440). As sketched above, Kant's thesis is that the nature of rational volition (say, the idea of pure practical reason informed by the conception of free rational agency) is the source of its own fundamental principle – the principle of pure practical reason – independently of any contingent interests. Particular categorical imperatives result from the application of this principle of pure practical reason to more specific volitions, and are in that sense principles that rational agents will for themselves through pure practical reason. (Both the categorical imperative and particular categorical imperatives are "autonomously legislated," though in somewhat different senses.) Second, the autonomy of the will so understood grounds the autonomy or sovereign standing of individual agents – that they are bound only to normative requirements that issue from their own reason. Third, agents with a good will can be said to "act autonomously," or realize the value of autonomy in their choices, when they act from principles that are autonomously legislated (through their own reason, independently of contingent desire-based interests) out of their understanding of the rational basis of these principles. All three forms of autonomy are seen in justice as fairness. First, the original position is based on the conception of free and equal moral persons plus the different requirements of practical reason. The original position represents citizens simply in terms of their freedom, equality, and moral personality, and the veil of ignorance excludes any factors external to their freedom, equality, and moral personality from influencing their choice of principles. Further, since the parties are moved by their higher order interests and the desire for primary goods, the abstract conception of their good likewise drops out of their moral personality. Once the original position as a procedure of construction is set up to model the conception of the person and the requirements of practical reason (compare: the will gives itself the categorical imperative), Rawls can say that citizens will the principles of justice for themselves simply as free and equal moral persons (compare: agents will particular categorical imperatives through pure practical reason). Second, Rawlsian citizens in a well-ordered society are bound in their political life only to the principles of justice that they have reason to choose simply as free and equal moral persons. And third, citizens realize an ideal of "full autonomy" when they affirm and act from principles of justice that they give to themselves simply as free and equal moral persons (independently of interests based on social and natural contingencies), out of their understanding of the public justification of these principles (*PL*, pp. 77–8).

10.4 The "Kantian Interpretation" of justice as fairness

In §40 of *TJ* we find Rawls's first discussion of several of the ideas developed in detail in "Kantian Constructivism." Rawls's first main point in this section is that justice as fairness uses the Kantian notion of autonomy to specify the content of justice. The argument from the original position is a way of rendering Kant's idea that moral principles derive from the free and purely rational willing of the agents subject to them, adapted to a conception of social justice for the basic structure. Rawls says that "the description of the original position is an attempt to interpret [Kant's] conception" that "moral legislation is to be agreed to under conditions that characterize men as free and equal rational beings" – here emphasizing the realm of ends formulation of the categorical imperative (*TJR*, p. 221). Toward the end of the section he writes:

> The original position may be viewed, then, as a procedural interpretation of Kant's conception of autonomy and the categorical imperative within the framework of an empirical theory. (*TJR*, p. 226)

The original position is a "procedural interpretation of Kant's conception of autonomy" in that it sets out a well-defined problem of choice and a procedure for resolving it in order to justify a specific conception of justice. Rational agents behind the veil of ignorance are to rank competing conceptions of justice for the basic structure in light of their desire for primary goods. The requirements of practical reason that bear on a conception of social justice are represented in different features of the descriptions of the parties and the original position, all of which can be enumerated as sketched in the previous section. In this way the original position sets out an explicit procedure for determining the content of the conception of justice most reasonably agreed to by free and equal moral persons as such.

Kant's theory of free agency and his aim of grounding the moral law in free agency is often thought to carry undesirable metaphysical baggage. For example, some readers interpret him to hold that moral principles are chosen by the transcendentally free noumenal self apart from the conditions of time.[15] Another feature of Rawls's "procedural interpretation" of Kantian autonomy is to steer clear of any such implications. In justice as fairness the idea of principles that represent the choice of free and equal moral persons as such is no longer "purely transcendent and lacking explicable connection with human conduct" (*TJR*, p. 226). For example, the freedom of citizens is "political not metaphysical," and the freedom of the parties is represented by the higher order interests in the exercise of their moral powers and the use of pure procedural justice in the original position. The "connection with human conduct" is achieved in part by introducing general empirical information into the original position (embedding "Kant's conception of autonomy... within the framework of an empirical theory"). For example, the parties are choosing principles to be employed in the circumstances of justice, which is a deep but empirical fact about human social life. Were that assumption changed, the content of or the need for a conception of justice

---

[15] For the record, I don't think that Kant should be read in this way, but I can't address that issue here.

would change.[16] Likewise, since the conception of justice is to be stable, the parties take general features of human psychology into account in ranking justice as fairness over the principle of utility (*TJR*, pp. 153–60 and chapter 8). Rawls says that among the "premises" of justice as fairness are "elementary facts about persons and their place in nature" (*TJR*, p. 226). In this respect, he departs from Kant, who held that the necessity and unconditional authority of morality is secured only if "the ground of obligation. . . [is] not sought in the nature of the human being or in the circumstances of the world in which he is placed, but a priori simply in concepts of pure reason" (*G* 4: 389).

Because the two principles of justice are reasonably agreed to by free and equal moral persons as such and thus represent normative commitments that follow from this conception of persons, Rawls says that the principles "are analogous to categorical imperatives" (*TJR*, p. 222). Categorical imperatives are a priori practical requirements that bind us simply as free rational agents, independently of our specific desires or ends. Granted, the parties choose the two principles in light of their higher order interests and the desire for primary goods, which model citizens' higher order interests in exercising their moral powers and pursuing their determinate conceptions of the good. But that does not make the principles hypothetical imperatives in Kant's sense. The applicability of a hypothetical imperative "depends on one's having an aim which one need not have as a condition of being a rational human being" (*TJR*, p. 223), but citizens have these higher order interests in virtue of their self-conception as free moral persons. The principles of justice thus apply to citizens simply as such persons, independently of their particular aims and conceptions of the good. But then one might ask, why are the principles only "analogous" to categorical imperatives? The answer may lie in empirical assumptions incorporated into the original position. The categorical imperative is based in pure practical reason strictly a priori and the particular categorical imperatives that it grounds inherit its unconditional authority. Because the choice of principles in the original position depends on some general empirical information about the conditions of human life, they would not have the unconditional rational necessity that Kant ascribes to categorical imperatives. I'll return to this point in concluding the final section.

A second important point that also first appears in *TJ* §40 is that in acting from principles that are rationally chosen in the original position, citizens

---

[16] Here compare Hume, *Treatise*, pp. 484–98, where he rejects the traditional view that principles of justice are eternal truths of reason since the utility of the conventions on which justice is based depend on contingent facts about human life.

"express their nature as free and equal rational beings subject to the general conditions of human life" (*TJR*, p. 222). For the most part, Part I of *TJ* is arguing for one conception of the content of social justice over alternatives. At this point, Rawls uses the Kantian idea of autonomy to take on an issue closer to Kant's aim of establishing the unconditional authority of morality – that it is reasonable to accept the deliberative priority of morality. The question here is whether there is good reason for citizens in a well-ordered society to recognize the deliberative priority of principles of justice as setting final limits on the pursuit of good – that is, to affirm their sense of justice as regulative of their life plans and the pursuit of their ends (*TJR*, pp. 497–8). Rawls addresses this question with the argument for the congruence of the right and the good, and the idea that citizens express their nature as free and equal moral persons by acting from the principles of justice is one component of the congruence argument.

Rawls explains the concept of "expression" as follows: "[T]o express one's nature as a being of a particular kind is to act on principles that would be chosen if this nature were the decisive determining element" (*TJR*, p. 222). The argument from the original position gives a clear sense to the claim that the two principles are what free and equal moral persons as such have reason to choose to regulate the terms of their association. Thus by acting on these principles citizens express their nature as free and equal moral persons. They realize the value of acting autonomously in a Kantian sense since they act from principles that they will for themselves simply as free and equal persons independently of social and natural contingencies.[17] Since expressing one's

---

[17] In explicating the concept of "expression" in this context, Rawls's aims to fill a lacuna in Kant's theory that Sidgwick's objection brings out – namely that Kant did not clearly explain why morally worthy choice expresses our nature as free and rational in ways that acting from morally indifferent or bad principles fails to. To show that acting from the principles of justice as regulative expresses our nature as free and equal persons, we first need to see (through the argument from the original position) that they are the principles endorsed by free and equal persons as such – "if this nature were the decisive determining element." The issue in Kant is due to an ambiguity in the idea of the noumenal self. Generally speaking, the noumenal self is the set of rational capacities in virtue of which we are active choosing selves. But is the "noumenal self" the purely rational self that wills the moral law as its fundamental principle of action, or is it the freely choosing self responsible for willing whatever maxims an agent adopts? It can be understood both ways. When Rawls says that the original position "is similar to the point of view from which noumenal selves see the world" or "resembles the point of view of noumenal selves, of what it means to be a free and equal person" (*TJR*, p. 225), he understands the noumenal self in the first sense – as the normative and rational capacities that define our rational nature, which make us active rational subjects. The argument from the original position spells out the normative commitments that are part of that self-conception.

nature as free and equal is part of one's good, it is rational for citizens from the point of view of their individual good to affirm the regulative priority of justice, and the stability of justice as fairness is secured.[18] This component of the congruence argument turns on a re-description of the content of the sense of justice that follows Kant's argumentative strategy in *Groundwork* II and III. As we saw above, the series of reformulations of the categorical imperative in *Groundwork* II contributes to the argument for the authority of morality in *Groundwork* III by showing that FUL, which expresses the fundamental demand of morality, is also the basic principle of free agency. Likewise, by accepting the regulative priority of and acting from principles of justice, citizens realize their nature as free and equal persons. As Rawls says, "the desire to act justly and the desire to express our nature as free moral persons turn out to specify what is practically speaking the same desire" (*TJR*, p. 501). In a well-ordered society that satisfies the full publicity condition, citizens' understanding of this equivalence would lead them to see just conduct as part of their good and would reinforce their commitment to upholding the demands of just institutions.

10.5 Further parallels and one possible difference

Earlier I said that the content of Kant's moral conception is constituted by what agents will under the direction of pure practical reason, but Rawls takes the CI-procedure to embody all the requirements of practical reason, both as pure and as empirically conditioned. Since these claims may seem to be in tension, some clarification is in order to see how in each theory normative content is generated by the way in which the "reasonable frames the rational."

The issue here is how much moral content can be derived a priori from pure practical reason in Kant's conception without introducing empirical information about human volition and interests. As suggested above, the condition of universal validity given by pure practical reason may be understood as the general principle that one is to act from maxims that are rationally willed as universal law for agents with autonomy in a community all of whose members are equally agents with autonomy. That is a substantial moral requirement, but it does not lead to a developed moral conception without

---

[18] See *TJR*, §86. This brief sketch of the congruence argument omits many details. For a thorough discussion (on which I have drawn), see Freeman, *Rawls*, Chapter 6. For discussion of why the requirements of a political conception of justice lead Rawls to abandon the congruence argument, see Freeman, *Rawls*, pp. 315–23.

more input. However further a priori features of rational agency are available to Kant that, in conjunction with the condition of universal validity, take us closer to a developed moral conception. It is an a priori feature of (at least) finite rational agency that agents set ends for themselves through their own practical judgments and have the end of happiness. Furthermore, rational agents *necessarily* act under the idea of freedom. That is to say that it is a necessary feature of practical self-consciousness that rational agents under-stand themselves to be free agents – that their judgments about practical reasons are determined only by their own application of relevant practical principles, and not by anything external to their use of their normative capacities.[19] In this way, rational agents understand themselves to be the sources of their ends and actions through their own practical judgments. If these a priori elements of the self-conception of free rational agency are incorporated into the categorical imperative, it becomes the principle of acting only from maxims that can serve as universal law for a community of agents with autonomy who set their own ends and necessarily act under the idea of freedom, that is, who conceive of themselves as the sources of their ends and actions through their own practical judgments. This is the basic normative commitment that follows from our self-conception as free rational agents with autonomy.

This principle of the pure will is a substantial moral requirement that regulates the more specific rational willing of human agents, both shaping and limiting their final ends and the means thereto. It contains enough to rule out maxims of action whose universal adoption undermines the conditions of autonomous agency and, moreover, undermines the self-conception of agents as acting under the idea of freedom. Universalization of such maxims is in contradiction with one's self-conception as a free agent with autonomy. Furthermore, I believe that this principle requires the end of supporting the possibility of autonomous conduct in others and oneself. Thus by incorpor-ating necessary features of our self-conception as rational agents into the condition of universal validity that comes from pure practical reason, we approach the outlines of Kant's moral conception – all on a priori grounds.[20]

---

[19] See *G* 4: 448. As stated there, the "idea of freedom" is that reason does not "consciously receive direction from any other quarter with respect to its judgments, since the subject would then attribute the determination of his judgment not to his reason but to an impulse. Reason must think of itself as the author of its principles, independently of alien influences; conse-quently, as practical reason or as the will of a rational being it must be regarded as of itself free."

[20] This idea is developed in Herman, *The Practice*, pp. 113–31 and Reath, *Agency*, pp. 211–20.

Still, to get all the way to the familiar prohibitions on interferences with freedom, coercion, and deception, and so on, and to the obligatory ends of our own perfection and the happiness of others, we need to introduce more of the material conditions of human agency, and one way to do this is to apply the principle of pure practical reason to the kinds of principles that agents are inclined to adopt as rational means to their final ends, including their own happiness. The full content of Kant's moral conception then comes from what is willed by agents in the business of leading human lives (with an interest in happiness, etc.) who follow all the requirements of practical reason, etc. It is what they will under the direction of pure practical reason in the sense that the basic moral requirement regulates (both shapes and limits) the pursuit of their discretionary final ends, that is, in the sense that the reasonable frames the rational.

If one accepts this reading of Kant, the structural parallels between the ways in which Kant's conception and the argument from the original position lead to substantive normative principles are very close indeed. The conception of persons as free persons with equal moral standing and the reasonable conditions on conceptions of justice by themselves lead to a very general requirement of social justice, e.g. that principles of social justice for the basic structure should establish terms of social cooperation that are fair to all citizens as free and equals, that justify the social order to each citizen and provide public recognition of each citizen's worth, that give each citizen equal opportunity to pursue their conception of the good, etc. But this requirement of the reasonable is not quite a *conception* of social justice. At this point justice as fairness advances by introducing the abstract conception of the good of each person (the rational) that is based on the conception of the person – that being the higher order interest in the exercise of their moral powers that leads to the interest in primary goods. The parties at this point also have general empirical information about the conditions of human life. We now have the set-up of the original position: that rational agents of construction with a desire to further their own good in abstract form choose a conception of justice under the fair conditions imposed by the reasonable. When the reasonable in this way constrains the rational deliberations of the parties, Rawls's two principles result.

Let me close by considering a possible difference between Kant's and Rawls's conceptions of the person. In each case, they are *self*-conceptions – ways in which persons understand themselves – with normative implications. Kant's conception of the person is a priori and rationally necessary in that it is based on necessary features of the practical standpoint. That is, in occupying the practical standpoint, we understand ourselves to be agents with both empirical and pure practical reason, who act under the idea of freedom, who regard ourselves as ends in themselves, etc. These are necessary features of practical self-consciousness with normative implications. In contrast, I do not think that Rawls takes citizens' self-conception as free and equal moral persons to be rationally necessary in this sense, nor does he need to as long as it reflects deep features of the way we think of ourselves in our social order. But certainly this conception of the person is not contingent and merely empirically given, or, say, rationally discretionary. Is it then a priori in some sense other than Kant's? Perhaps this question is misplaced. Rawls refers to the conception of the person (and society) as "ideas" or "conceptions of practical reason," and in explanation says only that "they characterize the agents who reason and they specify the context for the problems and questions to which principles of practical reason apply" (*PL*, pp. 107–8; cf. pp. 90, 109). This remark suggests that they are ways of thinking of ourselves and others that are "prior to" and that shape specific choices of action, ends, interaction with others, life plans, and so on. Some elements of Rawls's conception may be rationally necessary in Kant's sense (perhaps possession of the two moral powers or equal basic moral worth), but I take it that Rawls sees no need to maintain a sharp distinction between purely a priori features of citizens' self-conception and those drawn from general, empirically given conditions of human life (See *TJR*, pp. 226–7; *CP*, pp. 303–4).

I speculate that the difference in their views here is that while Kant's conception of the person contains necessary features of practical self-consciousness given to us simply by occupying the practical standpoint, for Rawls the conception of the person has a social and institutional basis. It is a conception that is reflected in our social structures and political institutions that is made available to us by our participation in those structures. This difference in the bases of their conception of the person is a question that is worth pursuing, but on another occasion.

11   Stability and the original position from *Theory* to *Political Liberalism*

Paul Weithman

A conception of justice is stable when members of a society adhere to it over time, so that their basic institutions remain in conformity with its principles of justice. Since Rawls argued that justice as fairness "generates its own supportive moral attitudes" (*TJ*, p. 350), his conception of justice would be *self*-stabilizing. He seems to suggest at one point that the part of his conception that would do the self-stabilizing is his principles of justice (*TJ*, p. 119). In this chapter, I shall argue that it is illuminating to think of stability as effected, not by Rawls's *principles*, but by *the agreement upon them*. More precisely, it is illuminating to read Rawls as arguing that justice as fairness would stabilize itself because the agreement reached in the original position is a special kind of what is sometimes called a "self-enforcing agreement."

One advantage of this reading, as we shall see in section 11.6, is that it offers a clear and economical way of understanding what it is for a conception to be self-stabilizing. Rawls averred that self-stabilization tells strongly in a conception's favor, but he does not say why (*TJ*, p. 154). The interpretation offered here suggests an answer to that question. Another advantage, which we shall see in section 11.7, is that it offers a precise understanding of Rawls's transition to political liberalism. Rawls said he made the turn to political liberalism because he came to think that the stability arguments of *TJ* failed. My reading explains that failure as the failure of the agreement reached in the original position to satisfy two of the conditions of self-enforcement. This reading also helps us understand the account of stability Rawls offered in *PL* by displaying new conditions of self-enforcement and by showing how the later Rawls could maintain that the agreement reached in the original position satisfied them. Finally, we shall see in section 11.8 that because this reading highlights the importance of the original position in Rawls's treatments of stability, it helps to answer the much-controverted question of whether the original position is

Thanks to David Estlund and Timothy Hinton for their comments on an earlier draft.

essential to Rawls's theory. It does so by identifying a crucial premise in both his accounts of stability that depends upon his reasons for devising it.

We shall see that for Rawls both early and late, the agreement reached in the original position is able to enforce itself because of its representative function. It will therefore be useful to begin by recalling what Rawls meant by saying that in *TJ*, the original position had been used as a "device of representation" (*PL*, p. xxxvi).

11.1 The original position as a device of representation

Rawls chose the characteristics with which he endowed the parties in the original position – their rationality, mutual disinterest, desire for primary goods, and interest in the subsequent development and exercise of their moral powers – and imposed a veil of ignorance on them – so that the original position would be "a state of affairs in which the parties are equally represented as moral persons" (*TJ*, p. 22). So in devising the original position, Rawls relied on and elaborated a basic intuitive idea of the human. The contents of that idea are not, as Rawls thought critics of *TJ* had charged, properties which are metaphysically necessary for counting as a human being. Rather, the idea was what we might call a basic intuitive "idea of moral personality." In *TJ*, the original position functioned as a device for representing the contents of that idea. More precisely, the original position functioned as a device for representing human beings as possessed of moral personality – for short: as a device for representing us as free and equal persons. The original position functioned that way because Rawls devised it for exactly that purpose. To see how the representative function of the original position figures in Rawls's treatment of stability, we need to see the conditions of self-enforcing agreements.

11.2 The conditions of self-enforcement

The notion of a self-enforcing agreement is drawn from the theory of non-cooperative games. These are games in which players can communicate, but in which agreements reached on the basis of communication are not binding because there is no mechanism – e.g. an agent with coercive power over the players – for enforcing whatever agreements they reach.[1] Crudely put, an

---

[1] The locus classicus of the distinction between cooperative and non-cooperative games is Harsanyi, "A General Theory," p. 616.

agreement reached under these conditions is *self-enforcing* when parties to the agreement freely uphold it, and when the agreement itself is what ensures that it is freely upheld.

While I am not aware of literature in which the conditions of self-enforcing agreements are explicitly laid out, there seem to be three that such agreements must satisfy. First, trivially:

> (1) The principles that the players are to follow – the strategies they are to play – must be specified by the terms of an agreement or contract among them.

Second, if the agreement is actually to be upheld, none of the parties to it can deviate from its terms. Since deviation is not prevented by an enforcement mechanism, the terms agreed to must be an equilibrium. So:

> (2) None of the parties to the contract referred to in (1) can have sufficient reason to deviate from its terms, at least so long as all the other parties comply with them.

But this condition is too weak. Games can have multiple equilibria. An agreement on terms which define one of them will enforce itself only if it is an agreement on the terms parties to the agreement actually honor. Indeed, the point of a pre-play agreement might be to coordinate on the selection of one equilibrium-state among many. This suggests a strengthened version of (2):

> (2′) None of the parties to the contract referred to in (1) can have sufficient reason to deviate from its terms, at least so long as all the other parties comply with them, and all the others do comply.

Third, an agreement to do what parties are going to do anyway is otiose, and is therefore not an agreement which brings about or enforces compliance with its own terms.[2] And so:

> (3) The fact that the terms were agreed to in the contract referred to in (1) must be what brings it about that all the parties comply with them.

The agreement that Rawls wanted to show would be self-enforcing is an agreement on principles of justice. These are moral principles, needed to play a public role and capable of moving us to act for their own sake. The conditions on self-enforcing agreements need to be strengthened for that special case.

---

[2] Aumann, "Nash Equilibria," pp. 615–20.

First, Rawls thought an agreement for the special case had to be reached in special circumstances. "[T]he guiding idea" of his theory says what those circumstances are: principles of justice "are the principles that free and rational persons concerned to further their own interests would accept in an initial position of equality" (*TJ*, p. 11). So while (1) is a trivial condition on self-enforcing agreements, the strengthened version of it is the non-trivial:

> (R1) The principles of justice that members of the well-ordered society are to follow must be specified by the terms of an agreement or contract among them, conceived as "moral persons, as creatures having a conception of their good and capable of a sense of justice" (*TJ*, p. 19).

To see how the second condition should be strengthened, recall the attraction of self-enforcing agreements. Self-enforcing agreements are attractive because they are maintained without coercion, and so are freely honored in some sense of "freely." The agreement reached in the original position is to be honored by members of a society whose basic institutions satisfy the principles. Rawls wants them to honor that agreement while exercising an especially robust kind of freedom, freedom which characterizes the lives of moral persons as such. The Rawlsian version of (2') has to require that the agreement be honored by conduct realizing freedom of that kind. This suggests that the strengthened version of (2') should be a conjunction, with one conjunct expressing the requirement:

> (R2') None of the members of the well-ordered society can have sufficient reason to deviate from the principles of justice, at least so long as all the others comply with them, and all do comply by conducting themselves as "moral persons, as creatures having a conception of their good and capable of a sense of justice" (*TJ*, p. 19).

Finally, the strengthened versions of (1) and (2) suggest a way of strengthening (3):

> (R3) The fact that the principles were agreed to in the contract referred to in (R1) must be what brings it about that members of the well-ordered society comply with it, as (R2') requires, and the connection between the contract and the conduct referred to by (R2') must be established in ways which treat members of the well-ordered society as "moral persons, as creatures having a conception of their good and capable of a sense of justice" (*TJ*, p. 19).

But Rawls insists that the agreement on his principles must be hypothetical rather than actual (*PL*, pp. 271ff.). The hypothetical character of the agreement poses a serious problem for this way of strengthening (3). To see why, it will help to recall (3)'s rationale.

As I said when introducing them, self-enforcing agreements cannot be otiose or redundant, as an agreement would be if it was simply a contract to do what parties were going to do anyway. Version (3) responds to the intuition that an agreement can be self-enforcing only if the agreement itself makes a difference to what parties do. That is (3)'s rationale. (R3) incorporates (3)'s response by requiring a connection between a self-enforcing agreement and the conduct maintaining it which is *efficacious*. Self-enforcing agreements are agreements in which payoffs provide the parties sufficient reasons to comply. Agreements can make a difference in what parties do by bringing it about that the expected payoffs of the agreement provide such reasons.[3] If an agreement makes this kind of difference, its connection with the conduct which maintains it is *causally* efficacious. But merely hypothetical agreements cannot exercise causal power. Since the connection (R3) requires is causal, it states a condition which the agreement reached in the original position cannot satisfy. Moreover, because hypothetical agreements cannot exercise causal power, they cannot enforce themselves. So the claim that the agreement reached in the original position would be self-enforcing seems mistaken, and the attempt to identify conditions under which it would be seems wrongheaded from the start.

Non-actual agreements cannot exercise causal powers, but institutions that are known to satisfy the terms of such an agreement, and that are modeled on the conditions in which such an agreement would be made, *can* exercise them. They can do so by educating those who live under them so that they come to find the payoffs of honoring the agreement high enough to comply. That education connects the hypothetical agreement with conduct that honors its terms. But there are constraints the connection must satisfy. And so the proper way to strengthen (3) yields not (R3) but:

> (R3') The fact that the principles would be agreed to in the contract referred to in (R1) must be what brings it about that members of the well-ordered society comply with them, as (R2') requires, and the connection between the hypothetical agreement and the conduct referred to by (R2') must itself be established in ways which treat members of the well-ordered society as "moral persons, as creatures having a conception of their good and capable of a sense of justice" (*TJ*, p. 19).

---

[3] Aumann's example is one in which a pre-play agreement affects each player's choice of strategy by conveying information about which strategies others intend to play.

Conditions (R1), (R2′) and (R3′) are jointly sufficient for an agreement to be what I shall call "Rawlsian self-enforcing." In the next three sections, I argue that an agreement reached in the original position meets these conditions. This will show that Rawls used the original position, not just to identify the right principles of justice, but also to say how those principles should be institutionalized so that they would be freely complied with. As we shall see, he was able to use the original position in these ways because it represents us as free and equal moral persons.

11.3 Satisfying (R1)

(R1) requires:

> (R1) The principles of justice that members of the well-ordered society are to follow must be specified by the terms of an agreement or contract among them, conceived as "moral persons, as creatures having a conception of their good and capable of a sense of justice" (*TJ*, p. 19).

Rawls's argument that his principles would be chosen in the original position has been examined as extensively as any argument in contemporary philosophy. I believe his positive arguments for the claim that the original position is the "philosophically most favored interpretation of th[e] initial choice situation for the purposes of a theory of justice" (*TJ*, p. 16) are well understood. The positive arguments that can be offered for thinking the agreement reached in the original position satisfies (R1) are therefore easy to see. Moreover, it is well understood that the original position is philosophically most favored, and hence that (R1) is satisfied, because the original position represents the features of moral personality. Since these points are well understood, I shall not belabor them.

Rawls's comparisons with philosophically *less* favored interpretations of the initial situation helpfully clarify his reasons for endorsing (R1), for thinking that agreements reached in the original position satisfy it, and for thinking they satisfy it because of what the original position represents.

Rawls contrasts the agreement reached in the original position with an equilibrium reached as a result of agreements made among willing traders with full information (*TJ*, pp. 119–20). He contends that the former agreements but not the latter are just "whatever they turn out to be" because of the conditions of the original position. In "Basic Structure as Subject," he contrasts the contract made in the original position with that made in Locke's state of nature. He argues that the latter unjustly deprives the property-less of suffrage because the well off in Locke's state of nature know, and so can use the power that accrues because of, their property holdings (*PL*, p. 287).

The problem with economic markets and a Lockean state of nature is that they allow agreements reached in them to be affected by differences in bargaining power.[4] This is true even of self-enforcing agreements reached in them, which is why condition (1) on self-enforcing agreements proved too weak for Rawls's purposes. The original position improves on markets and on Locke's state of nature by using the veil of ignorance to block the influence of power differentials. The agreement reached in the original position therefore satisfies the stronger and more plausible (R1). The conditions of the original position are appropriate for the choice of principles because they force the content of agreements reached in it to depend only upon the shared features of moral personality. As Rawls puts it in a passage to which I shall return, in the original position our "nature [is] the decisive determining element" of the choice (*TJ*, p. 253).

11.4 Satisfying (R2′)

(R2′) requires:

> (R2′) None of the members of the well-ordered society can have sufficient reason to deviate from the principles of justice, at least so long as all the others comply with them, and all do comply by conducting themselves as "moral persons, as creatures having a conception of their good and capable of a sense of justice" (*TJ*, p. 19).

(R2′) is a conjunction. The argument that the agreement reached in the original position satisfies it assumes what Rawls tries to show in *TJ*, Chapter 8: members of the well-ordered society have a sense of justice, including a powerful, standing desire to act from principles of justice. The argument proceeds in two steps, corresponding to the condition's two conjuncts.

To see how the first step goes, we need to see why members of the well-ordered society want to act from the principles. The answer, Rawls says, is that by acting from them, members of the well-ordered society express their nature as moral persons. Call this "the expression claim." Rawls does not say what he means by "express" and its cognates. I take the notion to be adverbial – more specifically, to characterize the way someone lives or conducts

---

[4] Rawls, *LHPP*, pp. 150–2.

herself. To express one's nature as a moral person is to live as one. It is to exercise the features of moral personality, and thus to live in ways characteristic of a being who has those features. So the expression claim says that to act from a desire to comply with principles of justice is to live as such a being. Since acting from a desire to comply with the principles is the same as acting on them, we can recast the expression claim as the claim that to act on the principles is to conduct oneself as a moral person.

Rawls's defense of the expression claim so construed depends on a premise he states in *TJ*, §40, on the Kantian interpretation:

> to express one's nature as a being of a particular kind is to act on the principles that would be chosen if this nature were the decisive determining element. (*TJ*, p. 253)

The abstractness of this premise makes it difficult to assess. We can get some purchase on it by thinking about the case which interests Rawls, moral persons. Moral persons express their nature as such, or live as such, when they act freely. Rawls thinks that the relevant kind of freedom is autonomy, hence that moral persons act freely when they act from principles they would give themselves. When their nature as moral persons determines the principles they choose, those principles are ones they choose or give themselves as persons with that nature. Since members of the well-ordered society are represented as moral persons in the original position, their nature as such persons is "the decisive determining element" in the choice of principles there.

This conclusion, together with the expression claim, implies that if human beings act on the principles, they express their nature – and so conduct themselves – as "moral persons ... capable of a sense of justice." This implication gets us part way toward showing that agreements reached in the original position satisfy the second conjunct of (R2′), which requires that members of the well-ordered society comply with the principles by conducting themselves as "moral persons ... having a conception of their own good and capable of sense of justice." But pursuing this implication would get us ahead of ourselves; we first have to see whether members of the well-ordered society would act on their sense of justice and comply with the principles. To see that they would, we need to see why the first conjunct of (R2′) is satisfied. Though members of the well-ordered society are assumed to have a sense of justice, they may have desires which provide sufficient reasons to deviate from the principles. Then their conceptions of their good would undermine the agreement reached in the original position.

Rawls addresses this worry late in *TJ*, in §86. His arguments are compli-cated, and I have laid them out elsewhere.[5] Very roughly, Rawls thinks members of the well-ordered society have a strong desire to be just persons under that description. They can satisfy it only by regulating their plans and conduct by their sense of justice. Since the desire is strong and since – like all their rational desires, it belongs to their good – their conceptions of their good move them to honor the principles. Rawls also argues that whatever else members of the well-ordered society want, they have a powerful desire to express their nature as free and equal rational beings under *that* descrip-tion. That desire, too, belongs to their good. Since desires are individuated by descriptions of their objects, it is a different desire from the desire to be a just person. But it follows from the expression claim that the desire to express one's nature – like the desire to be a just person – can be satisfied only by regulating one's plans by principles that would be chosen in the original position. Since members of the well-ordered society all have a "lucid grasp" of justice as fairness (*TJ*, p. 572), each would *know* she can express her nature only by treating principles of justice as regulative, at least if others do likewise. Rawls concludes that each member of the well-ordered society would plan to preserve and act from her sense of justice as regulative, at least if others do.

This argument is meant to show that in a well-ordered society, each person's plan to be just is what Rawls calls her "best reply" to the similar plans of others (*TJ*, p. 568). Since a Nash equilibrium is a strategy combin-ation in which each player's strategy is the best reply to the strategies of the other players, his use of "best reply" suggests that he thinks these plans or conceptions of the good – taken together – are such an equilibrium. The equilibrium supports the agreement that would be reached in the original position. For when it obtains, each affirms that the sense of justice is itself good for her. Then no one has sufficient reason to deviate from the demands of justice, as the first conjunct of (R2′) requires. Each reaffirms her plan to pursue her good justly and everyone complies with the principles, as the second conjunct requires.

The second conjunct of (R2′) requires not just that members of the well-ordered society comply with the principles, but that they do so "by conduct-ing themselves as 'moral persons, as creatures having a conception of their good and capable of a sense of justice.'" We have seen that when they comply

---

[5] Weithman, *Why Political Liberalism?*

with the principles, they conduct themselves as "moral persons ... capable of a sense of justice." What of the other feature of moral personality referred to in (R2′)? Do members of the well-ordered society who treat principles of justice as regulative comply by "conducting themselves as 'moral persons ... having a conception of their good'"?

The question assumes a distinction where there is no difference. What the principles of justice are regulative *of* is someone's pursuit of her plan of life. To treat the principles as regulative is therefore to pursue one's plan in a certain way, a way characteristic of a moral person. Each person's plan gives her conception of the good. Since members of the well-ordered society would comply with principles agreed to in the original position by conduct characteristic of creatures capable of a sense of justice, they *ipso facto* comply with them by conduct characteristic of creatures with conceptions of their good as well. The agreement that would be reached in the original position therefore satisfies (R2′).

11.5 Satisfying (R3′)

(R3′) requires:

> (R3′) The fact that the principles would be agreed to in the contract referred to in (R1) must be what brings it about that members of the well-ordered society comply with them, as (R2′) requires, and the connection between the hypothetical agreement and the conduct referred to by (R2′) must itself be established in ways which treat members of the well-ordered society as "moral persons, as creatures having a conception of their good and capable of a sense of justice" (*TJ*, p. 19).

We saw in the previous section that members of the well-ordered society comply with principles of justice by acting on their desires to be just persons and to express their nature as moral persons, as (R2′) requires. We will see that the agreement reached in the original position satisfies the first conjunct of (R3′) by seeing how those desires depend on the fact that the principles would be accepted in the original position. I said when introducing (R3′) that the dependence is causal and that hypothetical agreements lack causal powers. But I suggested that the *fact* that principles of justice would be the object of a hypothetical agreement could cause compliance, and that it could do so by educating citizens via institutions which satisfy the principles and are modeled on the hypothetical agreement. I want to elaborate that suggestion, arguing that the institutions of a well-ordered society educate its members by encouraging the desires that motivate compliance, and that they do so in ways which satisfy the second conjunct of (R3′).

I assume Rawls's argument that members of a well-ordered society would develop a sense of justice is familiar since it has attracted considerable critical attention. But one feature of the sense of justice has attracted surprisingly little notice, given its great importance. That is that the sense of justice includes not only a desire to comply with the principles, but also the aspiration to live up to various "ideals" – to various conceptions of what we might be (*TJ*, p. 473).

The ideals to which members of the well-ordered society aspire include that of a just person and that of someone whose conduct expresses her nature as a moral person. It was crucial to the arguments of the previous section that members of the well-ordered society desire to live up to both ideals and that they know they can live up to the second only by living up to the first. Yet beyond one remark which might be construed to imply that the second ideal "exercises a natural attraction upon our affections" (*TJ*, p. 478), Rawls says little about where the desire to live up to that ideal comes from. And beyond his remark that members of the well-ordered society have a "lucid grasp" of justice as fairness, he says little about how they know that the two ideals coincide in their demands. To show that the agreement reached in the original position satisfies (R3′), I need to supply the details.

The most important detail is that justice as fairness is subject to "the full publicity condition" (*CP*, pp. 324–6). This condition requires that all its aspects be part of the public culture of a well-ordered society. The original position, the ways in which it represents moral personality, and the necessity of acting from principles chosen there for the expression of our nature as moral persons, would all be "publicly available" to members of the well-ordered society (*CP*, p. 324). Public officials will appeal to these ideas to justify policies and court decisions as outcomes which could be arrived at by free and equal moral persons, concerned to implement principles chosen in the original position. These appeals reinforce the ideal of free and equal moral persons, already familiar from the public culture. They also suggest to members of the well-ordered society that they can live as such persons only if they comply with those policies and decisions. The justifiability of the outcomes makes the ideal underlying their justification attractive, and elicits a desire to live up to it.

The claim that this is what Rawls thinks – and the dependence of this line of thought on the representational function of the original position – can be substantiated by Rawls's discussion of the points of view from which political decisions are to be made and court cases to be decided. In §31 of *TJ*, Rawls introduced the "four-stage sequence" for arriving at and implementing his two principles. The first stage is the original position, the second a constitutional convention, the third the "legislative stage," and the fourth the judicial stage. The stages form a sequence because the conditions of later stages are specified with reference to those preceding them. Progressively more information is made available to parties at succeeding stages, and parties at later stages are faced with choice-problems which are constrained by choices made at earlier ones.

The original position enjoys a conceptual priority in the definition of the sequence. Since later stages can be viewed as its "descendants," the original position gives the sequence a "genetic" unity. But it may not be clear that Rawls gave the original position priority in virtue of its representing moral personality. Even if he did, it might seem clear that later stages in the sequence cannot "inherit" this representative function. For parties at later stages are not represented *just* as free and equal moral persons since they have access to information about themselves and their society. The four-stage sequence may be "a device for applying the principles of justice" (*TJ*, p. 200), but it seems not to be a device *of representation*.

But an important remark late in *TJ* suggests otherwise. At the end of the section on the "Unity of the Self," Rawls says "the notion guiding the entire construction [of the four-stage sequence] is the original position and its Kantian interpretation" (*TJ*, p. 566). The remark occurs in Rawls's argument for the claim that principles of justice and the rules that implement them do not establish a dominant end, but rather "approximate the boundaries" within which people are free to choose plans of life (*TJ*, p. 566). The implication of this claim is that while principles of justice, the constitution, laws and judicial decisions of a well-ordered society may all limit human conduct, in justice as fairness they do so consistently with human freedom.

If freedom is understood as "autonomy," as I believe it must be, this can be true only if at each stage, the rules adopted are in some sense ones we give or would give ourselves. They might not be ones we would give ourselves as free and equal rational beings – for while our nature as such beings might serve as the "decisive determining element" in the original position (*TJ*, p. 253), it is too indeterminate to guide the choice of legislation. But they are ones we would give ourselves as free and equal authors of a constitution or free and equal legislators. If this is correct, the core ideas of freedom and equality are adapted to the demands of each stage in the four-stage sequence.[6] The adaptation is *of* those ideas *as modeled in the original position.* That is why Rawls says the original position "guid[es]" construction of the sequence. So the original position is given definitional priority in that sequence, and gives it genetic unity, because it is a device for representing moral personality. The use of that device by public officials, public knowledge of its use, and its availability to citizens who want to think through political and judicial questions for themselves (*TJ*, p. 473), all educate citizens in the ideal of moral personality it represents. Members of the well-ordered society then incorporate that ideal into their conceptions of the good as an end desirable for its own sake.

Rawls describes this moral education near the end of his second Dewey Lecture, saying that when the full publicity condition is satisfied:

> The derivation of citizens' rights, liberties and opportunities invokes a certain conception of their person. In this way citizens are made aware of and educated to this conception. They are presented with a way of regarding themselves that otherwise they would most likely never have been able to entertain. Thus the realization of the full publicity condition provides the social milieu within which the notion of full autonomy can be understood and within which its ideal of the person can elicit an effective desire to be that kind of person. (*CP*, pp. 339–40)

The argument which I have imputed to Rawls in this section, and which is summarized in the quoted passage, shows that the agreement that would be reached in the original position satisfies the first conjunct of (R3′). In *TJ*, §78, Rawls offers what is, in effect, a sequence of powerful arguments for the conclusion that the second conjunct is satisfied. He says that in the well-ordered society, each person's "moral education itself has been regulated by the principles of right and justice he would consent to in an initial situation in which all have equal representation as moral persons" (*TJ*, pp. 514–15). He offers further argument for this conclusion in his defense of full publicity. He argues that the condition is "fitting" because a society's conception of justice shapes the characters of its citizens, and this is consistent with treating them as free persons only if they can examine the conception and understand its effects on them (*CP*, pp. 325–6). If these arguments are sound, as I believe

---

[6] As if to confirm, Rawls says that "the constitutional process should preserve the equal representation of the original position to the degree that this is practicable" (*TJ*, p. 222).

they are, then the agreement reached in the original position satisfies (R3′) as well as (R1) and (R2′). That agreement is *Rawlsian self-enforcing*.

11.6 Taking stock: the appeal of self-enforcement

The fact that the agreement which would be reached in the original position would be Rawlsian self-enforcing means that the citizens of the well-ordered society would honor the principles of justice over time and maintain the justice of their basic institutions. And so it means that the well-ordered society would be stably just, hence that justice as fairness would be stable. The concept of Rawlsian self-enforcement therefore provides a way of expressing precisely what is meant by the claim that justice as fairness would be self-stabilizing or self-supporting.

One advantage of this form of expression is that it suggests why it is "a strong point in favor of a conception of justice . . . that it generates its own support" (*TJ*, p. 154). For it may seem, and has seemed to many thinkers in the history of political philosophy, that the benefits of social cooperation can be had only at the cost of freedom. Hobbes seems most pointedly to have raised this worry by arguing that the agreement to enter into a social order can be sustained only if the parties to the agreement also submit themselves to an absolute sovereign. Self-enforcing agreements are attractive because they are honored without such a mechanism of enforcement. Instead, parties to these agreements honor them because of the payoffs of doing so, which they judge superior to the payoffs of deviation. So as I noted earlier, agreements which satisfy the conditions on self-enforcement are honored freely, in some sense of "freely." How valuable that kind of freedom is depends upon how the payoffs move parties to the agreement and how the parties have come to value those payoffs.

The conditions of Rawlsian self-enforcement strengthen those of self-enforcement *simpliciter* by adding significant moral demands. As we saw, agreements which are Rawlsian self-enforcing are upheld by parties who value being just persons and expressing their nature, and who regard the payoffs they could gain from violating the principles as being "without value" (*CP*, p. 106). Members of the well-ordered society have the payoff-structure they do because they have been educated to be persons with those values by processes which they can see to be consistent with their freedom and equality. Agreements which satisfy the Rawlsian conditions are therefore upheld by parties who conduct themselves as free and equal moral persons. Because of the conditions of the original position, the kind of freedom they realize in their conduct is freedom of an especially robust kind. For in regulating their pursuits by principles they would adopt there, members of the well ordered society act autonomously. So once self-support is understood using the concept of Rawlsian self-enforcement, we can see why it counts in favor of a conception of justice that it be self-supporting: when society is well ordered by such a conception, its members realize the benefits of cooperation without sacrificing their autonomy.

I said that the reading advanced here also offers a precise understanding of Rawls's transition to political liberalism. Let us now turn to that transition.

11.7 The turn to political liberalism

Rawls famously opens *TJ*, §1, by observing that "justice is the first virtue of social institutions." He continues immediately "as truth is of systems of thought. A theory however elegant and economical must be rejected or revised if it is untrue[.]" The remark was prescient. The social contract theory presented in *TJ* was elegant and economical; as should be clear by now, part of its elegance and economy was due to the fact that the contract drawn up in *TJ*, Part I was shown to be self-enforcing in *TJ*, Part III. But Rawls came to believe that not all the theory's claims could be true, since it suffered from an inconsistency between "the account of stability given in part III of *Theory*" and "the view as a whole" (*PL*, pp. xvii–xviii). Where is the inconsistency?

As we saw in the section on (R2′), Rawls's stability argument depends on his claim that everyone in the well-ordered society would want to express her nature as a moral person by conducting herself autonomously. And as we saw in the section on (R3′), Rawls thought that that desire would be elicited by public knowledge and institutionalization of the agreement reached in the original position. But that agreement supports free institutions, and free institutions encourage their citizens to adopt different views of the kind of persons they want to be. And so while the "account of stability given in part III of *Theory*" requires that members of the well-ordered society converge on the same partial conception of the good, "the view as a whole" encourages divergence.

Since Rawls was not going to give up his defense of free institutions or his claim that they encourage moral pluralism, the inconsistency required him to give up his claims about convergence. These are claims Rawls relied upon to argue that the agreement which would be reached in the original position satisfies (R2′) and (R3′), and so would be Rawlsian self-enforcing. The inconsistency therefore forced Rawls to think anew about whether members of the well-ordered society could uphold that agreement while conducting themselves autonomously.

Rawls's response was, of course, to re-present justice as fairness as a political liberalism. The re-presentation began with changes in the basic intuitive ideas on which justice as fairness was said to rely and in what the original position was said to represent. Whereas the Rawls of *TJ* relied on a basic intuitive idea of moral personality and used the original position to represent its contents, the later Rawls founded his view on a basic intuitive idea of political personality or citizenship. Since the features he said are definitive of citizenship are those he had previously used to define moral personality – the capacities for a conception of the good and for a sense of justice (*CP*, p. 398) – he could claim that the original position represented the contents of *this* basic idea instead (*PL*, pp. 103–4). And so instead of identifying principles of justice with those which would be agreed to by free and equal persons, he identified them with those that would be agreed to by free and equal citizens (*CP*, p. 399). Instead of arguing that the agreement reached in the original position would enforce itself because everyone in the well-ordered society would develop a desire to live as a moral person, he argued – in effect – that it would enforce itself because everyone would develop a desire to live up to the conception of citizenship the original position was now said to represent. But to see how the new arguments for self-enforcement go, and to see that they are less controversial than those of *TJ*, we need to see how the conditions of self-enforcement – and the arguments for their satisfaction – change because of the turn to political liberalism.

Since the later Rawls identified principles of justice with principles that would be accepted by those who live under them conceived as free and equal citizens, he can be read as endorsing a "political variant" of (R1):

> (PL1) The principles of justice that members of the well-ordered society are to follow must be specified by the terms of an agreement or contract among them, conceived as citizens having a conception of their good and capable of a sense of justice.

Because the powers definitive of citizenship are those which were previously said to be definitive of moral personality, and because the original position represented the latter, it also represents the former. Many of the arguments canvassed in section 11.3, which show that the agreement reached in the original position satisfies (R1), can be re-purposed to show that it satisfies (PL1). (R2') and (R3') are the conditions on self-enforcement which the agreement reached in the original position cannot satisfy because of the inconsistency Rawls found in *TJ*. So as we would expect, more interesting and significant departures from the arguments for Rawlsian self-enforcement come to light when we ask whether the agreement reached in the original position would satisfy their political variants:

> (PL2′) None of the members of the well-ordered society can have sufficient reason to deviate from the principles of justice, at least so long as all the others comply with them, and all do comply by conducting themselves as citizens having a conception of their good and capable of a sense of justice

and

> (PL3′) The fact that the principles would be agreed to in the contract referred to in (PL1) must be what brings it about that members of the well-ordered society comply with them, as (PL2′) requires, and the connection between the hypothetical agreement and the conduct referred to by (PL2′) must itself be established in ways which treat members of the well-ordered society as citizens having a conception of their good and capable of a sense of justice.

Start with (PL2′). The later Rawls, like the earlier, would maintain that members of the well-ordered society would develop a sense of justice by the processes outlined in *TJ*, Chapter 8. Indeed, I believe Rawls never revisited the arguments of that chapter because he thought they were successful as they stood. As we saw, the sense of justice is – in effect though not in intention – a desire to act from principles chosen in the original position. As I have stressed, the later Rawls used the original position to represent the defining features of citizenship. So for the later Rawls, the sense of justice is, in effect, a desire to act from principles chosen in a situation which represents one's nature as a citizen. I believe he also accepted a political version of what I referred to as "the expression claim," according to which members of the well-ordered society express their nature as citizens by acting from principles chosen in the original position. If this is correct, then Rawls could conclude that by acting from the principles, members of the well-ordered society can express their nature as citizens capable of a sense of justice.

As we also saw, Rawls moved to the further conclusion that the agreement reached in the original position satisfied both conjuncts of (R2′) by showing that when members of the well-ordered society all plan to regulate their pursuits of their good by the principles of justice, their plans are in a

Nash-type equilibrium. The argument for *that* conclusion depended upon each person's attaching a very high value to the expression of her nature as a moral person. If the later Rawls could show that members of the well-ordered society would all value the expression of their citizenship highly enough that it would outweigh contrary desires, he could move – by parity of reasoning – to the conclusion that the agreement reached in the original position satisfies (PL2′). Since the conception of citizenship represented in the original position is strictly political and does not apply to all of life, the new argument would not depend upon convergence on a comprehensive conception of the good – even a partially comprehensive one. It *would* require convergence on a political conception of justice. Rawls seemed to think that such convergence would come about, and that all members of the well-ordered society "would want to realize in their person, and have it recognized that they realize, that ideal of citizens" (*PL*, p. 84). But under what conditions would they converge on that desire? Under what conditions would they attach enough value to satisfying it to get Rawls the conclusion he needs?

Rawls's answer is that they would if an overlapping consensus obtains. For when an overlapping consensus obtains, "[r]easonable conceptions [of the good] endorse the political conception, each from its own point of view" (*PL*, p. 134). When an overlapping consensus on justice as fairness obtains, reasonable comprehensive doctrines all recognize its values, including the value of living up to its ideal of citizenship. If members of the well-ordered society all follow their comprehensive doctrines, they all "will judge (by their comprehensive doctrine) that political values" – including the value of living as free and equal citizens – "outweigh or are normally (though not always) ordered prior to whatever non-political values may conflict with them" (*PL*, p. 392). Then each person's plan to live up to the ideal of citizenship – as represented in the original position – is her best reply to the similar plans of others. A Nash-type equilibrium obtains, each regulates her pursuit of her good by her sense of justice, and the agreement that would be reached in the original position satisfies (PL2′).

What of (PL3′)?

When I argued that the agreement reached in the original position would satisfy (R3′), and would do so in virtue of the original position's representational function, I devoted most of my effort to arguing that it would satisfy the first conjunct. Now it is the second conjunct that merits the most attention. For the argument that the first conjunct would be satisfied depended upon showing that members of the well-ordered society would come to aspire to two ideals: the ideal of a just person and that of someone whose life expresses her moral personality. The turn to political liberalism meant shifting from talk of the latter ideal to talk of an ideal of citizenship. But despite this shift, the argument that the agreement reached in the original position would satisfy the first conjunct of (PL3′) would be much the same as the argument that it would satisfy the first conjunct of (R3′). For the later argument like the earlier one depends upon claims about the educative effect of full publicity and about the educational value of adopting different points of view in the four-stage sequence.[7]

Those are claims I believe Rawls continued to endorse after his turn to political liberalism. As if to confirm this, the summary remark from the original Deweys Lectures which I quoted earlier appears virtually word for word in the revised version of the Deweys Lectures which appears in *PL*. The only difference which the turn made is that Rawls replaced the sentence

> Thus the realization of the full publicity condition provides the social milieu within which the *notion of full autonomy* can be understood and within which its ideal of the person can elicit an effective desire to be that kind of person. (*CP*, p. 340, emphasis added)

with:

> To realize the full publicity condition is to realize a social world within which *the ideal of citizenship* can be learned and may elicit an effective desire to be that kind of person. (*PL*, p. 71, emphasis added)

Of course, members of the well-ordered society will comply with the principles of justice only if the desire to realize the ideal of citizenship is "effective." Showing that the agreement reached in the original position would satisfy the second conjunct of (PL3′) requires showing something about the process by which the fact of agreement in the original position educates members of the well-ordered society into an effective desire. It must show that that process treats them as citizens. We saw above that that desire will be effective if an overlapping consensus obtains and reasonable comprehensive doctrines support that ideal. So to show that the agreement reached in the original position satisfies the second conjunct of (PL3′), Rawls would need to show that the fact that the principles would be agreed to helps bring about an overlapping consensus in a way which satisfies the requirement that conjunct expresses. How does an overlapping consensus come about? Does its coming about depend upon the representative function of the original position?

---

[7] For the latter, see *PL*, pp. 397–8.

Rawls conjectured that many members of the well-ordered society will endorse comprehensive doctrines which "are not seen by them as fully general and comprehensive" (*PL*, p. 160). These citizens will not take their views about the good life to have clear implications for politics, or at least clear implications regarding which conception of justice they should endorse. Rawls implied that an overlapping consensus obtains when reasonable comprehensive doctrines "understand the wider realm of values to be congruent with, or supportive of, *or else not in conflict with*, political values as these are specified by a political conception of justice" (*PL*, p. 169, emphasis added). "Slippage" between comprehensive doctrine and political conception (*PL*, p. 160) opens the possibility that many members of the well-ordered society can view their comprehensive doctrines as participating in an overlapping consensus simply by virtue of their doctrines' consistency with justice as fairness. Rawls conjectured that these citizens will acquire desires to be just and to express their citizenship from the public culture, and that their desires will be effective because their conceptions of the good are not comprehensive enough to encourage political ideals which conflict with them (see *PL*, p. 168). Since the educational processes of the public culture treat members of the well-ordered society as citizens with the two moral powers, the agreement reached in the original position satisfies (PL3′) in these cases.

More complicated questions arise with citizens who *do* see their comprehensive doctrines as "fully general and comprehensive." These doctrines include ideals of political conduct and encourage their adherents to desire to live up to those ideals. These doctrines can take part in an overlapping consensus on justice as fairness only if they are "congruent with, or supportive of" its political values. The question of how an overlapping consensus comes about, and whether it comes about in a way that satisfies the second conjunct of (PL3′), are questions about how fully and generally comprehensive doctrines come to be "congruent with or supportive of" justice as fairness.

Rawls ventured that this can happen because "a reasonable and effective political conception may bend comprehensive doctrines toward itself, shaping them if need be from unreasonable to reasonable" (*PL*, p. 246). But he said little about how this bending might take place. Perhaps he said little because the processes depend upon complex cultural and sociological forces which would be at work in a just society. These processes are not well understood, they are likely to operate differently on different comprehensive doctrines, and understanding them lies outside the expertise of political philosophy. What matters for now is that doctrines which are comprehensive enough to require such shaping are articulated in large and systematic bodies of thought. Their content and implications develop – and are "ben[t]" – through the intellectual work of their theoretically inclined adherents. Those adherents, like other members of the well-ordered society, may be attracted to justice as fairness by the workings of a public culture which satisfies the full publicity condition and treats them as free and equal citizens. Their education, the formation of their views, and the arguments they offer, all go some way toward sustaining the causal connection from the fact that principles would be agreed to in the original position – via an overlapping consensus – to compliance with the principles by adherents of their comprehensive doctrine. It therefore goes some way toward insuring that the agreement reached in the original position satisfies (PL3′).

But compliance by adherents of fully comprehensive doctrines is not just brought about by the arguments of their intellectual leaders. It is also brought about by education in their doctrines – including, perhaps, education by authority. That education may not enable them to realize the full autonomy of moral persons as initially modeled in the original position. It must, however, treat them as free and equal citizens (*PL*, pp. 199–200). And so the way in which the agreement reached in the original position enforces itself in political liberalism has to be qualified accordingly. That qualification is reflected in the kind of freedom that members of the well-ordered society realize when they comply with the principles of justice.

When I introduced (R1), (R2′), and (R3′), I said they are jointly sufficient for Rawlsian self-enforcement. I did not say they are necessary, for I take (PL1), (PL2′), and (PL3′) also to be jointly sufficient: because the agreement that would be reached in the original position satisfies them, that agreement enforces itself. I said that when an agreement is Rawlsian self-enforcing because it satisfies (R1), (R2′), and (R3′), those who uphold it realize freedom of an especially robust kind. In the original Dewey Lectures, Rawls called it "full autonomy" (*CP*, p. 340). An agreement satisfying (PL1), (PL2′), and (PL3′) is not upheld by conduct which realizes such autonomy, since the conduct by which members of the well-ordered society uphold it does not express their nature as moral persons. Rather, the principles which they would agree to in the original position are principles they would give themselves as political persons, and they comply with the principles by conducting themselves as such. In complying with an agreement on those principles which is self-enforcing, they realize an autonomy which Rawls was still willing to describe as "full" but which he insisted is "political not ethical" (*PL*, p. 77).

11.8 Is the original position essential?

At the outset, I said that my reading of Rawls would help to answer the question of whether the original position is essential to Rawls's theory. That question is usually understood as asking whether the justification of Rawls's principles depends upon his argument that they would be chosen by rational and mutually disinterested parties who maximin behind a veil of ignorance. The answer is often thought to be negative. But the maximin argument for the principles is just one part of Rawls's theory. The original position might be indispensable to his theory without being indispensable to that part of it.

As we have seen, *TJ*'s treatment of stability depends upon Rawls's claim that members of the well-ordered society would have a desire to express their nature together with what I called "the expression claim," according to which they can satisfy that desire by acting from principles chosen in the original position. The expression claim is not self-evident. It needs defense. We saw that Rawls defended it by appealing to the premise:

> to express one's nature as a being of a particular kind is to act on the principles that would be chosen if this nature were the decisive determining element. (*TJ*, p. 253)

This premise seems to be *needed* to support the expression claim, and the expression claim seems to be needed to show that the agreement that would be reached in the original position satisfies (R2′). Since the premise refers to principles – and the relevant principles are, of course, principles of justice – which are the object of a hypothetical choice, the claim that principles of justice would be the object of a hypothetical choice seems to be needed to show that (R2′) is satisfied. Moreover, the premise requires that the outcome of that choice be made on the basis of the nature that is expressed by acting on the chosen principles. The argument that (R2′) is satisfied – and that justice as fairness would be self-supporting – therefore seems to require the prior argument that Rawls's principles would be the object of a hypothetical choice, the outcome of which is determined by the choosers' nature as free and equal rational beings.

Perhaps that prior argument can be provided without appeal to a choice situation. If so, then the original position is not essential to the argument for Rawlsian self-enforcement. By itself, however, this would not be an especially telling or interesting point. Rawls himself concedes that arguments from the original position could be dispensed with in favor of other, albeit more cumbersome, arguments (*TJ*, p. 138). What really matters is what considerations those more cumbersome arguments would appeal to. The conclusion that the original position is not essential to Rawls's view is sometimes said to support the conclusion that Rawls's appeals to one or another element of our nature, such as our rational self-interest, are not essential to his account of justice.[8] That conclusion cannot be sustained. For the requirement cited at the end of the previous paragraph cannot be satisfied without appeals to the elements of our nature that various features of the original position represent. Even if the device of the original position is not essential to Rawls's theory as presented in *TJ*, the deep point he devised it to make – that principles of justice are rooted in moral personality as he understood it – *is* essential to it.

Is the original position essential to Rawls's theory once it is re-presented as a political liberalism? The argument which shows that the agreement reached in the original position satisfies the first conjunct of (PL2′) depends upon a political version of the expression claim. I believe that that version, like the original version, needs to be supported by the premise I quoted just above. If that is right, then the argument which shows that the point the later Rawls used the original position to make – that principles of justice are rooted in the nature of citizenship – is essential to his later treatment of stability, and so to his re-presented theory of justice.

---

[8] Thanks to Samuel Freeman for conversation about this point.

12 The original position in *The Law of Peoples*

Gillian Brock

12.1 Introduction

What kinds of principles should guide liberal peoples in their international affairs, especially when dealing with people who are not apparently committed to liberal values? If they are true liberals, should they insist, wherever possible and likely to prove effective, that other peoples conform to liberal standards or at least gradually evolve in a liberal direction? Alternatively, should they be tolerant of others who hold non-liberal commitments and not attempt to steer them towards liberal democratic ideals? How are we to identify the limit for any appropriate tolerance that we ought to exercise? What responsibilities do affluent developed societies have to those that are poor and developing? What form should any assistance take when advantaged countries try to help disadvantaged ones?

Clearly, these are important questions worthy of considerable reflection. And these are the sorts of issues that Rawls attempts to address in his highly influential work *The Law of Peoples* (*LP*). The original position plays a central role in deriving the principles that should guide liberal foreign policy. In this chapter we discuss Rawls's original position argument in *LP*. In the next section I outline the argument Rawls offers for the principles that constitute his Law of Peoples, highlighting the role played by the original position in arriving at guidance in international affairs. Section 12.3 covers some critical engagment with those arguments while section 12.4 discusses some ways in which Rawls, or rather those who would defend him, might address key challenges. Section 12.5 takes stock of the debate between the two sides and emphasizes the strengths of both Rawls's peoples-focused and cosmopolitan perspectives in pursuing a global realistic utopia. I show how Rawls's position on duties to address global poverty and his views concerning how to interact with non-liberal societies contain considerable insights that are not adequately acknowledged.

12.2 Rawls's *Law of Peoples*: some highlights featuring the original position

To appreciate the dynamics of the debate surrounding *LP* we must very briefly highlight several key moves Rawls makes in his earlier ground-breaking work, *TJ*. There he sets out to derive the principles of justice that should govern liberal societies. He makes use of the innovative original position technique to craft an ingenious thought experiment. The original position is a theoretical device often used to test the fairness of principles that aim at justice. It is a hypothetical device which aims to place us in a particular choosing situation that shields us from well-known distortive influences. Features of our situation (especially whether we occupy a position of advantage or disadvantage) can radically influence what we consider to be fair. The veil of ignorance attempts to shield us from these biasing factors, by stripping us of such relevant knowledge. Rawls invites us to consider which principles we might chose in the original position to govern the basic structure of society if we do not know what position we will occupy in that society. Rawls famously argued that it would be rational to select two principles: one protecting equal basic liberties and a second permitting social and economic inequalities when (and only when) they are both to the greatest benefit of the least advantaged (the difference principle) and attached to positions that are open to all under conditions of fair equality of opportunity (the fair equality of opportunity principle).

In *TJ*, Rawls's focus is on the principles that should govern closed communities – paradigmatically, nation states. Cosmopolitans (first Charles Beitz, *Political*, and then Thomas Pogge, *Realizing*) argued that these two principles should apply globally, because the same kind of reasoning that led to their endorsement at the domestic level should apply to the global case. After all, if the point of the veil of ignorance is to exclude us from knowledge of factors that are morally arbitrary, where one happens to have been born (or one's citizenship) qualifies as one of those quintessentially arbitrary factors from the moral point of view.

It was a disappointment, then, when Rawls later explicitly rejected such a suggestion.[1] He argued that, though the two principles should apply within

---

[1] Though Rawls does discuss principles for a "law of nations" (which applies to all nations) in *TJ*, § 58, the treatment there is extremely brief and focused in any case on the justification for conscientious refusal to participate in war. As it is his later treatment that constitutes his considered views on the topic of international justice and that critics target, this earlier treatment need not detain us here. But it may be worth observing that there is significant overlap between the earlier and later treatments, though the later one importantly adds two principles concerning human rights and aid to burdened societies.

liberal societies, they should not apply across them. Rather, in the international arena, Rawls argues that "well-ordered peoples" (that is, roughly, those that have institutions of self-governance or of consultation in their internal set-up) would choose eight principles (which constitute his Law of Peoples). These are principles acknowledging peoples' independence, their equality, that they have a right to self-defense, that they have duties of non-intervention, to observe treaties, to honor a limited set of human rights, to conduct themselves appropriately in war, and to assist other peoples living in unfavorable conditions. In addition, Rawls believes three international organizations would be chosen: one aimed at securing fair trade among peoples, one which enables peoples to borrow from a cooperative banking institution, and one which plays a similar role to that of the United Nations (*LP*, pp. 37–42).

There is considerable debate over whether Rawls's position should be applauded or rejected. Relevant to any assessment are Rawls's own views about what he is trying to achieve in this work. In *LP*, Rawls aims to derive the laws to which well-ordered peoples would agree. For Rawls, well-ordered peoples include reasonable liberal peoples and "decent peoples," that is, peoples who, though they are not liberal, have a "decent consultation mechanism," among other features to be discussed below. Rawls argues that the Law of Peoples he endorses is a realistic utopia. It is realistic because it takes account of many real conditions, by (for instance) acknowledging a fair amount of diversity in the world; not all peoples of the world do or can reasonably be made to endorse liberal principles. Furthermore, the view he offers is realistic because it takes people as they actually are, and "its first principles and precepts" must be "workable and applicable to ongoing political and social arrangements" (*LP*, p. 13).

Rawls's derivation occurs in several stages. Rawls makes use of multiple original positions in efforts to arrive at what liberal and decent people would agree to guide them as principles governing international relations. He says:

> Each of these agreements is understood as hypothetical and nonhistorical, and entered into by equal peoples symmetrically situated in the original position behind an appropriate veil of ignorance. Hence the undertaking between peoples is fair. (*LP*, p. 10)

Rawls first concerns himself only with liberal peoples and the principles they would endorse, deploying both a domestic and an international original position device to arrive at his position. Thereafter, he focuses on the principles decent peoples would choose, using a further original position scenario in which to do so. Let us consider these three parts of the argument in turn.

Rawls employs two original positions to derive his Law of Peoples for liberal peoples: the first grounds the social contract of the liberal political conception of a constitutionally democratic regime while the second operates among representatives of liberal peoples. The parties in the first original position must decide the fair terms of cooperation that will regulate the domestic basic structure of society. They are modeled as rational and "their aim is to do the best they can for citizens whose basic interests they represent, as specified by the primary goods, which cover their basic needs as citizens" (*LP*, p. 31). Since parties are behind a veil of ignorance, they will be motivated to choose a basic structure of society that reflects the freedom and equality of persons, and so they choose Rawls's famous two principles of justice.

After the principles governing the internal affairs of the liberal society have been derived, Rawls moves to the international level. Now a second original position is employed to derive the foreign policy that liberal peoples would choose. The representatives of peoples are subject to an appropriate veil of ignorance for the situation. For instance, they do not know the size of the territory or its "relative strength" (*LP*, p. 33). Representatives then "select from among available principles for the Law of Peoples guided by the principles of justice for a democratic society" (*LP*, p. 32). Rawls argues first that they would reject utilitarianism "since no people organized by its government is prepared to count, as a first principle, the benefits for another people as outweighing the hardships imposed on itself. Well-ordered peoples insist on equality among themselves as peoples, and this insistence rules out any form of the principle of utility" (*LP*, p. 40). Rather, he argues that they would choose principles 1–8 of his Law of Peoples, namely:

1 Peoples are free and independent, and their freedom and independence are to be respected by other peoples.
2 Peoples are to observe treaties and undertakings.
3 Peoples are equal and are parties to the agreements that bind them.
4 Peoples are to observe a duty of non-intervention.
5 Peoples have the right to self-defense but no right to instigate war for reasons other than self-defense.
6 Peoples are to honor human rights.
7 Peoples are to observe certain specified restrictions in the conduct of war.
8 Peoples have a duty to assist other peoples living under unfavorable conditions that prevent their having a just or decent political and social regime. (*LP*, p. 37)

In addition, Rawls believes three organizations would be chosen: one aimed at securing fair trade among peoples, one which enables people to borrow from a cooperative banking institution, and one which plays a similar role to that of the United Nations, which he refers to as "a Confederation of Peoples (not states)" (*LP*, p. 42). Rawls contends that "the eight principles of the Law of Peoples are superior to any others" (*LP*, p. 41). How does Rawls arrive at these eight principles? He informs us that he takes "[t]hese familiar and largely traditional principles ... from the history and usages of international law and practice" (*LP*, p. 41).[2] He adds later on that "in proposing a principle to regulate the mutual relations between peoples, a people or their representatives must think not only that it is reasonable for them to propose it, but also that it is reasonable for other peoples to accept it" (*LP*, p. 57).

Having made his argument concerning what liberal peoples would select as the eight principles and three organizations governing international affairs, he moves on to maintain that decent peoples would make the same selection. This raises the question of what Rawls has in mind in speaking of a "decent people." Rawls specifies that for a people to count as a decent one, at least four central conditions must be met. First, the society must conduct its affairs in ways that are peaceful and respectful of other societies. Second, the system of law and its idea of justice must secure basic human rights for all members of the people. However, it is important to realize that at this stage in the argument, the indicative list of particular rights that Rawls offers is very short (*LP*, p. 65). In describing these, Rawls specifies only the following: (a) the right to life, by which he means the rights to the means of subsistence and security; (b) the right to liberty, which equates to freedom from slavery or forced occupation but also includes some liberty of conscience, enough to ensure freedom of religion and thought; (c) the right to personal property; and (d) the right to formal equality, by which he means that similar cases be treated similarly. The third condition a decent people must satisfy is that judges and others who administer the legal system must believe that the law incorporates an idea of justice according to which there is a common good. Fourth, a decent people must have a "decent consultation mechanism" whereby constituent groups are consulted in an attempt to reflect all groups' significant interests.

Rawls's derivation of his Law of Peoples continues with a third original position, this time an international original position reserved only for decent

---

[2] Rawls adds that while the eight principles are open to different interpretations, these "*interpretations*, of which there are many... are to be debated in the second-level original position" (*LP*, p. 42).

non-liberal peoples that parallels the international original position for liberal societies. Rawls briefly argues that a decent people would accept the same Law of Peoples he earlier derived. Reflecting on the advantages of these principles for promoting equality among peoples, decent peoples "see no reason to depart from them or to propose alternatives" (*LP*, p. 41).

Rawls then turns to describe a case of a hypothetical decent people, Kazanistan, that he believes fulfills his requirements. Kazanistan is an idealized Islamic people in which only Muslims are eligible for positions of political authority and have influence in important political matters, though other religions are otherwise tolerated and encouraged to pursue a flourishing cultural life (*LP*, p. 76). Rawls believes Kazanistan can be admitted to the society of well-ordered peoples. Liberal societies should tolerate states such as Kazanistan. For those who have trouble with the idea that such a society should be considered as a member of the Society of Peoples,[3] Rawls believes that "something like Kazanistan is the best we can realistically – and coherently – hope for" (*LP*, p. 78). Moreover, he thinks that liberal peoples should "try to encourage decent peoples and not frustrate their vitality by coercively insisting that all societies be liberal" (*LP*, p. 62). By way of further defense of the view, Rawls argues that it is crucial that we maintain "mutual respect among peoples" (*LP*, p. 62).

Critics of Rawls's account of international justice – especially those identified as cosmopolitans – often challenge Rawls's views concerning duties of assistance, so it is worth understanding these in more detail. According to Rawls, some societies "lack the political and cultural traditions, the human capital and know-how, and, often, the material and technological resources needed to be well-ordered" (*LP*, p. 106). Well-ordered peoples have a duty to assist such societies to become part of the society of well-ordered peoples. The aim of assistance is to "help burdened societies to be able to manage their own affairs reasonably and rationally and eventually to become members of the society of well-ordered peoples. This defines the target of assistance. After it is achieved, further assistance is not required, even though the now well-ordered society may still be relatively poor" (*LP*, p. 111). The aim is to realize and preserve just (or decent) institutions that are self-sustaining.

According to Rawls, the political culture of a burdened society is all important to the levels of prosperity experienced in particular societies: wealth owes its origin and maintenance to the culture of the society rather

---

[3] By "Society of Peoples" Rawls means all those peoples who follow the principles of the Law of Peoples in their relations.

than (say) to its stock of resources. He says: "I believe that the causes of the wealth of a people and the forms it takes lie in their political culture and in the religious, philosophical, and moral traditions that support the basic structure of their political and social institutions, as well as in the industriousness and cooperative talents of its members, all supported by their political virtues" (*LP*, p. 108).

Rawls does engage directly with central claims made by some (though by no means all) cosmopolitans, who maintain that the principles of justice that applied in *TJ*, particularly the difference principle, should apply globally. He takes up Beitz's claim that, since a global system of cooperation already exists between states, a global difference principle should apply across states as well. Rawls argues against this for a couple of reasons, but notably, as we have just seen, because he believes that wealth owes its origin and maintenance to domestic factors such as the political culture of the society rather than (say) to its stock of resources. Furthermore, any global principle of distributive justice we endorse must have a target and a cut-off point, which are secured by ensuring the requirements of political autonomy. That is to say, what we should focus on with our assistance is to target measures that will enable states to be self-determining. And when states have the necessary ingredients to be self-determining, we will have discharged our duties of assistance. When it comes to other common cosmopolitan complaints that Rawls fails to be sufficiently attentive to inequalities between the lowest income groups in different societies, Rawls's central response is similar. Any principles of global redistribution must have a target and a cut-off point. For Rawls, these are achieved when just institutions are in place that can ensure political autonomy. By contrast, Rawls believes that since cosmopolitans are concerned with the well-being of *individuals*, there is no obvious cut-off point at which redistribution ceases in the global arena, and this result is problematic for several reasons, for instance, in undermining proper incentives for a people to take responsibility for its own well-being.

12.3 Some critical responses to Rawls's *LP*

In this section I consider some of the more important or commonly advanced critical responses made to *LP*, focusing particularly on challenges made to the way delegates might reason in the original position in this crucial decision-making position. One of the most frequently raised objections is that the background picture forming part of the set-up of Rawls's international original positions depends on outmoded views of relations between states, peoples, and individuals of the world. In describing these original positions, Rawls presupposes that states are (sufficiently) independent of one another, so that each society can be held responsible for the well-being of its citizens. Furthermore, according to Rawls, differences in levels of prosperity are largely attributable to differences in domestic factors such as political culture and the virtuous nature of a state's citizens. Critics point out, however, that Rawls ignores both the extent to which unfavorable conditions may result from factors external to the society and the fact that there are all sorts of morally relevant connections between states, notably that they are situated in a global economic order that perpetuates the interests of wealthy, developed states with little regard for the interests of poor, developing ones. Those who live in the affluent, developed world cannot thus defensibly insulate themselves from the misery of the worst off in the world, since they are complicit in keeping them in a state of poverty.

One prominent advocate of such a view is Pogge (e.g. "An Egalitarian," "Priorities," and *World Poverty*). According to Pogge, two international institutions are particularly worrisome: the international borrowing privilege and the international resource privilege. Any group that exercises effective power in a state is recognized internationally as the legitimate government of that territory, and the international community is not much concerned with how the group came to power or what it does with that power. Oppressive governments may borrow freely on behalf of the country (the international borrowing privilege) or dispose of its natural resources (the international resource privilege) and these actions are legally recognized internationally. These two privileges have enormous implications for the prosperity of poor countries because they provide incentives for *coup* attempts, often influence what sorts of individuals are motivated to seek power, help maintain oppressive governments, and, should more democratic governments get to be in power, they are saddled with the debts incurred by their oppressive predecessors, thus significantly draining the country of resources needed to firm up fledgling democracies. All of this is disastrous for many poor countries. Because foreigners benefit so greatly from the international resource privilege, they have an incentive to refrain from challenging the situation (or worse, to support or finance oppressive governments). For these reasons, the current world order largely reflects the interests of wealthy and powerful states. Local governments have little incentive to attend to the needs of the poor, because their being able to continue in power depends more on the local elite, foreign governments, and corporations. Those in affluent developed countries have a responsibility to stop imposing this unjust global order and to mitigate the harms inflicted on the world's most vulnerable people. As one initial proposal for making progress in the right direction, Pogge suggests that we impose a global resources tax of roughly 1 per cent to fund improvements to the lives of the worst off in developing societies.

Another aspect of the Rawlsian set-up for his international original position that has been attacked by critics concerns his view of the boundedness and separateness of political communities. Rawls assumes we can talk coherently of bounded political communities that constitute self-sufficient schemes of political cooperation. However, critics argue this is an untenable assumption due to phenomena such as globalization and integration (Hurrell, "Global Inequality"). Some authors argue that we have a system of global cooperation between societies and this gives rise to obligations to the worst off (Hinsch, "Global Distributive Justice"). Several critics argue that the basic global structure is a scheme of coercive institutions that importantly affects individuals' life prospects. That structure should be transformed so that it becomes a fair scheme of cooperation among all citizens of the world (Forst, "Towards a Critical Theory").

In addition, critics question one of the key concepts in Rawls's international original position arguments, namely that of a people, asking whether the notion is sufficiently clear or important to do the work Rawls thinks it can do (Pogge, "An Egalitarian," p. 197; Kuper, "Rawlsian Global"). Rawls often takes the boundaries of states to mark off distinct peoples, which leads his view into difficulties. If we take a people to be constituted by commonalities such as shared language, culture, history, or ethnicity, then the official state borders and peoples do not coincide well. National territories are not typically comprised of a single people, nor is it clear that individuals belong to one and only one people.

Furthermore, critics charge that Rawls's original position based reasons for excluding greater socioeconomic equality are unconvincing (Moellendorf, *Cosmopolitan*; Pogge, *Realizing*; Tan, *Tolerance*). As Pogge notes, Rawls assumes that representatives of peoples are interested in the justice of domestic institutions and care nothing about the well-being of members beyond what is essential for just domestic institutions. But why assume this? It is more plausible to assume that each delegate is interested not only in just domestic institutions but also, all else being equal, in having "a higher rather than a lower average standard of living" (Pogge, "An Egalitarian," p. 208). Even if this interest is only slight, the representatives would be inclined to adopt at the very least something like Pogge's global resources tax proposal. However, if delegates also know that great international inequality can negatively affect the institutions of domestic justice in poor countries, representatives would have at least a "tie-breaking reason to favor a more egalitarian Law of Peoples over Rawls's" (Pogge, "An Egalitarian," p. 214). It would also seem that there is substantial tension in the reasoning Rawls offers for our interest in socioeconomic equality at the domestic level and our apparent lack of interest in this at the international level, claiming that the reasons for our interest in equality at the domestic level apply as well to the global.

Critics also charge that Rawls provides little argument for why representatives of decent societies in an original position would endorse even the limited set of human rights that Rawls offers initially (Pogge, "An Egalitarian," pp. 214–15). Delegates from liberal societies, by contrast, would want to add more to the list of human rights; for instance, freedom of speech, democratic political rights, and equal liberty of conscience. In the case of neither decent peoples nor liberal ones would the precise list Rawls offers be chosen, and moreover it is noted that the attempt to find a politically neutral Law of Peoples acceptable to both peoples is not promising (Pogge, "An Egalitarian," p. 215). Rawls's failure to include democratic rights is often remarked upon as a mistaken move (Kuper, "Rawlsian Global," pp. 655–8). Amartya Sen, for instance, provides extensive evidence to support the claim that non-democratic regimes have severely adverse consequences for the well-being and human rights of those over whom they rule (Sen, *Development*, pp. 147–8 and 154–5). Sen also argues that respect for human rights and ideas of democracy are not confined to liberal societies, but rather that substantial elements of these ideas can be found in all major cultures, religions, and traditions.

Rawls employs the original position to argue for a respectful relationship between states (as representatives of peoples). Indeed, he argues that liberal democratic regimes have an obligation to deal with illiberal decent regimes as equals, and not to endeavor to impose their values on them. Some might think that Rawls's views appropriately acknowledge the importance of our cultural or national affiliations. Andrew Kuper in "Rawlsian Global" argues that Rawls may take cultural pluralism seriously, but he does this at the expense of taking less seriously the reasonable pluralism of *individual persons*. Decent societies may well contain individuals who hold liberal ideas. Rawls's account incorporates the wrong kind of toleration for such societies at the expense of liberal values. Indeed, it would seem that Rawls, in defending non-liberal states as he has, would be forced to defend the rights of states to impose inegalitarian policies on its citizens, even if a majority of the citizens were vigorously against such policies (Blake and Smith, "International

Distributive"). Rawls gets into this kind of bind, according to some, because of a mistaken view about what tolerance demands. There is also a debate about what the appropriate unit of toleration should be: legitimate differences among individuals or among peoples. Liberalism does, in certain cases, require commitment to tolerating views that are not liberal. However, critics argue that the only appropriate object of toleration should be legitimate differences among individuals, not peoples, as this ensures better tolerance of legitimate differences where they matter, namely, among individual persons (Pogge, "An Egalitarian"; Tan, *Tolerance*).

Rawls aims at a realistic utopia, but critics charge that the result is neither sufficiently realistic nor utopian (Kuper, "Rawlsian Global," p. 383). It is insufficiently realistic, they claim, because it fails to take account of interdependence or domination in the global arena. And the view is challenged as being insufficiently utopian as the ideals are not much of an advance over the status quo. Rawls has tried to ensure that the Law of Peoples results in stability yet, critics charge, the Law of Peoples might be quite unstable because it involves tolerance of unjust regimes, which are potentially much less stable than just ones. Critics also claim that Rawls's focus on getting consent from diverse societies leads him to tailor steps in his argument to produce a result that enjoys wide agreement. Indeed, according to Darrel Moellendorf, Rawls "sacrifices full justice for wider agreement" (Moellendorf, *Cosmopolitan*, p. 15). According to Bruce Ackerman, Rawls has offered us nothing more than a modus vivendi with oppressor states (Ackerman, "Political," p. 383).

12.4 Defending Rawls's *Law of Peoples*

Many philosophers have tried to defend Rawls against this litany of criticisms.[4] Several lines of defense have been attempted. It is often pointed out that critics have failed to appreciate some salient issues that orient *LP*. As Samuel Freeman emphasizes, *LP* is commonly misunderstood to be asking questions like: what is the nature of global justice? What would a globally just world order look like? According to Freeman, Rawls's Law of Peoples addresses a less ambitious question, namely, what should the foreign policy of liberal peoples be? In particular, how should liberal peoples relate to non-liberal peoples? Should they tolerate and cooperate with non-liberal peoples, or should they try to convert non-liberal peoples to liberal ones? What are the

---

[4] For some notable attempts see Freeman, "The Law of Peoples"; Heath, "Rawls on Global"; Mandle, "Tolerating"; Reidy, "Rawls on International."

limits of what liberal peoples should tolerate with respect to non-liberal peoples? Indeed, Rawls's primary aim in *LP* is to dislodge realism, the view that states should pursue their rational interests without attending to normative issues. This constitutes a more limited project than trying to come up with an entire theory of global justice (Heath, "Rawls on Global").

To address these less ambitious questions, Rawls needs to distinguish the concept of a decent society from that of a fully just one (in the liberal democratic sense), with the idea of a decent society playing the role of a theoretical construct. While liberal peoples should tolerate decent peoples, this is not the case with so-called outlaw regimes. It is not reasonable to expect all decent societies to conform to all the norms of a constitutional democracy as a requirement of peacefully coexisting and cooperating with them (Freeman, "Introduction," p. 46). If we reject Rawls's way of addressing the issues, it appears the only alternative is to intervene constantly in the affairs of other states, which seems unattractive and destabilizing. According to Freeman, this stance does not entail that citizens of liberal states must refrain from criticizing illiberal societies. However, there is a key difference between liberal citizens engaging in criticism and their "government's hostile criticisms, sanctions, and other forms of coercive intervention. The Law of Peoples says that liberal peoples, as peoples represented by their governments have a duty to cooperate with, and not seek to undermine, decent non-liberal societies" (Freeman, "Introduction," pp. 46–7).

While the Rawls of *LP* is certainly trying to work out what the foreign policy of a liberal peoples should be (see *LP*, p. 10), in parts of the text he also indicates that an alternative interpretation of his project is a plausible one which has aspirations to be an account of global justice. This is especially true of the many passages in which he describes himself as offering a realistic utopia. The phrase suggests that Rawls is trying to determine the conditions under which a utopian world order might be possible, albeit with the caveat that he wants it to be realistic (*LP*, pp. 5–6). Defenders of the more modest reading of Rawls's aims are quick to point out that on this interpretation of Rawls's project, Rawls is trying to establish under what conditions we can secure a *peaceful and stable* world order, rather than one which is *just* (Audard, "Cultural Imperialism," p. 73). This is the proper ambition, it is maintained, because of the constraints provided by wide diversity, reasonable pluralism, and respect for peoples' self-determination. If securing a peaceful world order is our primary objective, we should permit coercion only in the most essential cases. And so it is proper that Rawls's work is concerned with the legitimacy of global coercive political power, rather than with a range of other ideas that occupied him in earlier works, such as the arbitrariness of initial positions in determining one's fate, distributive justice, and other matters concerning a more robust conception of justice as fairness.[5]

Defenders of the more limited project frequently claim that cosmopolitans (who endorse the more ambitious project concerning global distributive justice) underestimate the importance of global political stability and peace. Without peace there can be no justice, so establishing a peaceful order does seem to be the first crucial step in an international Law of Peoples.

If Rawls's aim were to establish the conditions for a peaceful and stable world order, rather than a just one, the concepts of legitimacy and respect for legitimate governments would play a key role. But even if we accept the significant role that legitimacy plays, critics argue that that would still not explain away other puzzling features of Rawls's Law of Peoples. One criterion by which we gauge legitimate governments is how well they respect human rights. Critics frequently remark that Rawls endorses a very concise list of human rights. Would his commitment to legitimacy not require him to embrace several of the rights he notably excludes, such as freedom of expression, association, political participation, and non-discrimination?

Much has been said in attempting to defend Rawls's abbreviated list of human rights. Two approaches are standardly used: one revolves around a concern with wide acceptability and the other draws attention to the way violations of human rights can function to justify the use of coercion in Rawls's account.[6] According to the first line of defense, Rawls is concerned with how one might find a widely acceptable list of human rights in the face of a wide range of views about conceptions of valuable lives in the international community. Given this constraint, only the most essential of human entitlements would gain the relevant international consensus. According to the other common line of defense, attention is drawn to the status of violations of human rights in underwriting the use of coercion in the international order.[7] Intervention in the affairs of a sovereign people being such a weighty matter, the argument goes, we should reserve space on the list of human rights for only those rights for which non-compliance could adequately justify considering the full force of international interventive measures. This might

---

[5] The concern with legitimacy is present in earlier works, so there is more continuity in Rawls's body of work than critics have so far acknowledged. See Wenar, "Why Rawls."

[6] Indeed, Rawls says as much in *LP* at p. 65, and p. 80, and, more generally, section 10.

[7] Rawls says this in *LP* at p 80. See also, Tasioulas, "From Utopia"; Hinsch and Stepanians, "Human Rights," pp. 126–7.

explain why certain rights, such as the right to belong to a trade union or free speech, are not included.

Some argue that there is a widespread misconception about Rawls's views on human rights. David Reidy maintains that Rawls's endorsed list of human rights is much fuller than his critics seem to appreciate. In the commonly identified passages in which Rawls presents his list, Rawls offers only an incomplete sketch of what he has in mind. Reidy notes that most readers mistakenly think Rawls's list is excessively minimalist, but he draws attention to the fact that Rawls begins his list with the words "Among the human rights are" and therefore leaves open the possibility that what he presents is not an exhaustive treatment (Reidy, "Political Authority," p. 170).[8]

What might Rawls's defenders have to say to the charges that there is a global basic structure and that Rawls has ignored the unjust global economic order (which includes privileges such as the international resource and borrowing privileges, as Pogge discusses)? Joseph Heath argues that there is no *global* basic structure because key characteristics of such an order are absent, notably, a way to guarantee reciprocity and mutually beneficial cooperation. A shared framework provided by the rule of law is a necessary condition for this, and such a framework is clearly absent at the international level (Heath, "Rawls on Global," pp. 201–5). Without some international authority or means of enforcing global rules, we cannot talk of a global basic structure. Freeman also argues that there is no global *basic* structure and that all global norms supervene on those of states. For instance, contracts are specified and enforced according to the laws of one or other society. There are no basic global institutions – no world state and no independent legal order (Freeman, "The Law of Peoples," pp. 243–60; Freeman, "Introduction," p. 39).

Freeman also maintains that Rawls recognizes the many injustices to which Pogge refers. Rawls himself says that given current injustices, the appeal of something like a Global Difference Principle, as a transitional principle to establishing a well-ordered Society of Peoples, is easy to understand (*LP*, p. 117). Furthermore, Freeman maintains that the states Pogge describes as taking advantage of international resource and borrowing privileges are not well formed but rather outlaw states. As outlaws, they are not to be tolerated and it would be "wrong for well-ordered peoples to do anything to perpetuate them" (Freeman, "The Law of Peoples," p. 251).

---

[8] For some further analysis of Rawls's view on human rights see Brock, "Human Rights."

Rex Martin argues that we can find space to accommodate duties to change unfair features of the global order (such as international resource and borrowing privileges) by examining the duty of assistance in more detail. He argues that this duty entails a requirement to assist burdened societies to become self-supporting in a variety of ways, including economically. This duty therefore entails the need to revise "the financial and economic environment in which formerly burdened societies interact with wealthier and more technologically advanced societies" (Martin, "Rawls on International," p. 238). On this view, we can include fairly onerous duties to reform the existing global order to promote the goal of helping burdened societies achieve political autonomy (Freeman, "The Law of Peoples," p. 35).

12.5 The strengths of both perspectives in pursuing a global realistic utopia

Both critics and defenders of Rawls's peoples-centered account make many reasonable points and both have valuable perspectives to offer as we develop a realistic utopia applicable to international affairs. In the space remaining I aim to cover two important sets of concerns that are raised in this debate and show how Rawls presents subtle approaches that can usefully inform models of global justice.

We have canvased two central strands of criticism of Rawls's view which run through much of the debate:

1 Rawls's approach to our duties to assist with addressing global poverty is alleged to be inadequate.
2 Rawls's toleration of non-liberal societies is said to be problematic.

I believe both these critiques are unfair and fail to appreciate Rawls's sophisticated perspective on some complex problems. I start by attempting to defend his views on our duties to assist since this will enable us to appreciate his views on toleration.

Consider two questions that are important to address when we discuss our duties to assist. What are the causes of prosperity? How can we help promote prosperity in countries struggling with widescale poverty? There is an enormous literature on these topics and a lively debate continues on these themes.[9] One plausible answer stresses the quality of institutions in particular

---

[9] For an introduction to these debates see Brock, *Global*, Chapter 5.

states, no matter what other factors are also found to play a role.[10] So on this view, those institutions that promote (for instance) respect for the rule of law and accountability make for an environment conducive to innovation and investment in education, health, and infrastructure, all key ingredients for lifting people out of poverty.

Because Rawls is a strong proponent of this institutional thesis, he holds the view that the simple transfer of resources is not necessarily an effective way to assist developing countries. The simple transfer of wealth (without adequate and strategic focus) is not what will transform burdened societies. What such burdened societies need is reformed domestic institutions so that members can make effective use of resources and opportunities. On this account, we need to target domestic institutional reform if we aim to assist effectively. There are sound normative and empirical grounds for focusing on robust domestic institutions. As Rawls himself notes, the institutions that govern the basic structure have profound and pervasive effects on people's life prospects. And the body of empirical literature that identifies institutions as key to beneficial development is also vast.[11] Effective states capable of self-determination, the protection of citizens' basic rights, and the promotion of citizens' well-being all require adequate institutional capacity.

While Rawls is (rightly) committed to the importance of institutions in promoting beneficial development, his approach to issues of development also permits a great deal of scope for societies to explore and embrace novel solutions to their own circumstances. The approach is less prescriptive, more open minded, and therefore more flexible about what form those solutions may take. Rawls does not assume that developing societies *must* adopt a particular formula (such as the so-called Washington Consensus) though as we see below, he does not shy away from offering advice about what courses of action are likely to yield important gains for beneficial development, such as when he highlights the important role attending to the fundamental interests of women is likely to play.

In what ways is Rawls more open minded about the possibility of a multiplicity of successful ways towards beneficial development? One example is that Rawls does not require that non-liberal societies must commit to democratization, as a condition of receiving development assistance or as a condition of being considered legitimate by the international community. He is open to the possibility that burdened societies may be able to develop in

[10] For more on this topic see ibid.   [11] For some of that literature see ibid.

ways that differ from liberal societies, exploring alternative paths in which a self-determining people may plausibly arrange their affairs consistent with their own non-liberal worldviews and traditions. And, on his view, a certain range of alternative non-liberal societies deserve respect from liberal peoples and therefore deserve to be tolerated by liberal societies.

Is it conceivable that forms of governance might exist that are capable of protecting basic human rights and other important interests of members of those societies, but are not democratic as we have come to characterize democracy in liberal societies? Perhaps a form of governance might be deliberative, consultative, and responsive to citizens' views, and therefore include liberal democratic elements, without specifically including rights to stand for office and to vote in elections? These questions are worthy of genuine consideration, and I believe there is considerable merit in Rawls's entertaining them.

A charitable interpretation of Rawls's project might also emphasize other elements, such as concern with effectiveness of assistance or a sense of humility about what we can claim to know about the way human beings ought to live. If we are concerned about the effectiveness of assistance, it is not irrelevant that societies are often more likely to arrive at liberal positions if they follow their own internal reform processes in their own ways and at their own pace. And we should be appropriately cautious about what we can claim as "the truth about how we ought to live." This humility about our own knowledge should ground an attitude of considerable openness to alternative ways of life that are worthy of respect. As Catherine Audard says, Rawls offers "a truly 'critical' theory of international justice ... avoiding both the dogmatism of cosmopolitans and the skepticism of both realists and cultural relativism. This is a difficult and courageous position" (Audard, "Cultural Imperialism," p. 273).

Having said much in defense of Rawls, let me also point to the ways in which his arguments seem weak and vulnerable to attack. Rawls makes some strong claims about tracing the origins of prosperity. In an influential passage Rawls boldly states that:

> I believe that the causes of the wealth of a people and the forms it takes lie in their political culture and in the religious, philosophical, and moral trad-itions that support the basic structure of their political and social insti-tutions, as well as in the industriousness and cooperative talents of its members... The crucial elements that make the difference are the political culture, the political virtues and civic society of the country. (*LP*, p. 108)

As it stands, Rawls's claim is a relatively easy one to rebut given the strength of what is being asserted. Note that Rawls does not say that the wealth of a people is *influenced by* or *correlated with* political culture, philosophical traditions, characteristics of members (and so forth). As Rawls states this position, the causal origins of the wealth of a people are entirely attributable to local factors.[12] This position is much too strong and ignores other important factors that influence the prosperity nations are able to achieve, namely, all the factors outside of local control that also undeniably play a role. Thomas Pogge helpfully indicates some of these. For instance, international institutions (such as international borrowing and resource privileges) can play an important role in explaining persistently high levels of local poverty. Pogge often talks about this phenomenon in terms of the international institutions creating a headwind against which nations must struggle.[13] So Pogge does not deny that domestic factors play a role, but he shows that those efforts render more obvious the strong headwind against which many nations must struggle and, importantly, a wind that is within the power of developed countries to alter (at low cost to the globally advantaged). So, in responding to Rawls's overly strong claim, Pogge usefully draws attention to the ways in which international institutions, policies, and practices also contribute to domestic prosperity. Both the claim that global poverty is the result *exclusively* of international political and economic factors and the claim that it is exclusively the result of domestic factors are surely false.

The debate between Pogge and Rawls raises a number of very interesting questions which deserve further consideration. These would include: what factors are important in sustaining such currently high levels of global poverty? No doubt the factors are complex and multidimensional and we would do well to understand more of this complexity. Relatedly, what strategies and mechanisms prove to be effective in addressing poverty? Which proposals for reform might be most normatively desirable, feasible, and effective?

We might interpret Rawls's controversial views as motivated by reflections on these kinds of topics. In fairness to Rawls, when he does make the bold assertions about the causes of wealth it is in a context where his target is a view that access to resources is a crucial feature which importantly determines prospects for prosperity. It is in contrast to such a view that he makes a plea –

---

[12] Rawls does indeed mean to convey a strong claim, by bolstering it with other assertions that the factors he picks out are "all-important" (*LP*, p. 108).

[13] See for instance, Pogge, "Priorities," p. 17.

certainly in language that is too strong – for the under-appreciated role of political culture and local factors. And he goes on to reflect on how difficult it is to change destructive patterns that may be found in political culture. Simply dispensing funds won't change political culture. But, he says, an "emphasis on human rights may work to change ineffective regimes and the conduct of rulers who have been callous about the well-being of their own people" (*LP*, p. 109). After a very interesting discussion on prospects and challenges with discharging the duty of assistance, he concludes: "there is no easy recipe for helping a burdened society to change its political culture. Throwing funds at it is usually undesirable. . . But certain kinds of advice may be helpful, and burdened societies would do well to pay particular attention to the funda-mental interests of women" (*LP*, p. 110). He also emphasizes again the important role discourse about human rights can play in improving the political culture and its institutions.

So here Rawls is acknowledging the important role human rights can play in changing political culture and reforming unjust societies, contra his critics. And in emphasizing that particular attention should be paid to the funda-mental interests of women, Rawls indicates that he thinks there is a role for criticism, albeit criticism that might be embedded in carefully worded, diplo-matic, and strategic conversations. The impression that critics have that Rawls is overly tolerant of non-liberal societies is, I think, mistaken. Rather, as I have been suggesting, we might interpret Rawls's position as one in which he is sensitive to a range of important considerations that must be balanced in international affairs. We should be particularly attentive to when and how we offer advice, if we are concerned about which courses of action are likely to be effective and which are likely to prove counterproductive in trying to assist constructively in any reform process. Rawls identifies an important role for political leaders, particularly "the statesman," to play in this process. The statesman must make judgments assessing when opportunities are ripe for offering advice that might prove to be constructive and when it would be more appropriate to refrain from doing so. Altogether then, if we reflect on the problems Rawls was grappling with, particularly the issues of how we can appropriately discharge our duties of assistance given obstacles blocking prospects for promoting robust institutions, we see that Rawls offers subtle advice that critics have been too quick to dismiss.

References

Ackerman, B., "Political Liberalisms," *Journal of Philosophy* 91 (1994) 364–86.
  Social Justice in the Liberal State (New Haven, CT: Yale University Press, 1980).
  "What Is Neutral about Neutrality?" *Ethics* 93 (1983) 372–90.
Adorno, T., *Metaphysics: Concept and Problems* (Stanford University Press, 2001).
Alexander, S., "Social Evaluation through Notional Choice," *The Quarterly Journal of Economics* 88 (1974) 597–624.
Alstott, L., *No Exit: What Parents Owe Their Children and What Society Owes Parents* (New York: Oxford University Press, 2004).
Anderson, E., "Toward a Non-Ideal, Relational Methodology for Political Philosophy: Comments on Schwartzman's *Challenging Liberalism*," *Hypatia* 24 (2009) 130–45.
Arendt, H., *The Origins of Totalitarianism* (New York: Harcourt, Brace, Jovanovich, 1979).
Arneson, R., "Distributive Justice and Basic Capability Equality: 'Good Enough' Is Not Good Enough" in A. Kaufman (ed.) *Capabilities Equality: Basic Issues and Problems* (London: Routledge, 2005), pp. 17–43.
  "Justice Is Not Equality" in B. Feltham (ed.) *Justice, Equality and Constructivism: Essays on G. A. Cohen's Rescuing Justice and Equality* (Oxford and Malden, MA: Wiley-Blackwell, 2009).
Attas, D., "Fragmenting Property," *Law and Philosophy* 25 (2006) 119–49.
Audard, C., "Cultural Imperialism and 'Democratic Peace'" in R. Martin and D. Reidy (eds.) *Rawls's Law of Peoples* (Malden, MA: Blackwell, 2006), pp. 59–75.
Aumann, R., "Nash Equilibria Are Not Self-Enforcing" in Aumann, *Collected Papers: Volume I.* (Cambridge, MA: MIT Press, 2000), pp. 615–20.
Baehr, A. R., "Liberal Feminism" in Edward N. Zalta (ed.) *The Stanford Encyclopedia of Philosophy* (Winter 2013 Edition), http://plato.stanford.edu/archives/win2013/entries/feminism-liberal/.
  "Liberal Feminism: Comprehensive and Political" in R. Abbey (ed.) *Feminist Interpretations of Rawls* (College Park, PA: Pennsylvania State University Press, 2013), pp. 150–66.
Barry, B., *Theories of Justice* (Berkeley, CA: University of California Press, 1989).
Beitz, C., *Political Theory and International Relations* (Princeton University Press, 1976).
Bhandary, A., "Dependency in Justice: Can Rawlsian Liberalism Accommodate Kittay's Dependency Critique?" *Hypatia* 25 (2010) 140–56.
  "Liberal Dependency Care," *Journal of Philosophical Research*, forthcoming (2016).

Binmore, K., *Game Theory: A Very Short Introduction* (Oxford University Press, 2007).
  Natural Justice (New York: Oxford University Press, 2005).
  Rational Decisions (Princeton University Press, 2009).
Blake, M. and P. T. Smith, "International Distributive Justice" in Edward N. Zalta
  (ed.) *The Stanford Encyclopedia of Philosophy* (Winter 2013 edition), http://
  plato.stanford.edu/archives/win2013/entries/international-justice/.
Brake, E., *Minimizing Marriage: Marriage, Morality, and the Law* (New York: Oxford
  University Press, 2012).
Brink, D. O., "The Separateness of Persons, Distributive Norms, and Moral Theory"
  in C. Morris and R. Frey (eds.) *Value, Welfare, and Morality* (New York:
  Cambridge University Press, 1993), pp. 252–389.
Brock, G., *Global Justice: A Cosmopolitan Account* (Oxford University Press, 2009).
  "Human Rights" in J. Mandle and D. Reidy (eds.) *A Companion to Rawls* (Malden,
  MA: Wiley-Blackwell, 2014), pp. 346–60.
Brock, G. and H. Brighouse (eds.), *The Political Philosophy of Cosmopolitanism*
  (Cambridge University Press, 2005).
Casal, P., "Why Sufficiency Is Not Enough," *Ethics* 117 (2007) 296–326.
Christman, J., *The Myth of Property: Toward an Egalitarian Theory of Ownership*
  (New York: Oxford University Press, 1993).
Clark, B. and H. Gintis, "Rawlsian Justice and Economic Systems," *Philosophy &
  Public Affairs* 7 (1978) 302–25.
Clayton, M., "Liberal Equality: Political not Erinaceous," *Critical Review of Inter-
  national Social and Political Philosophy*, forthcoming 2015.
  "The Resources of Liberal Equality," *Imprints* 9 (2000) 63–84.
Cohen, G. A., *On the Currency of Egalitarian Justice, and Other Essays in Political
  Philosophy*, ed. M. Otsuka (Princeton University Press, 2011).
  "On the Currency of Egalitarian Justice," *Ethics* 99 (1989) 906–44.
  "Expensive Taste Rides Again" in J. Burley (ed.) *Dworkin and His Critics* (Oxford:
  Blackwell, 2004), pp, 3–29.
  "Incentives, Inequality, and Community," *The Tanner Lectures on Human Values*
  13 (1992).
  Lectures on the History of Moral and Political Philosophy, ed. J. Wolff (Princeton
  University Press, 2014).
  "Robert Nozick and Wilt Chamberlain: How Patterns Preserve Liberty," *Erkenntnis*
  11 (1977) 5–23.
  Rescuing Justice and Equality (Cambridge, MA: Harvard University Press, 2008).
  Self-Ownership, Freedom and Equality (Cambridge University Press, 1995).
  "The Structure of Proletarian Unfreedom" in Cohen, *History, Labour and Freedom:
  Themes from Marx* (Oxford University Press, 1988), pp. 255–85.
  "Where the Action Is: On the Site of Distributive Justice," *Philosophy and Public
  Affairs* 26 (1997) 3–30.
Cohen, J., "Democratic Equality," *Ethics* 99 (1989) 727–51.
Crisp, R., "Equality, Priority, and Compassion," *Ethics* 113 (2003) 745–63.
Cudd, A. E., *Analyzing Oppression* (New York: Oxford University Press, 2005).

Dworkin, R., *Justice for Hedgehogs* (Cambridge, MA: Harvard University Press, 2011).

"The Original Position" in N. Daniels (ed.) *Reading Rawls* (Palo Alto, CA: Stanford University Press, 1989), pp. 16–52.

"The Original Position," *The University of Chicago Law Review* 40 (1973) 500–33.

"Rawls and the Law" in *Justice in Robes* (Cambridge, MA: Harvard University Press, 2006).

Taking Rights Seriously (London: Duckworth, 1977).

Sovereign Virtue: The Theory and Practice of Equality (Cambridge, MA: Harvard University Press, 2000).

Eaton, A. W., "A Sensible Anti-Porn Feminism," *Ethics* 117 (2007) 674–715.

Estlund, D., "Human Nature and the Limits (if any) of Political Philosophy," *Philosophy and Public Affairs* 39 (2011) 207–37

Fisk, M. "History and Reason in Rawls' Moral Theory" in N. Daniels (ed.) *Reading Rawls* (Palo Alto, CA: Stanford University Press, 1989), pp. 53–80.

Forst, R., "Towards a Critical Theory of Transnational Justice," *Metaphilosophy* 32 (2001)160–79.

Frankfurt, H., "Equality as a Moral Ideal," *Ethics* 98 (1987) 21–43.

Freeman, S., "Introduction: John Rawls – An Overview" in S. Freeman (ed.) *The Cambridge Companion to Rawls* (Cambridge University Press, 2003), pp. 1–61.

"The Law of Peoples, Social Cooperation, Human Rights, and Distributive Justice," *Social Philosophy and Policy* 23 (2006) 29–68.

"The Original Position" in Edward N. Zalta (ed.) *The Stanford Encyclopedia of Philosophy* (Winter 2013 edition) http://plato.stanford.edu/archives/win2013/entries/original%20position/.

Rawls (London and New York: Routledge, 2007).

Freeman, S. (ed.), *The Cambridge Companion to Rawls* (Cambridge University Press, 2003).

Gauthier, D., *Morals by Agreement* (Oxford University Press, 1987).

Gibbard, A., "Natural Property Rights," *Nous* 10 (1976) 77–86.

Gorr, M., "Rawls on Natural Inequality" in J. A. Corlett (ed.) *Equality and Liberty: Analyzing Rawls and Nozick* (New York: St. Martin's Press, 1991), pp. 19–36.

Hampton, J., "Feminist Contractarianism" in L. Antony and C. Witt (eds.) *A Mind of One's Own* (Oxford: Westview, 1993), pp. 227–56.

Harsanyi, J., "Bayesian Decision Theory, Subjective and Objective Probabilities, and Acceptance of Empirical Hypotheses," *Synthese* 57 (1983) 341–65.

"Bayesian Decision Theory and Utilitarian Ethics," *The American Economic Review* 68 (1978) 223–8.

"Can the Maximin Principle Serve as a Basis for Morality? A Critique of John Rawls's Theory," *The American Political Science Review* 69 (1975) 594–606.

"Cardinal Utility in Welfare Economics and in the Theory of Risk-Taking," *The Journal of Political Economy* (1953) 434–5.

"Cardinal Welfare, Individualistic Ethics, and Interpersonal Comparisons of Utility," *The Journal of Political Economy* August (1955) 309–21.

"A General Theory of Rational Behavior in Game Situations," *Econometrica* 34 (1966) 613–34.

"Morality and the Theory of Rational Behavior" in A. Sen and B. Williams (eds.) *Utilitarianism and Beyond* (Cambridge University Press, 1982), pp. 39–62.

Rational Behavior and Bargaining Equilibrium in Games and Social Situations (Cambridge University Press, 1977).

Hart, H. L. A., *The Concept of Law*, 3rd edn (Oxford University Press, 2012).

"Rawls on Liberty and Its Priority," reprinted in N. Daniels (ed.) *Reading Rawls* (Oxford: Blackwell, 1974), pp. 230–52.

Hart, H. M. and A. M. Sacks, *The Legal Process: Basic Problems in the Making and Application of Law*, ed. W. Eskridge and Philip Frickey (Westbury, NY: Foundation Press, 1994).

Hartley, C. and L. Watson, "Is a Feminist Political Liberalism Possible?" *Journal of Ethics and Social Philosophy* 5 (2010) 1–21.

Heath, J., "Rawls on Global Distributive Justice: A Defence," *Canadian Journal of Philosophy* Supp. Vol. 31 (2005) 193–226.

Herman, B., *The Practice of Moral Judgment* (Cambridge, MA: Harvard University Press, 1993).

Hill, T., *Dignity and Practical Reason in Kant's Moral Theory* (Ithaca: Cornell University Press, 1992).

Respect, Pluralism, and Justice: Kantian Perspectives (Oxford, New York: Oxford University Press, 2000).

Hinsch, W., "Global Distributive Justice," *Metaphilosophy* 32 (2001) 58–78.

Hinsch, W. and M. Stepanians, "Human Rights as Moral Claims" in R. Martin and D. Reidy (eds.) *Rawls's Law of Peoples* (Malden, MA: Blackwell, 2006), pp. 117–33.

Hinton, T., "Equality, Self-Ownership and Individual Sovereignty," *Philosophical Forum* 44 (2013) 165–78.

"Liberalism, Feminism and Social Tyranny," in *Public Affairs Quarterly* 21 (2007) 235–53.

Hume, D., *A Treatise of Human Nature*, ed. L. A. Selby-Bigge (Oxford University Press, 1978).

Hurrell, A., "Global Inequality and International Institutions," *Metaphilosophy* 32 (2001) 34–57.

James, A., "Constructing Justice for Existing Practice: Rawls and the Status Quo," *Philosophy and Public Affairs* 33 (2005) 281–316.

Kant, I., *Critique of Practical Reason* in *Kant: Practical Philosophy*, trans. and ed. Mary J. Gregor (Cambridge University Press, 1996). Abbreviated as *KpV*, citations to volume and page number in the Berlin Academy edition of Kant's *Gesammelte Schriften*.

Groundwork of the Metaphysics of Morals in *Kant: Practical Philosophy*, trans. and ed. Mary J. Gregor (Cambridge University Press, 1996). Abbreviated as *G*, citations to volume and page number in the Berlin Academy edition of Kant's *Gesammelte Schriften*.

Religion within the Boundaries of Mere Reason, trans. George di Giovanni, in *Kant: Religion and Rational Theology*, trans. and ed. Allen W. Wood and George di Giovanni (Cambridge University Press, 1996). Citations are to volume and page number in the Berlin Academy edition of Kant's *Gesammelte Schriften*.

Kittay, E., *Love's Labor* (New York: Routledge, 1999).

Kohlberg, L., *The Philosophy of Moral Development* (New York: Harper and Row, 1981).

Korsgaard, C., *Creating the Kingdom of Ends* (Cambridge and New York: Cambridge University Press, 1996).

   The Sources of Nonnativity (Cambridge and New York: Cambridge University Press, 1996).

Kukathas, C. and P. Pettit, *Rawls: A Theory of Justice and Its Critics* (Palo Alto, CA: Stanford University Press, 1990).

Kuper, A., "Rawlsian Global Justice: Beyond the *Law of Peoples* to a Cosmopolitan Law of Persons," *Political Theory* 28 (2000) 640–74.

Lichtenstein, A., "The Past and Present of Marxist Historiography in South Africa: An Interview with Martin Legassick," *Radical History Review* 82 (2002) 111–30.

Lloyd, S. A., "Toward a Liberal Theory of Sexual Equality," *Journal of Contemporary Legal Issues* 9 (1998) 203–24.

Luce, R. D. and H. Raiffa, *Games and Decisions* (New York: Wiley and Sons, 1957).

Mandle, J., "Tolerating Injustice" in G. Brock and H. Brighouse (eds.) *The Political Philosophy of Cosmopolitanism* (Cambridge University Press, 2005), pp. 219–33.

Martin, R., "Rawls on International Distributive Justice" in R. Martin and D. Reidy (eds.) *Rawls's Law of Peoples* (Malden, MA: Blackwell, 2006), pp. 226–42.

Martin, R. and D. Reidy (eds.), *Rawls's Law of Peoples: A Realistic Utopia?* (Malden, MA: Blackwell, 2006).

McClennen, E. F., *Rationality and Dynamic Choice* (Cambridge University Press, 1990).

Meadowcroft, J., "Nozick's Critique of Rawls: Distribution, Entitlement and the Assumptive World of *A Theory of Justice*" in R. M. Bader and J. Meadowcroft (eds.) *The Cambridge Companion to Nozick's Anarchy, State and Utopia* (Cambridge University Press, 2011), pp. 168–96.

Metz, T., "Arbitrariness, Justice, and Respect," *Social Theory and Practice* 26 (2000) 25–45.

Miller, R., "Rawls and Marxism," *Philosophy & Public Affairs* 3 (1974) 167–9, reprinted in N. Daniels (ed.) *Reading Rawls* (Palo Alto, CA: Stanford University Press, 1989), pp. 206–30.

Mills, C., *The Racial Contract* (Ithaca, NY: Cornell University Press, 1999).

   "Rawls on Race/Race in Rawls," in *The Southern Journal of Philosophy* 47 (2009) 161–84.

Moellendorf, D., *Cosmopolitan Justice* (Boulder, CO: Westview Press, 2002).

Moehler, M., "Contractarian Ethics and Harsanyi's Two Justifications of Utilitarianism," *Politics, Philosophy & Economics* 12 (2013) 24–47.

Murphy, L. and T. Nagel, *The Myth of Ownership: Taxes and Justice* (Oxford University Press, 2002).

Nagel, T., "Rawls on Justice," *The Philosophical Review* 82 (1973) 220–34.

Narveson, J., *The Libertarian Idea* (Philadelphia, PA: Temple University Press, 2001).

Narveson, J. and J. Sterba, "Are Liberty and Equality Compatible?" Special Issue, *Journal of Social Philosophy* 42 (2011) 403–15.

Neufeld, B. and C. van Schoelandt, "Political Liberalism, Ethos Justice, and Gender Equality," *Law and Philosophy* 33 (2014) 75–104.

Nozick, R., *Anarchy, State, and Utopia* (New York: Basic Books, 1974).

Nussbaum, M., *Sex and Social Justice* (New York: Oxford University Press, 1999).

Okin, S., *Justice, Gender and the Family* (New York: Basic Books, 1989).

"*Political Liberalism*, Justice, and Gender," *Ethics* 105 (1994) 23–43.

O'Neill, M. and T. Williamson (eds.), *Property-Owning Democracy* (Malden, MA: Wiley-Blackwell, 2014).

O'Neill, O., *Constructions of Reason: Explorations of Kant's Practical Philosophy* (Cambridge and New York: Cambridge University Press, 1990).

Otsuka, M., "Self-Ownership and Equality: A Lockean Reconciliation," *Philosophy and Public Affairs* 27 (2006) 65–92.

Pateman, C., *The Sexual Contract* (Palo Alto, CA: Stanford University Press, 1988).

Paul J., (ed.), *Reading Nozick: Essays on Anarchy, State and Utopia* (Oxford: Blackwell, 1981).

Plato, *Euthyphro* in *Plato: Complete Works*, ed. J. M. Cooper (Indianapolis: Hackett, 1997).

Pogge, T., "Cohen to the Rescue!" *Ratio (new series)* 21 (2008) 454–75.

"An Egalitarian Law of Peoples," *Philosophy and Public Affairs* 23 (1994) 195–224.

John Rawls: His Life and Theory of Justice (Oxford University Press, 2007).

"Priorities of Global Justice," *Metaphilosophy* 32 (2001) 6–24.

Realizing Rawls (Ithaca, NY: Cornell University Press, 1989).

World Poverty and Human Rights (Cambridge: Polity, 2002).

World Poverty and Human Rights, 2nd edn. (Cambridge: Polity, 2008).

Rawls, J., *Collected Papers*, ed. S. Freeman (Cambridge, MA: Harvard University Press, 1999).

"Distributive Justice" in P. Laslett and W. G. Runciman (eds.) *Philosophy, Politics, and Society* (Oxford: Blackwell, 1967), pp. 58–82, reprinted in *Collected Papers*, pp. 130–53.

"Distributive Justice: Some Addenda," *Natural Law Forum* 13 (1968), reprinted in *Collected Papers*, pp. 154–75.

"The Idea of Public Reason Revisited," *University of Chicago Law Review* 64 (1997) 765–807, reprinted in *Collected Papers*, pp. 573–615.

"Justice as Fairness," *Journal of Philosophy* 54 (1957) 653–62, reprinted in *Collected Papers*, pp. 47–72.

Justice as Fairness: A Restatement, ed. Erin Kelly (Cambridge, MA: Harvard University Press, 2001).

"Justice as Fairness: Political not Metaphysical," *Philosophy and Public Affairs* 14 (1985) 223–51, reprinted in *Collected Papers*, pp. 388–414.

"Kantian Constructivism in Moral Theory," *Journal of Philosophy* 77 (1980) 515–72, reprinted in *Collected Papers*, pp. 303–58.

The Law of Peoples: With the Idea of Public Reason Revisited (Cambridge, MA: Harvard University Press, 1999).

Lectures on the History of Moral Philosophy, ed. Barbara Herman (Cambridge, MA: Harvard University Press, 2000).

Lectures on the History of Political Philosophy, ed. Samuel Freeman (Cambridge, MA: Harvard University Press, 2007).

"Outline of a Decision Procedure for Ethics," *Philosophical Review* 60 (1951), reprinted in *Collected Papers*, pp. 1–19.

Political Liberalism (New York: Columbia University Press, 1993).

Political Liberalism, paperback edition (New York: Columbia University Press, 1996).

"Reply to Alexander and Musgrave," *Quarterly Journal of Economics* 88 (1974) 633–55, reprinted in *Collected Papers*, pp. 232–53.

"Social Unity and Primary Goods" in A. Sen and B. Williams (eds.) *Utilitarianism and Beyond* (Cambridge: Harvard University Press, 1982), pp. 159–86, reprinted in *Collected Papers*, pp. 359–87.

"Some Reasons for the Maximin Criterion," *American Economic Review* 64 (1974) 141–6, reprinted in *Collected Papers*, pp. 225–31.

A Theory of Justice (Cambridge, MA: Harvard University Press, 1971).

A Theory of Justice, rev. edn (Cambridge, MA: Harvard University Press, 1999).

Reath, A., *Agency and Autonomy in Kant's Moral Theory* (Oxford University Press, 2006).

"Kant's Conception of Autonomy of the Will" in Oliver Sensen (ed.) *Kant on Moral Autonomy* (Cambridge University Press, 2013), pp. 32–52.

Reidy, D., "Political Authority and Human Rights" in R. Martin and D. Reidy (eds.) *Rawls's Law of Peoples* (Malden, MA: Blackwell, 2006), pp. 169–88.

"Rawls on International Justice: A Defense," *Political Theory* 32 (2004) 291–319.

"Three Human Rights Agendas," *Canadian Journal of Law and Jurisprudence* 19 (2006) 237–54.

Robeyns, I., "Gender, Care and Property-owning Democracy" in M. O'Neill and T. Williamson (eds.) *Property-Owning Democracy: Rawls and Beyond* (Malden, MA: Wiley-Blackwell, 2012), pp. 163–79.

Rousseau, J. J., *Basic Political Writings*, ed. D. Cress (Indianapolis, IN: Hackett, 1987).

Ryan, C. C., "Yours, Mine, and Ours: Property Rights and Individual Liberty," *Ethics* 87 (1977) 126–41.

Savage, L. J., "The Theory of Statistical Decision," *Journal of the American Statistical Association* 46 (1951) 55–67.

Scanlon, T. M., "Contractualism and Utilitarianism" in A. Sen and B. Williams (eds.) *Utilitarianism and Beyond* (Cambridge University Press, 1982), pp. 103–28.

"Rawls on Justification" in S. Freeman (ed.) *The Cambridge Companion to Rawls* (Cambridge University Press, 2003), pp. 139–67.

What We Owe to Each Other (Cambridge, MA: Harvard University Press, 1998).

Scheffler, S., "Is the Basic Structure Basic?" in C. Sypnowich (ed.) *The Egalitarian Conscience: Essays in Honour of G. A. Cohen* (New York: Oxford University Press, 2006), pp. 102–29.

Sen, A., *Development as Freedom* (Oxford University Press, 1999).

Shields, L., "The Prospects for Sufficientarianism," *Utilitas* 24 (2012) 101–17.

Stark, C., "How to Include the Severely Disabled in a Contractarian Theory of Justice," *Journal of Political Philosophy* 15 (2007) 127–45.

Sterba, J., "In Defense of Rawls against Arrow and Nozick," *Philosophia* 7 (1978) 293–303.

Street, S., "What is Constructivism in Ethics and Metaethics?" *Philosophy Compass* 5 (2010) 363–84.

Tasioulas, J., "From Utopia to Kazanistan: John Rawls and the Law of Peoples," *Oxford Journal of Legal Studies* 22 (2002) 367–93.

Tan, K. C., *Tolerance, Diversity, and Global Justice* (University Park, PA: Pennsylvania State University Press, 2000).

Thompson, J., "What Do Women Want? Rewriting the Social Contract," *International Journal of Moral and Social Studies* 8 (1993) 257–72.

Valentini, L. and M. Ronzoni, "On the Meta-Ethical Status of Constructivism: Reflections on G. A. Cohen's 'Facts and Principles,'" *Politics Philosophy Economics* 7 (2008) 403–22.

Vallentyne, P. and H. Steiner (eds.), *Left-Libertarianism and Its Critics: The Contemporary Debate* (London: St. Martins Press, 2000).

Von Mises, L., *Socialism* (New Haven, CT: Yale University Press, 1951).

Von Neumann, J. and O. Morgenstern, *Theory of Games and Economic Behavior*, 3rd edn (Princeton University Press, 1953).

Waldron, J., "How Law Protects Dignity," *Cambridge Law Journal* 71 (2012) 200–22.
    "John Rawls and the Social Minimum," *Journal of Applied Philosophy* 3 (1986) 21–33, reprinted in Waldron, *Liberal Rights*, pp. 250–70.
    Liberal Rights: Collected Papers 1981–1991 (Cambridge University Press, 1993).
    "Theoretical Foundations of Liberalism," *Philosophical Quarterly* 37 (1987) 127–50, reprinted in Waldron, *Liberal Rights*, pp. 35–62.

Weithman, P., *Why Political Liberalism?* (Oxford University Press, 2010).

Wenar, L., "Why Rawls Is not a Cosmopolitan Egalitarian" in R. Martin and D. Reidy (eds.) *Rawls's Law of Peoples* (Malden, MA: Blackwell, 2006), pp. 95–113.

Williams, A., "Equality for the Ambitious," *The Philosophical Quarterly* 52 (2002) 377–89.

Wolff, R. P., *Understanding Rawls: A Reconstruction and Critique of a Theory of Justice* (Princeton University Press, 1977).

Wolpe, H., "Capitalism and Cheap Labour-Power in South Africa: From Segregation to Apartheid," *Economy and Society* 1 (1972) 425–56.

Wood, A., *Karl Marx*, 2nd edn (London and New York: Routledge, 2004).

Index